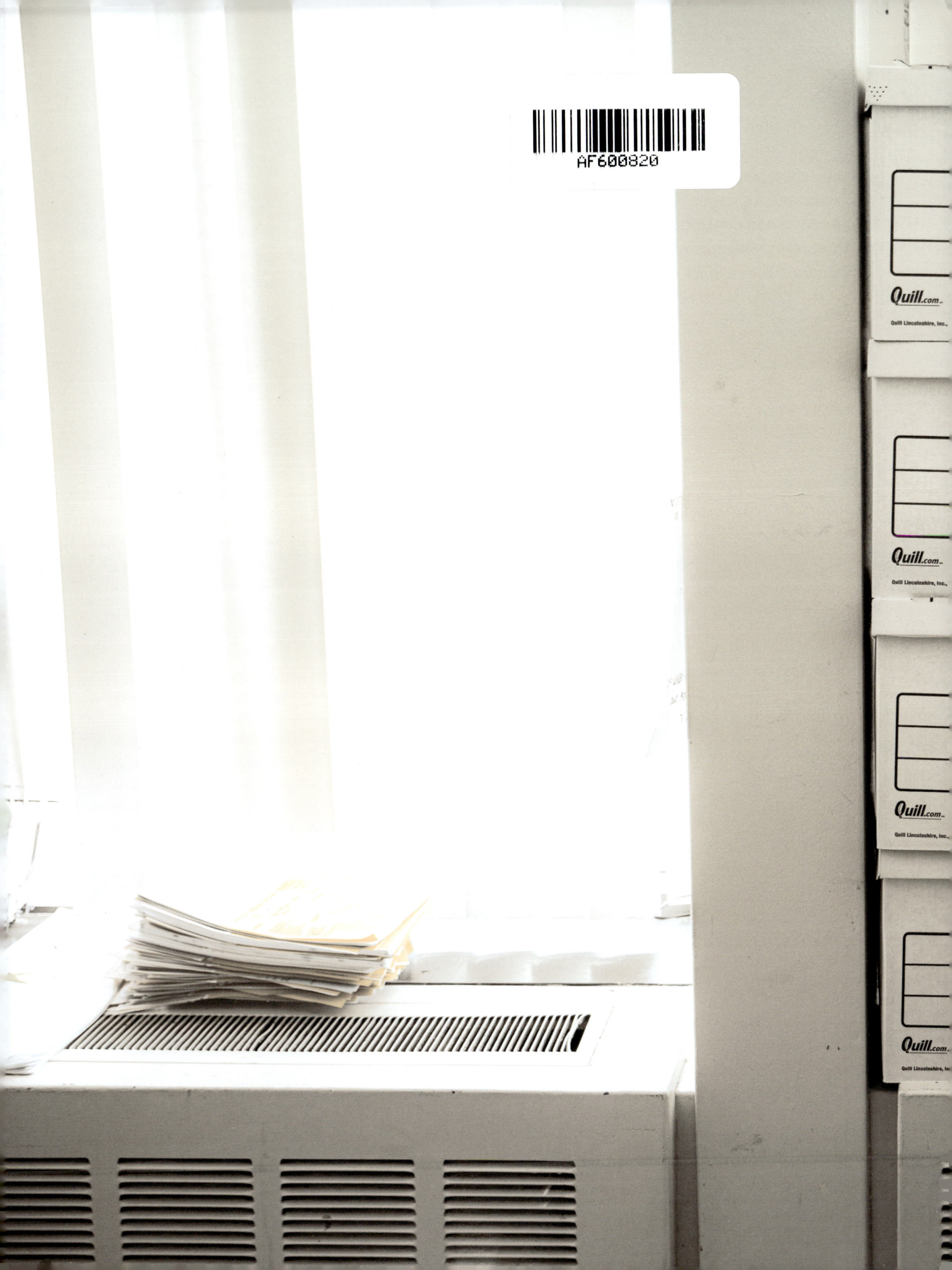

Banker Boxes located in an office in a Ludwig Mies van der Rohe-designed building in Chicago's Brownsville neighborhood. The racially segregated Mecca Flats apartments and surrounding properties were flattened in 1952 to create Mies van der Rohe's expansive structures with curtain walls on what is now the Illinois Institute of Technology campus.

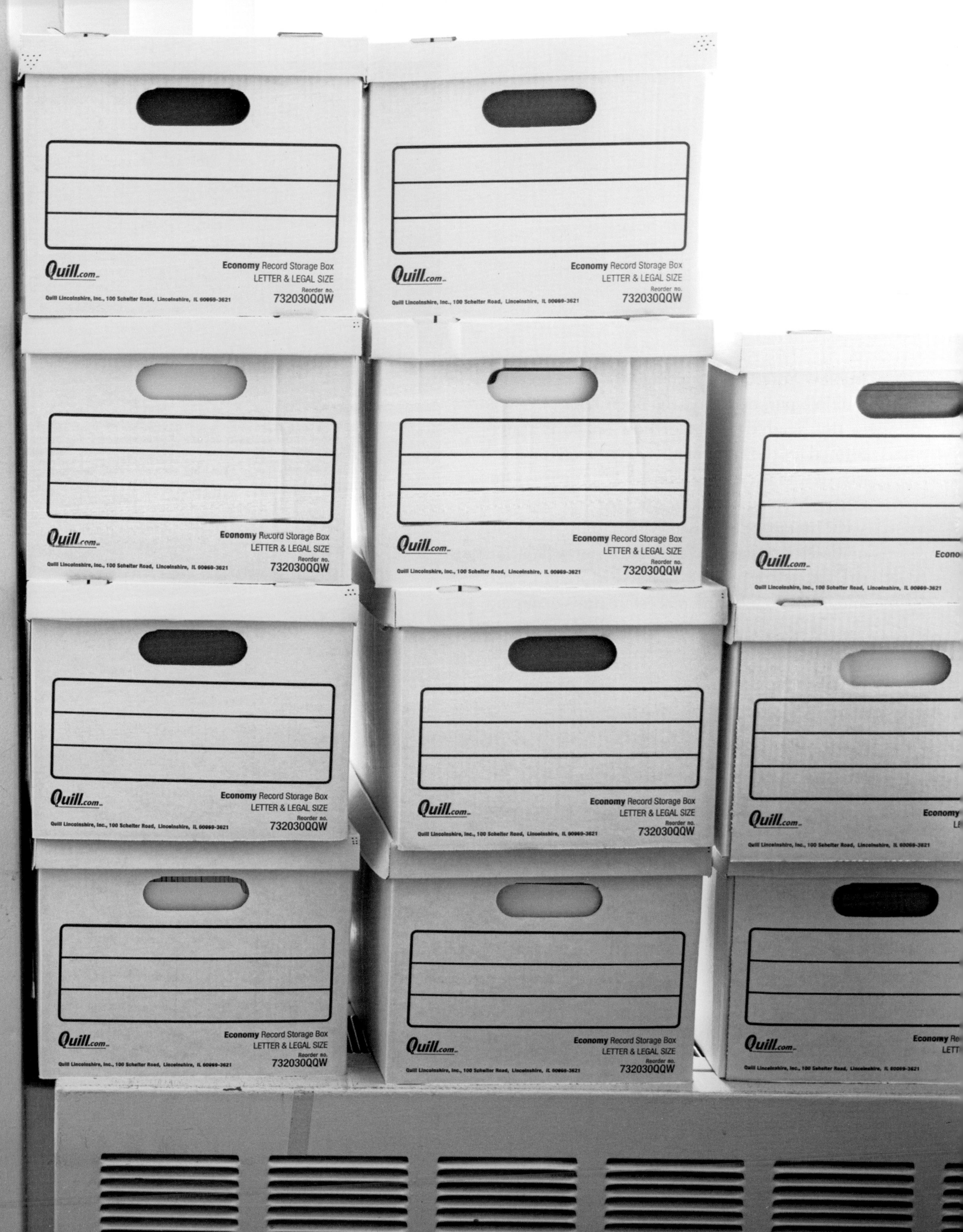
Quill.com
Economy Record Storage Box
LETTER & LEGAL SIZE
Reorder no.
732030QQW
Quill Lincolnshire, Inc., 100 Schelter Road, Lincolnshire, IL 60069-3621

In New York City, buildings are often used for multiple purposes, and the open floor plan aids in this seamless shift of how space is transformed for the labor market. Pictured is an interior view of the building formerly known as One Chase Manhattan Plaza, the first International style building in Lower Manhattan. With an open floor design and executive suites flanking the periphery of each floor, JPMorgan Chase and other finance and real estate firms occupied this building from 1961–2010s before it was sold to an international investment company. For a period in 2015 and 2016 artist workspaces were located on the 15th floor of the building, known now as 28 Liberty Street.

By 2018 the investment firm finished its renovations, transforming the building into high-end luxury residential, dining and retail spaces.

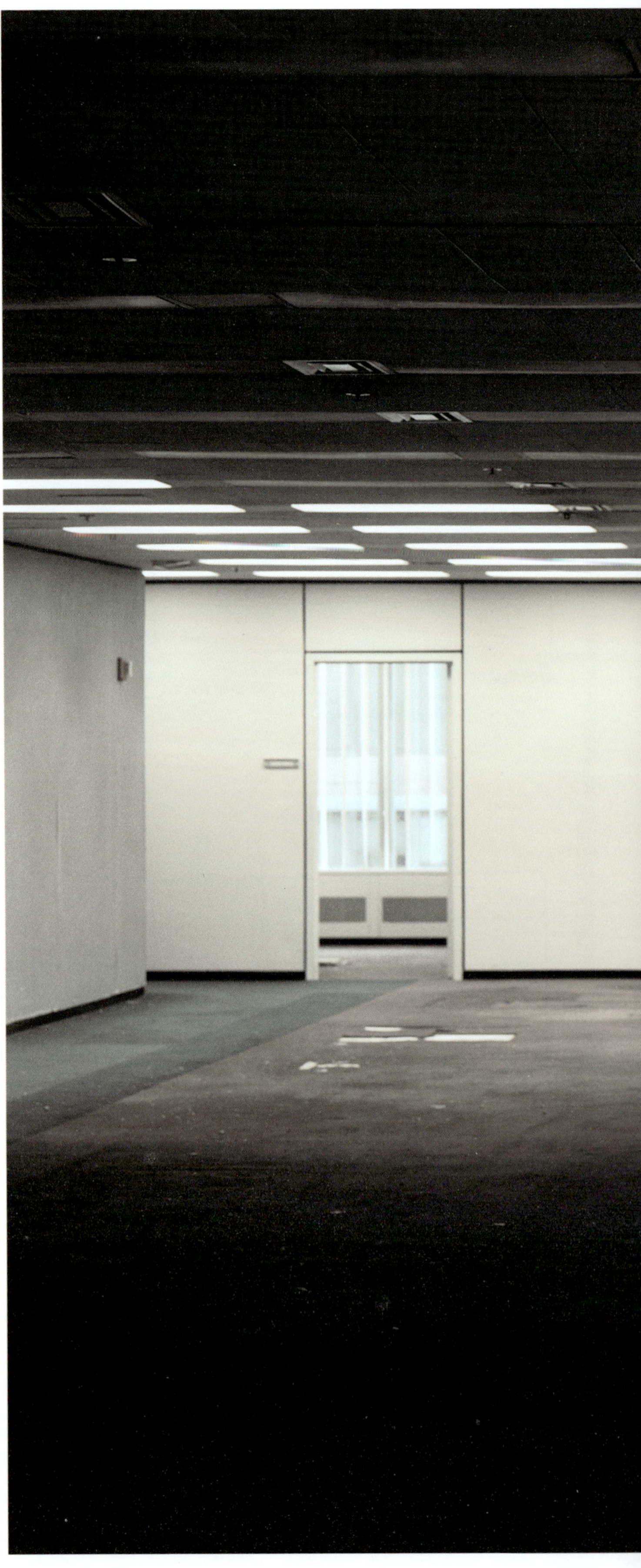

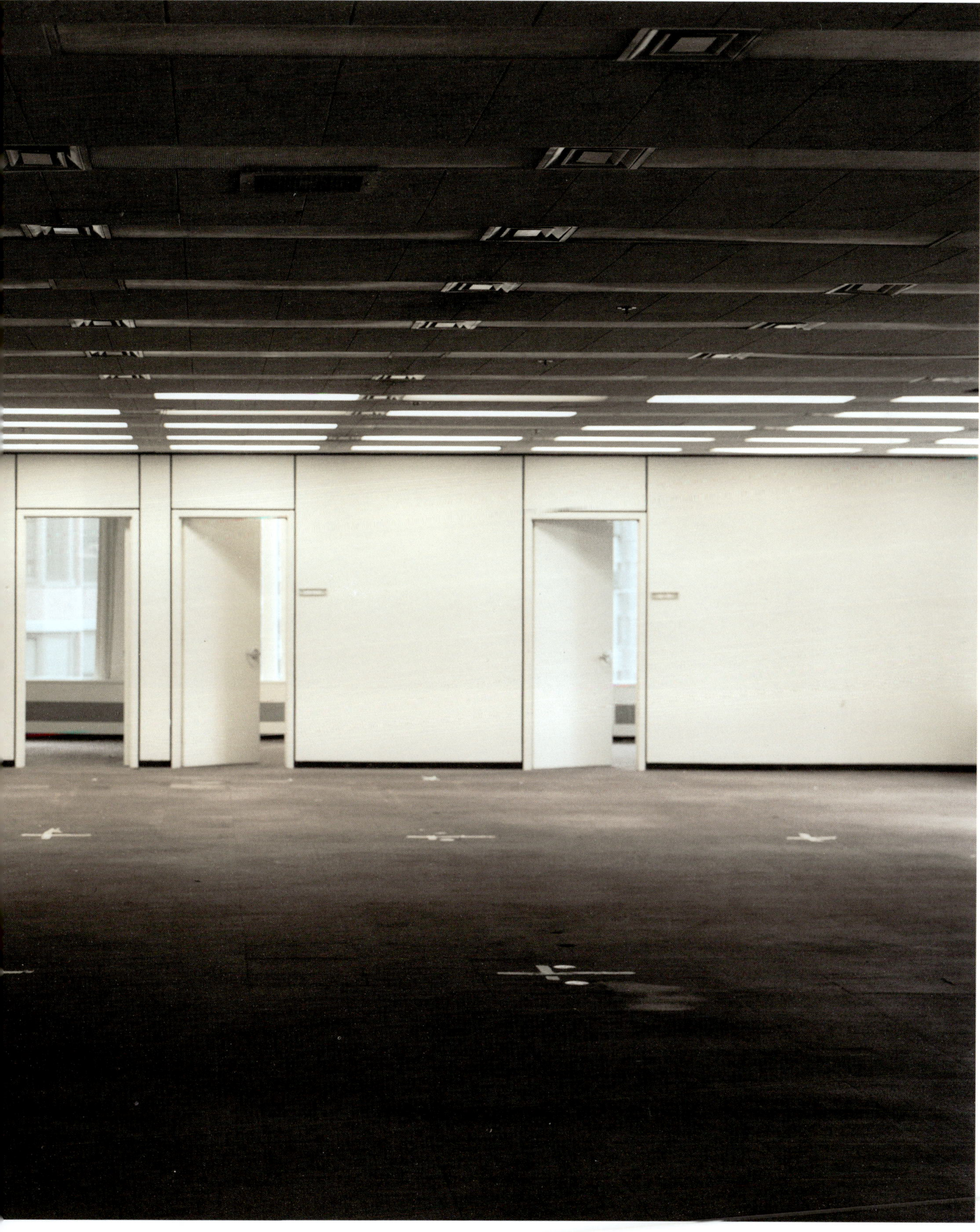

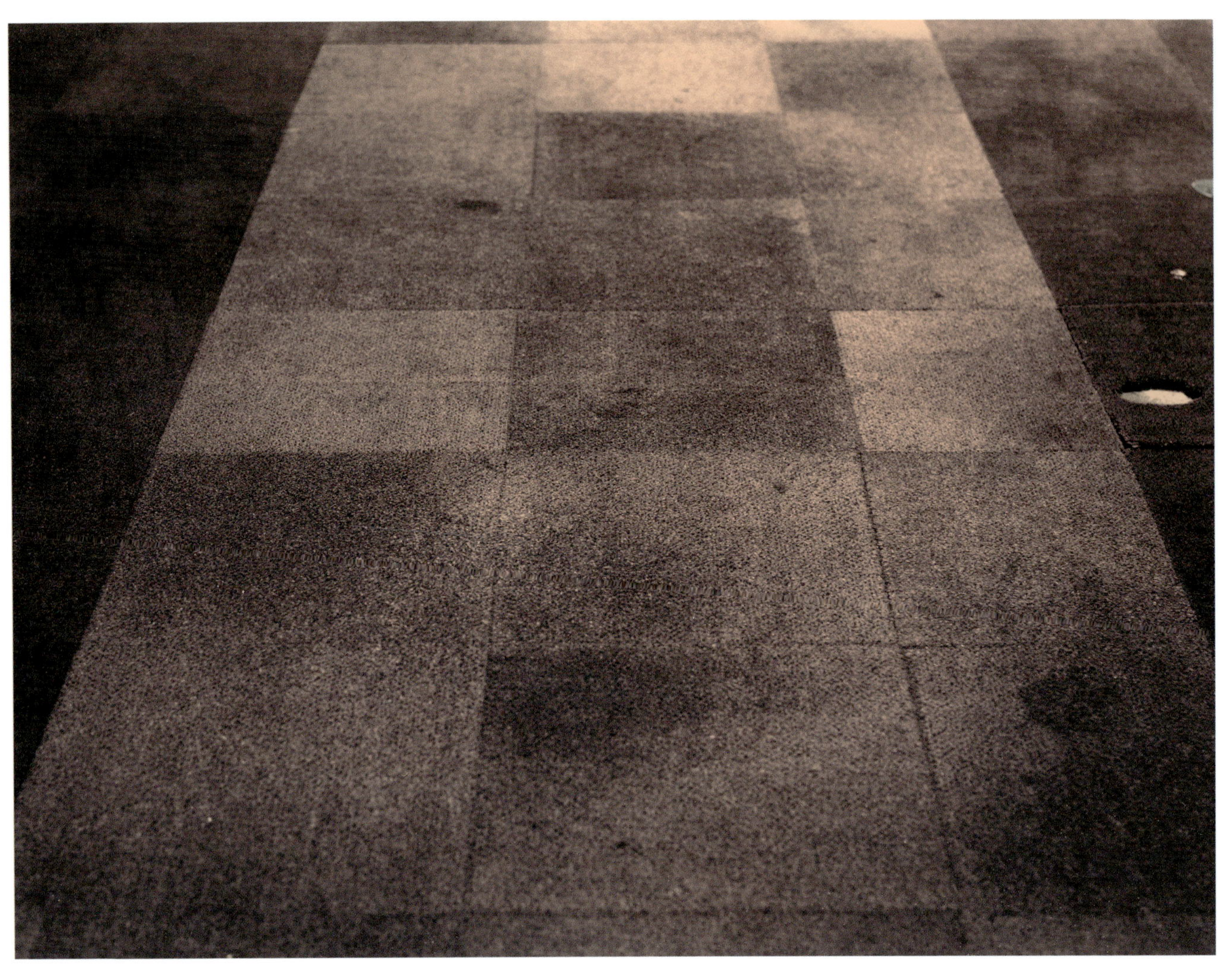

Pictured here are carpet tiles located at 28 Liberty Street. Several were removed from the floor and are ready for disposal.

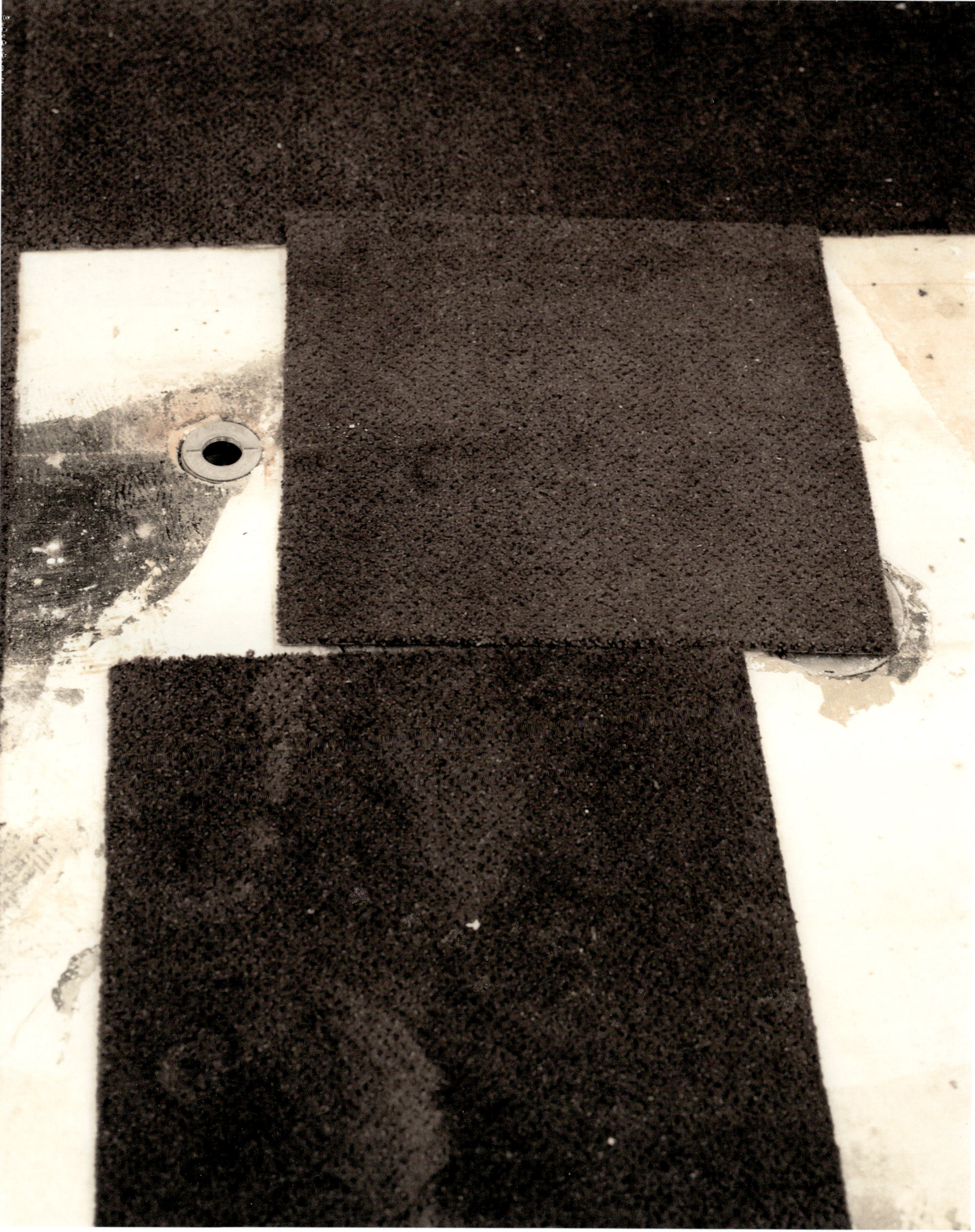

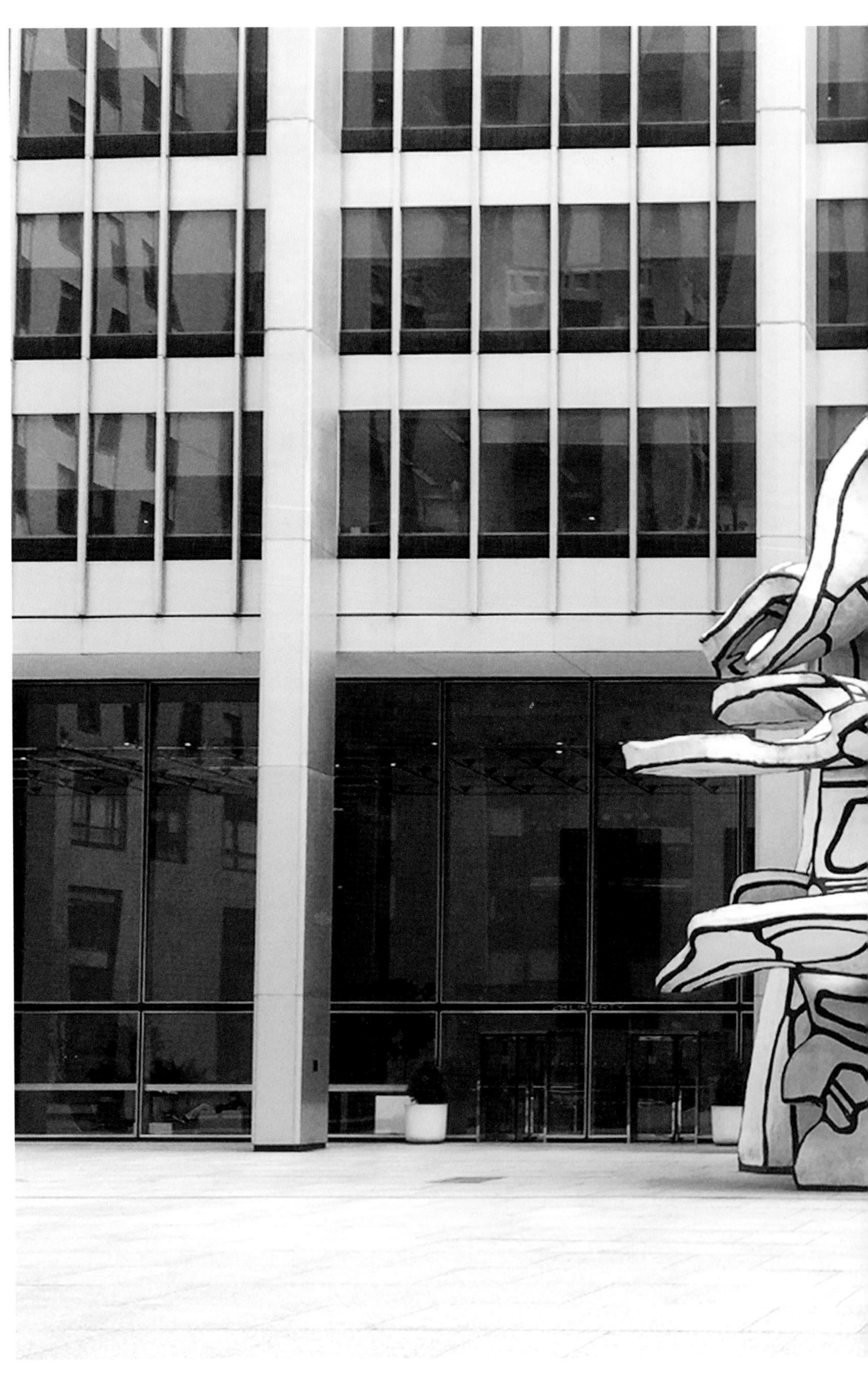

Group of Four Trees by French artist Jean Dubuffet in front of 28 Liberty Street.

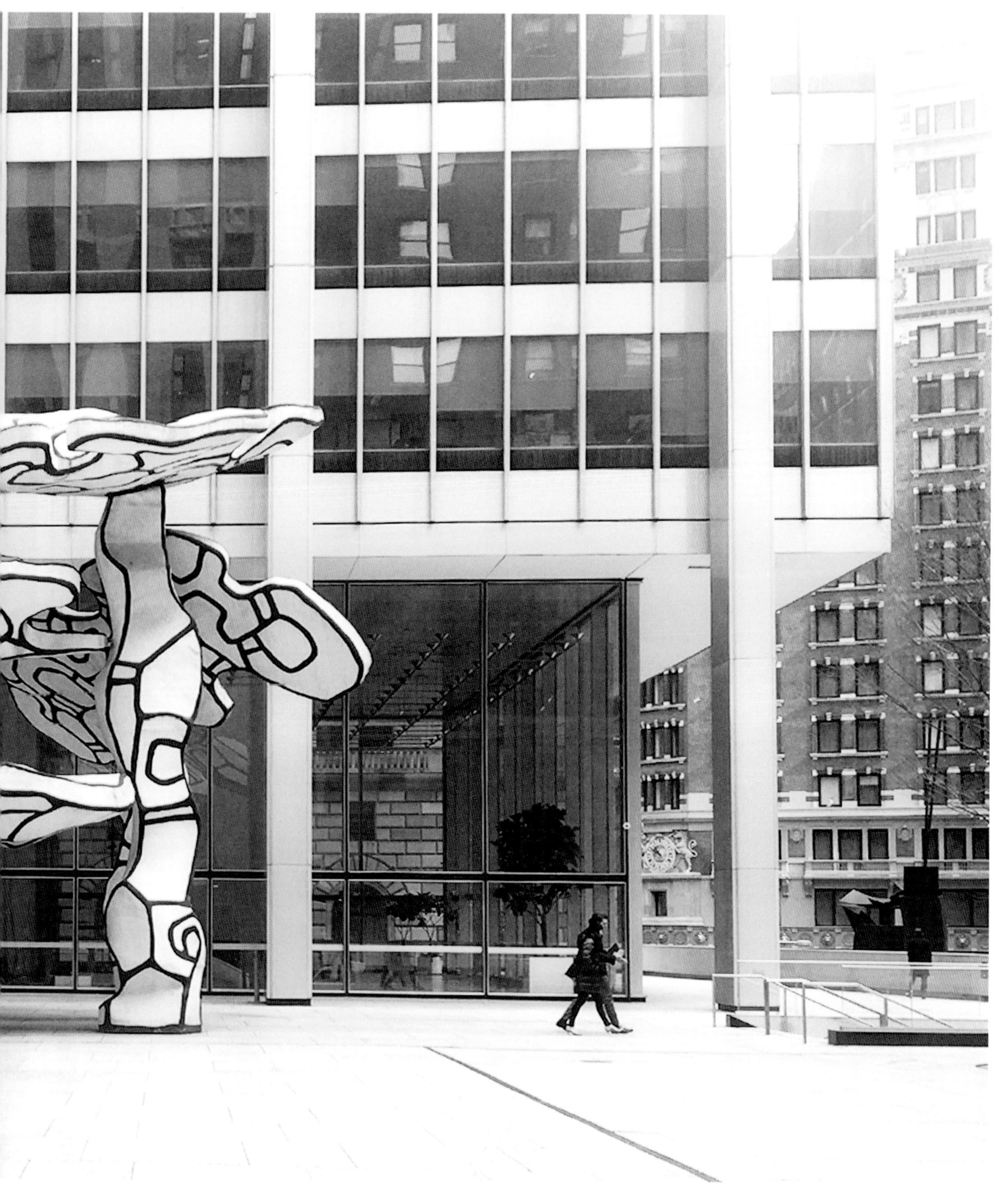

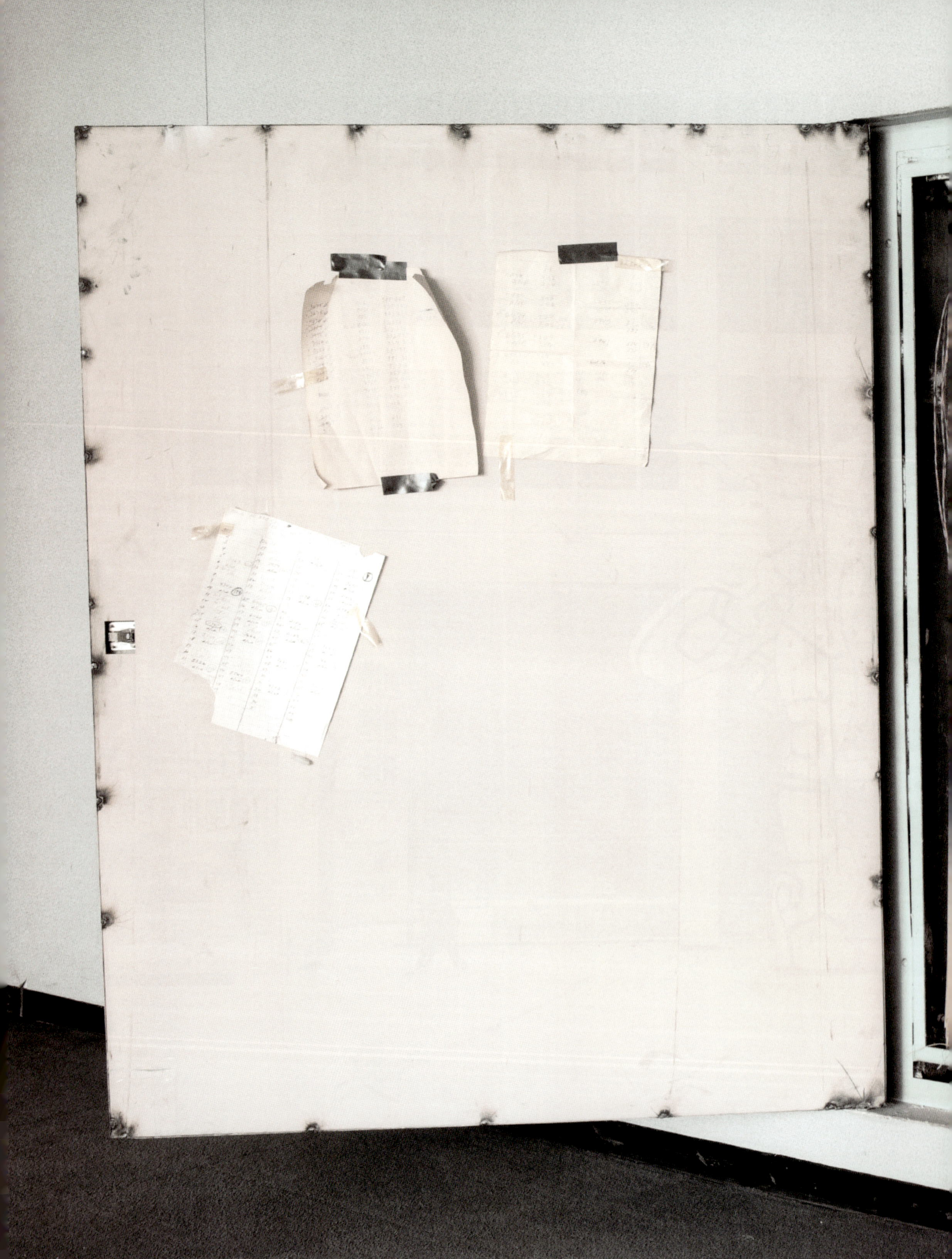

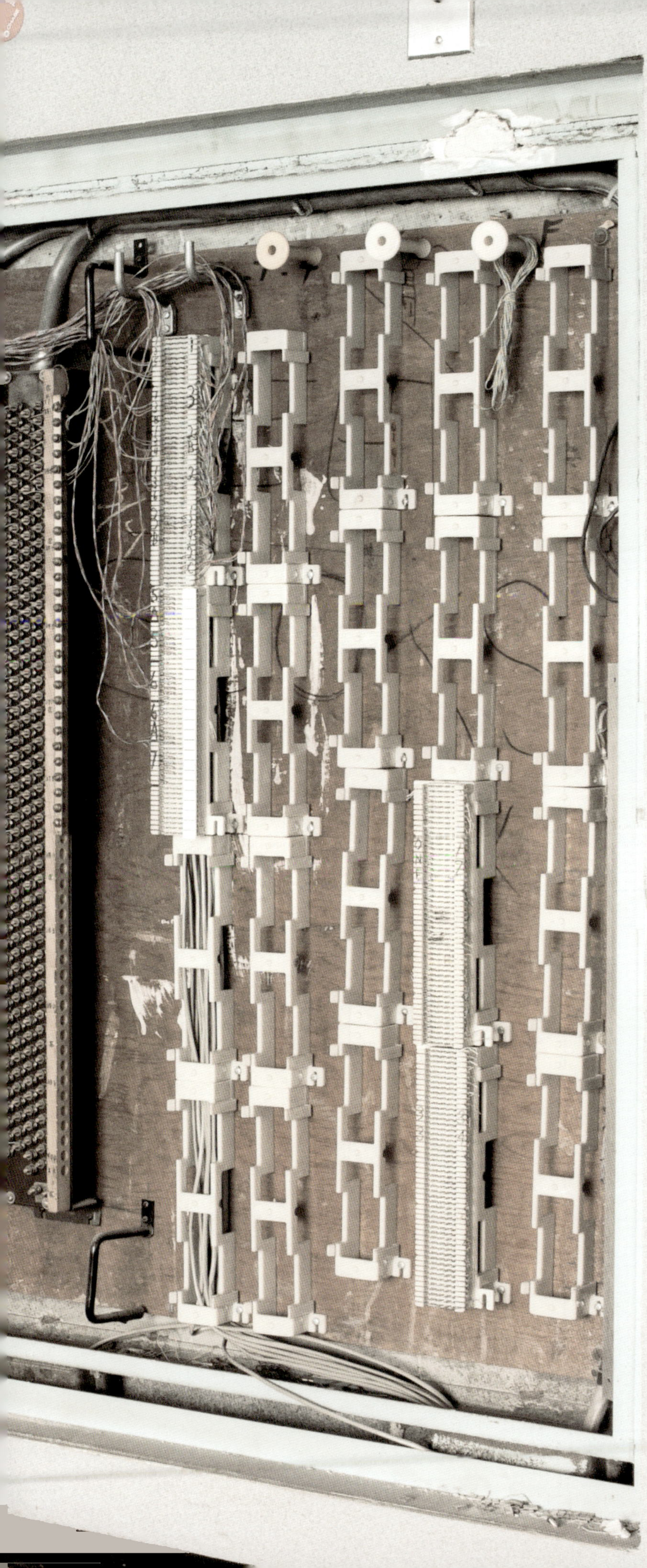

This photograph of a circuit board with defunct electrical wiring was taken in a former office space on the 15th floor of 28 Liberty Street. Inoperable and indicative of a downward turn, this internal network infrastructure once kept communication and power moving for the corporation that occupied the floor.

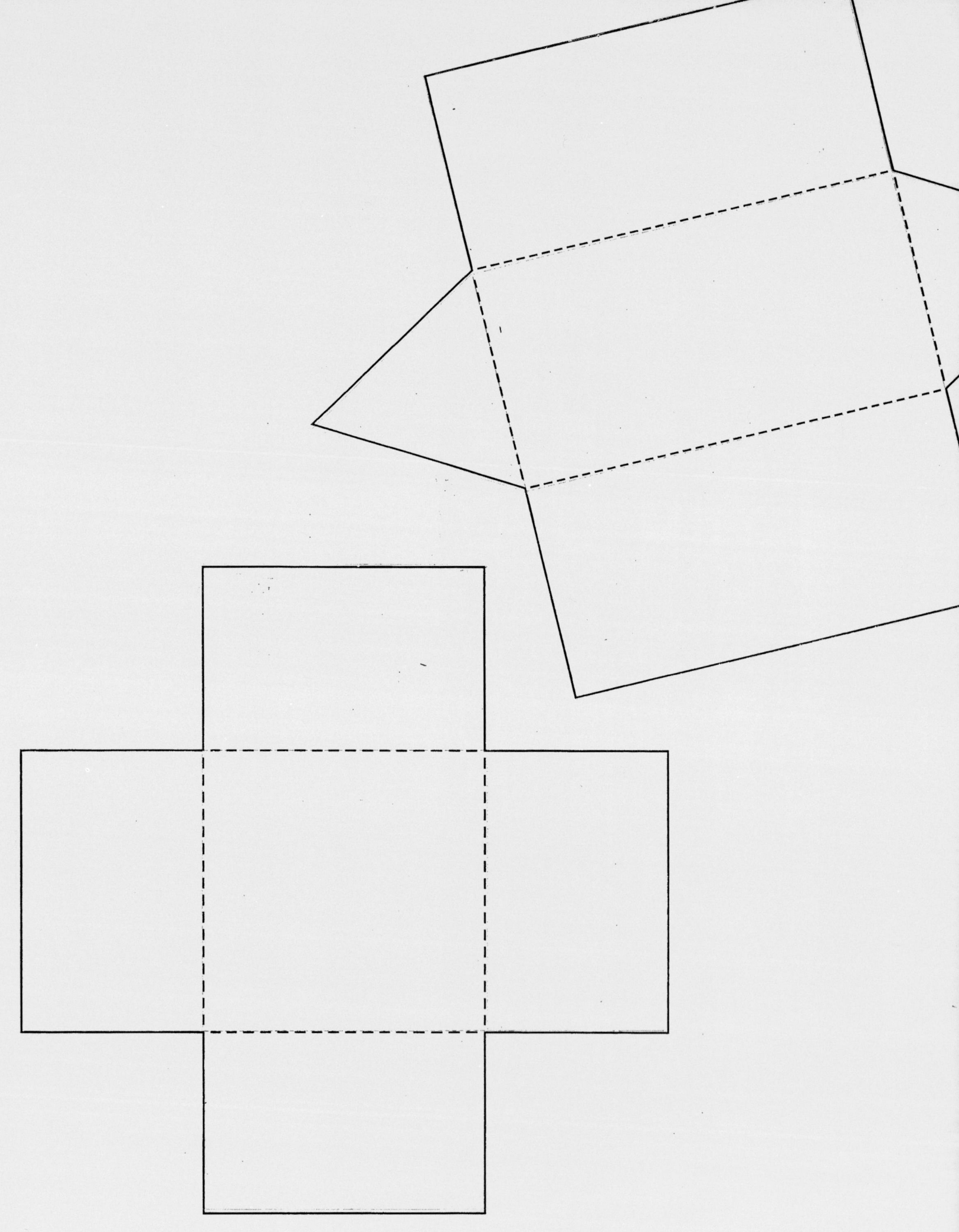

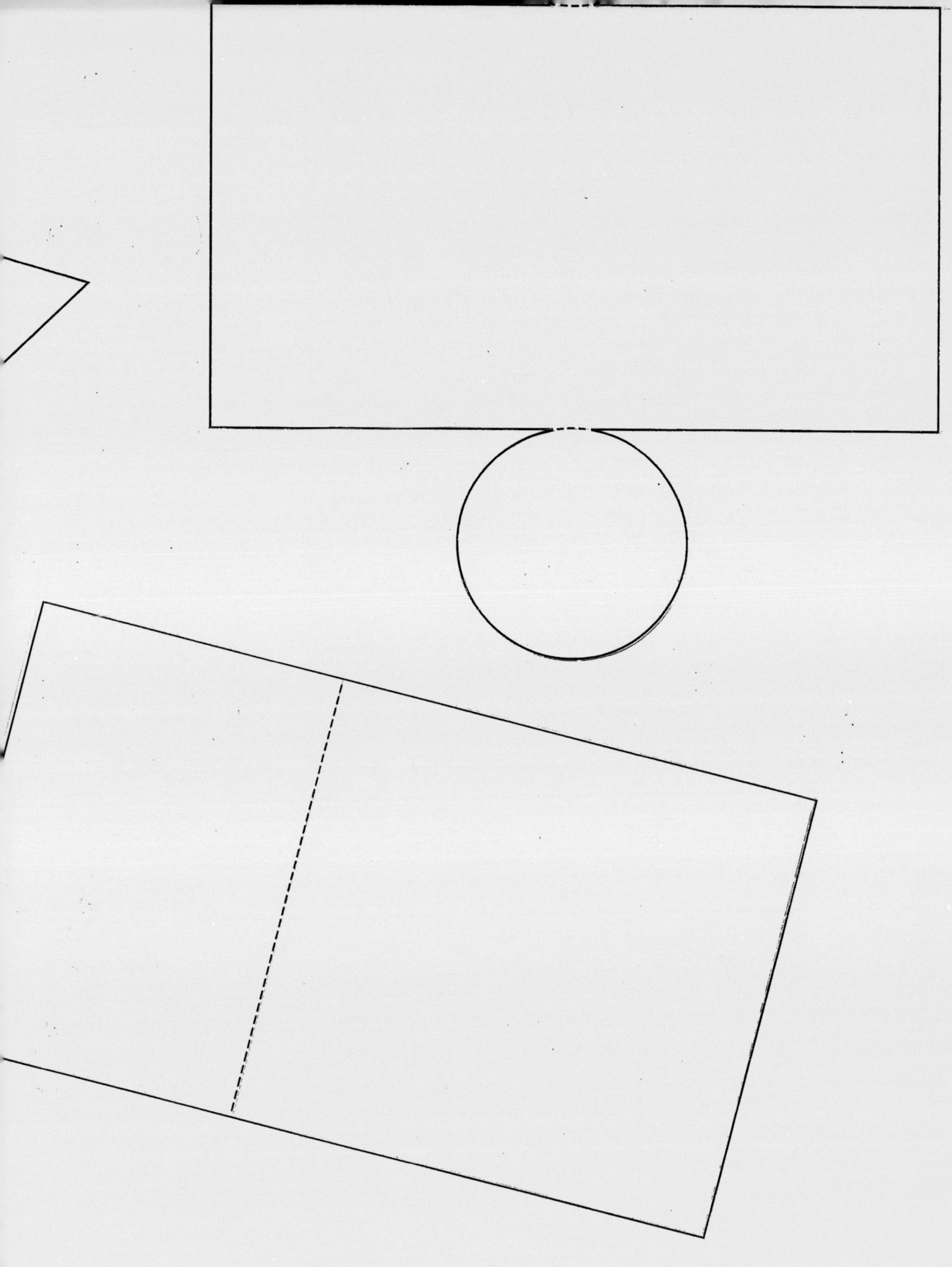

“In the years following the financial crisis, a cultural ‘turn to passion’ may be observed in the sphere of work as masses of newly unemployed workers are advised by career guides to take the opportunity to pause and consider their passions and dreams. ‘What do you like: what makes your heart sing’ are the various therapeutic cliches offered to workers who have to re-enter a job scarce marketplace.”
Renyi Hong, “Finding passion in work: Media, passion and career guides”

This photo was taken in a co-working office space in Brooklyn, NY. Pictured are a number of pattern and color elements for furniture and interior design, evoking leisure, domestic comfort in the workspace and work as a lifestyle. The ethos of this co-working venture espoused community, social and career networking. After a failed public buyout in 2019, the company that managed this space announced the outsourcing of roughly 1,000 cleaning and building maintenance staffers whose work was to maintain the upkeep of the interior and exterior facade. They were given the opportunity to take new jobs at any of the outsourcing partners.

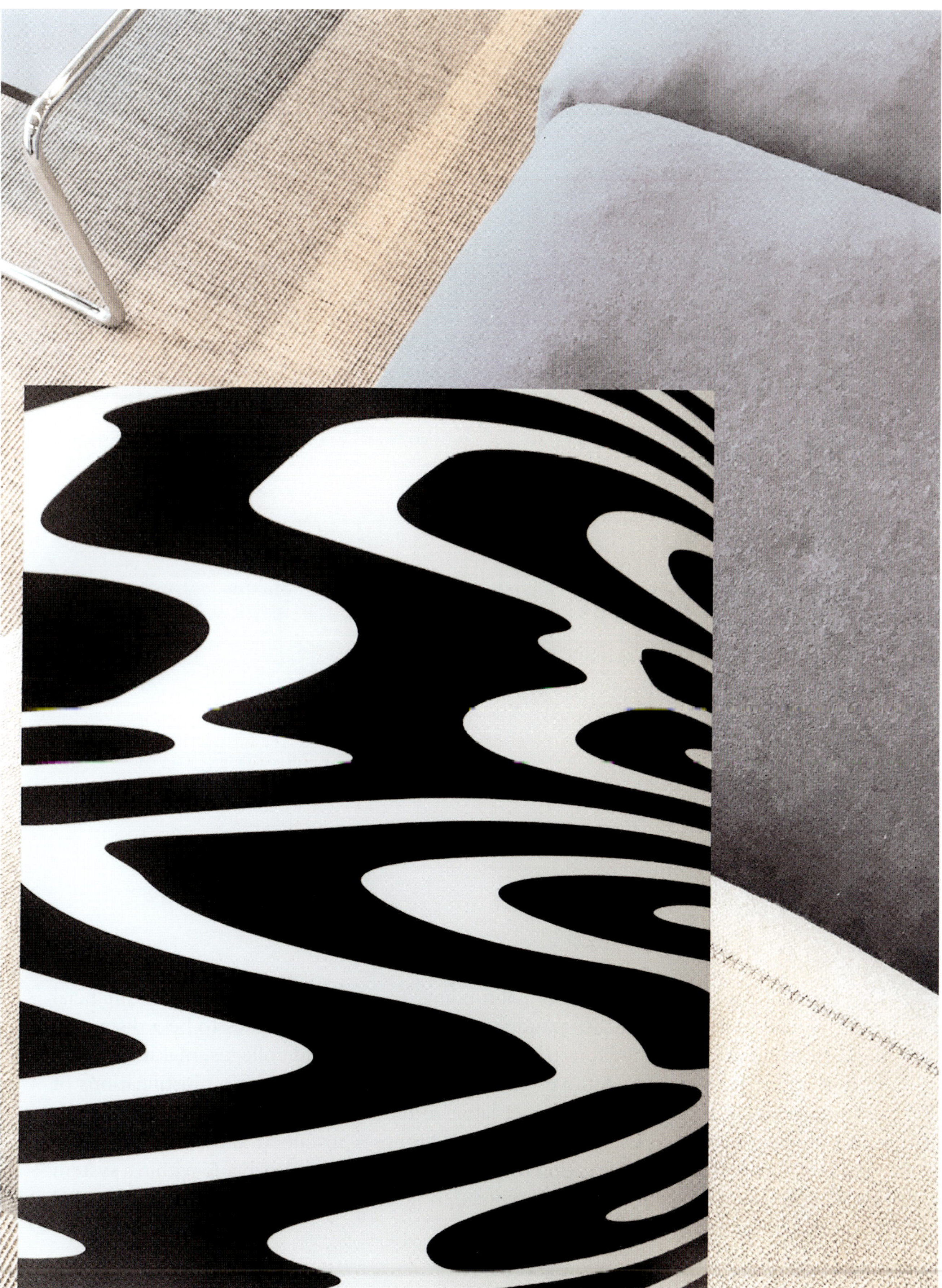

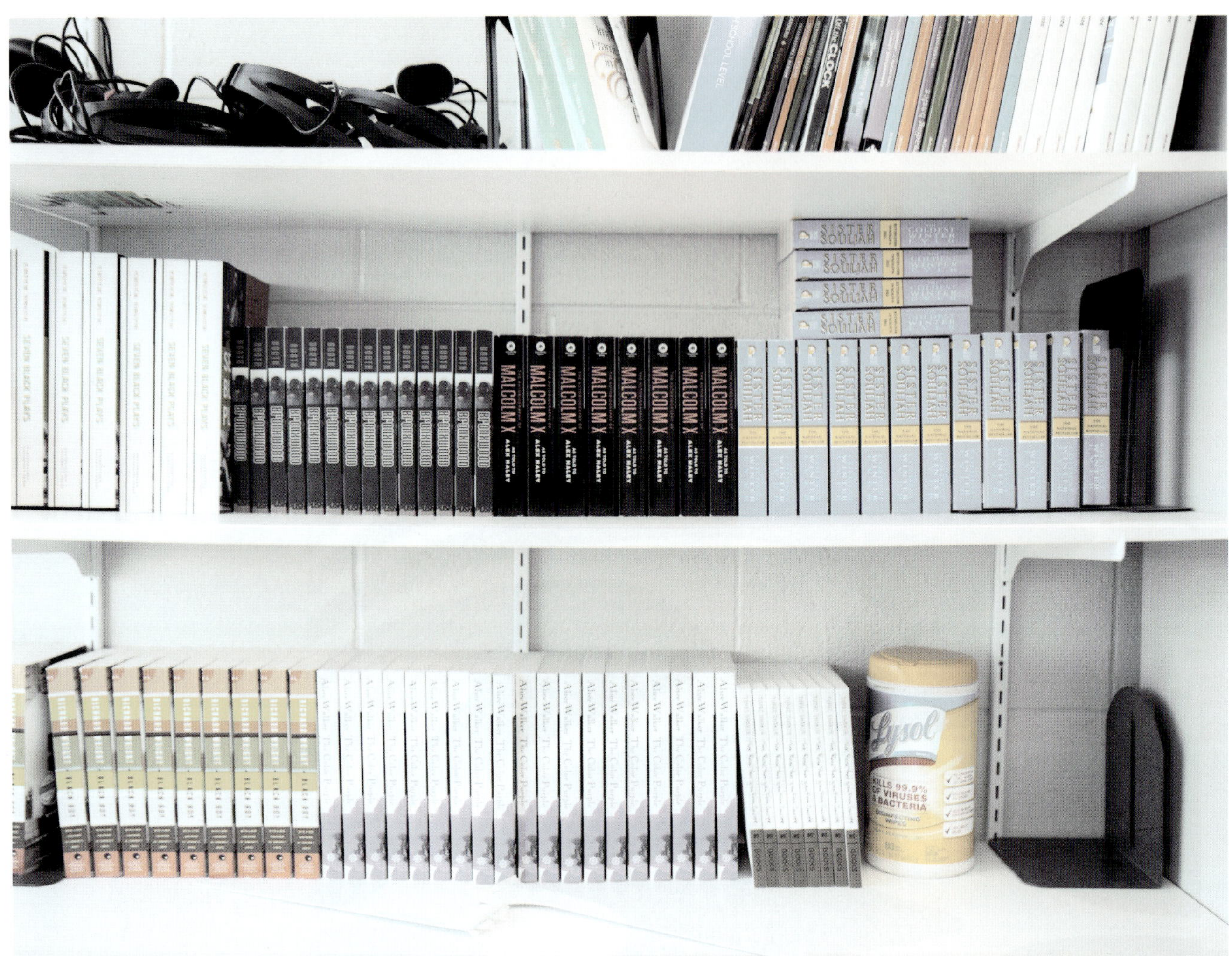

Due to reductions in federal educational funding, accelerated by the 2007–08 financial crisis and an international health pandemic in 2020, there continues to be a disinvestment in tenure track teaching positions in US universities and colleges, making the job market strikingly more competitive for long-term employment. Using justifications of financial restraint for employing adjunct labor to fill the void, many institutions do not make hiring people from racially marginalized groups a sustained and focused priority outside of satisfying affirmative action requirements. These choices made within a system focused on appeasing white guilt, or privilege, is destined to fail regardless of the global economic circumstances.

108861

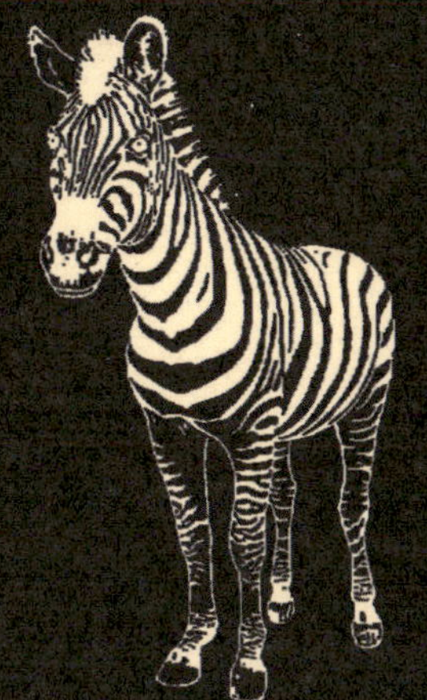

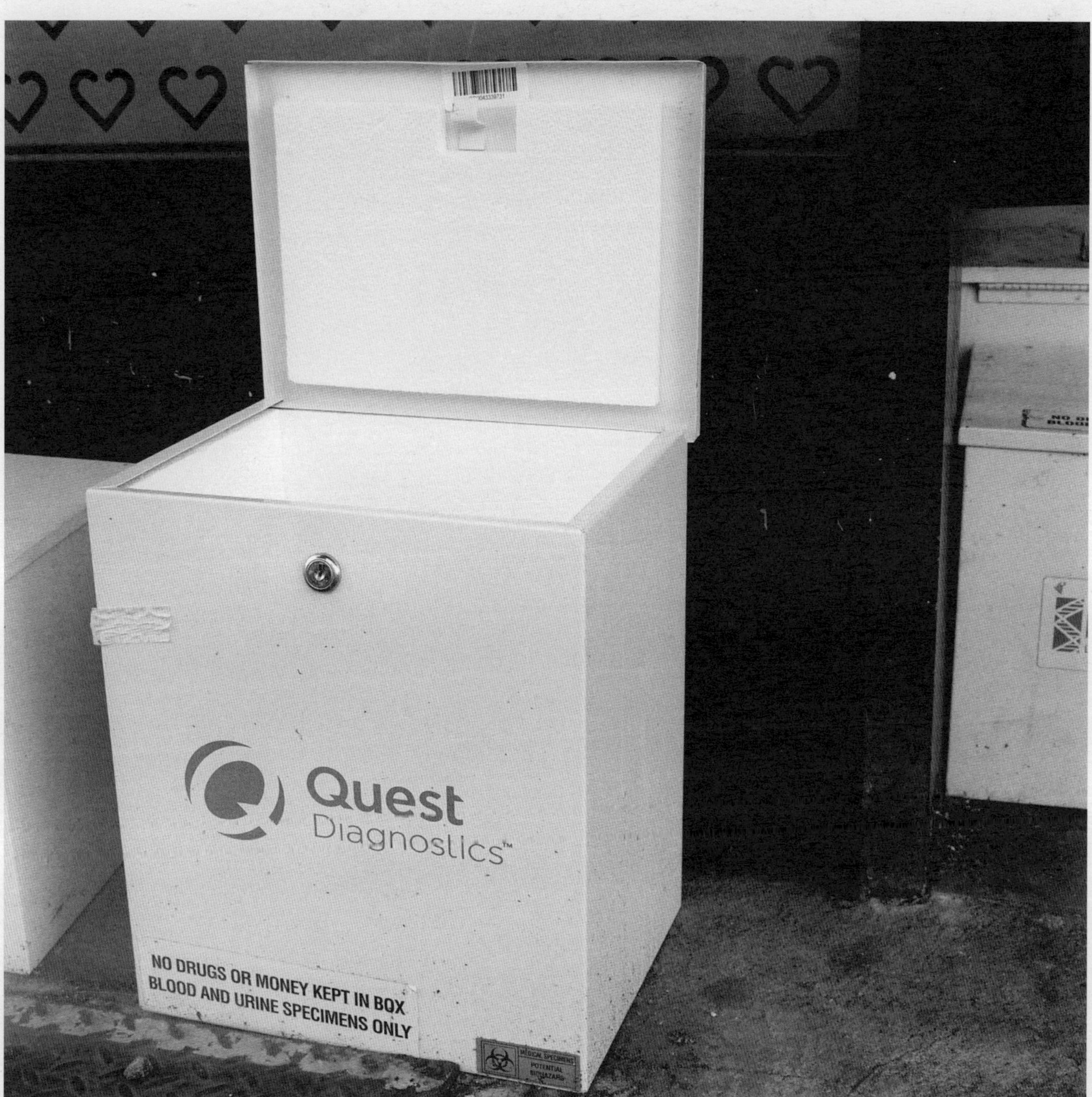
Quest
Diagnostics™
NO DRUGS OR MONEY KEPT IN BOX
BLOOD AND URINE SPECIMENS ONLY

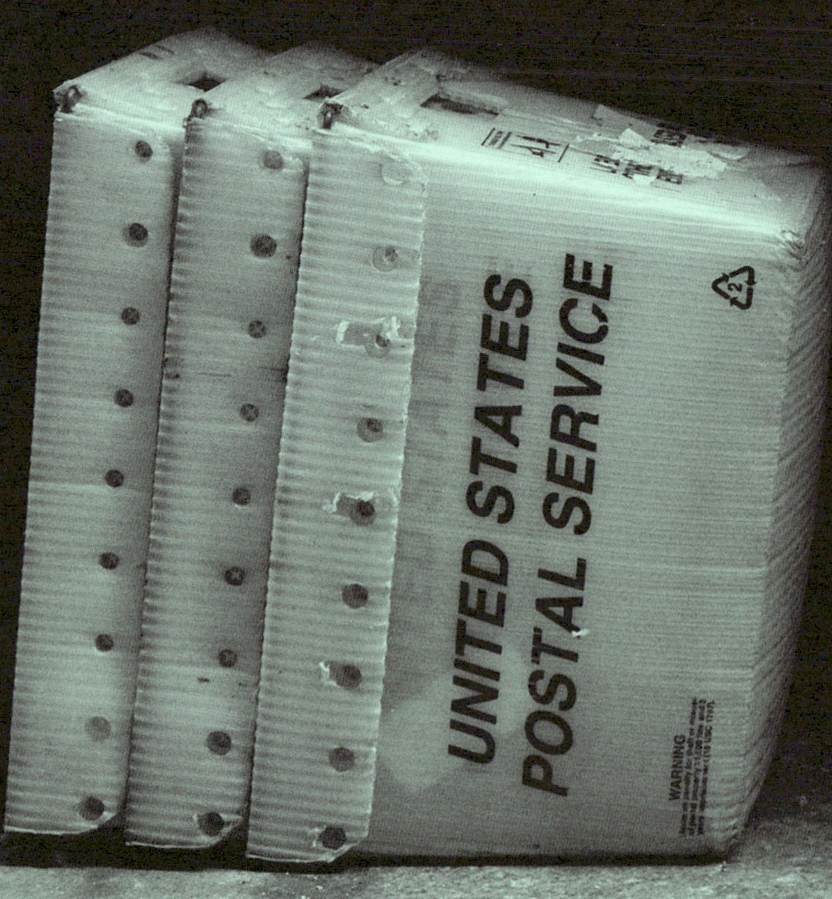
UNITED STATES
POSTAL SERVICE
WARNING

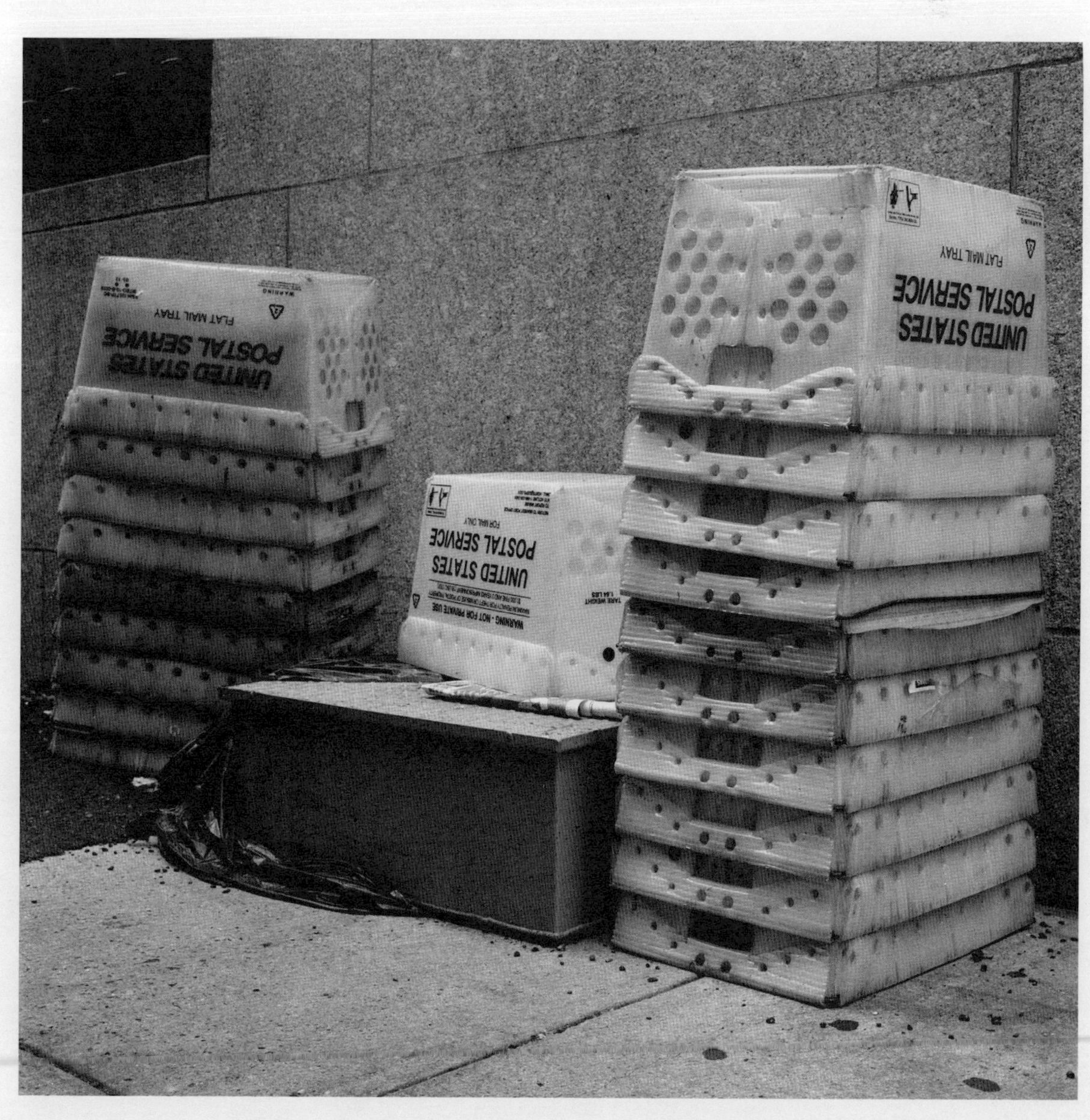
UNITED STATES
POSTAL SERVICE
FLAT MAIL TRAY
UNITED STATES
POSTAL SERVICE
FLAT MAIL TRAY
WARNING - NOT FOR PRIVATE USE
UNITED STATES
POSTAL SERVICE
FOR MAIL ONLY

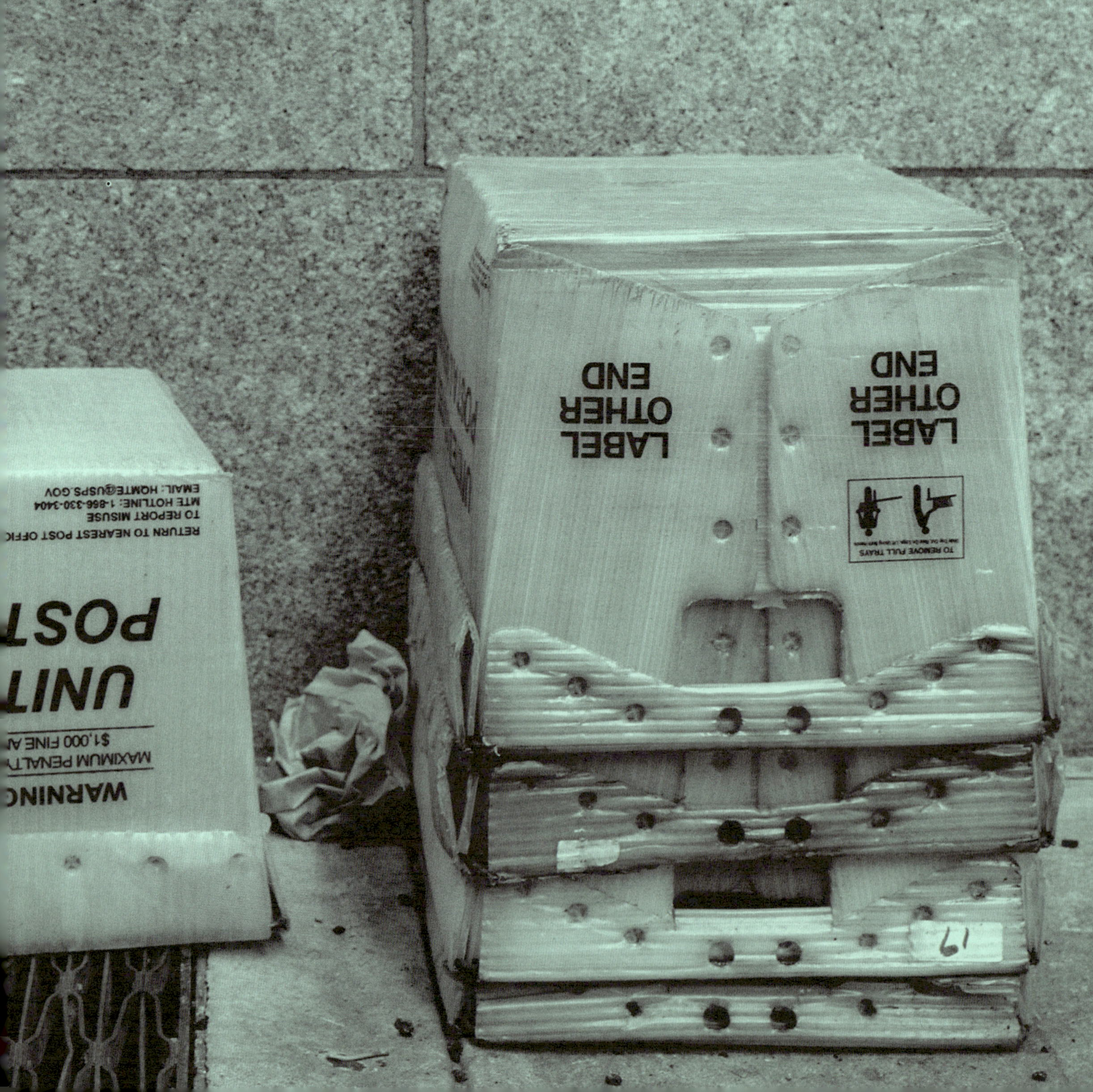
LABEL OTHER END
LABEL OTHER END
TO REMOVE FULL TRAYS
TO REPORT MISUSE
MTE HOTLINE: 1-866-330-3404
EMAIL: HOMTE@USPS.GOV
17

103861

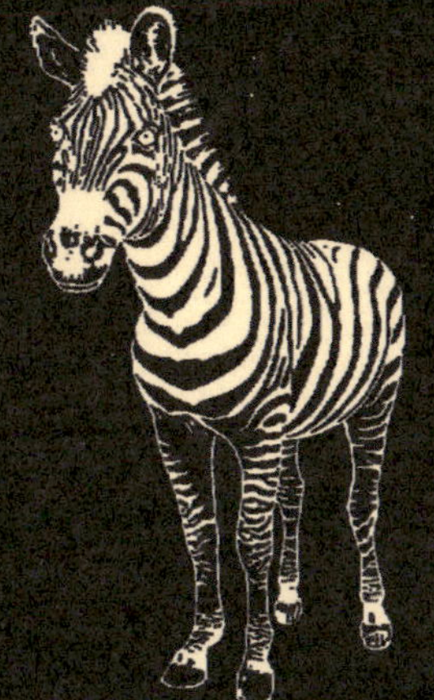

ober 1987

UNITED STATES
GENERAL ACCOUNTING OFFICE

GAO

[illegible]
Parren J. Mitchell, House of Representatives

January 1987

AFFIRMATIVE ACTION:

Social Security Can Do More to Improve Blacks' Rep[illegible]ntation [illegible] Its Wo[illegible]

037[illegible]

GAO/[illegible]D-87-[illegible]

United States General Accounting Office

GAO

Fact Sheet for the Honorable Julian C. Dixon, House of Representatives

September 1994

EQUAL EMPLOYMENT OPPORTUNITY

Displacement Rates, Unemployment Spells, and Reemployment Wages by Race

United States General Accounting Office

GAO

Testimony

Before the Committee on Governmental Affairs
United States Senate

For Release on Delivery
Expected at
9:30 a.m. EDT
Wednesday
May 26, 1993

FEDERAL EMPLOYMENT

Progress of Women and Minorities in Key Federal Jobs and Handling of EEO Complaints at the Bureau of Alcohol, Tobacco, and Firearms

Statement of
Nancy Kingsbury, Director,
Federal Human Resource Management Issues,
General Government Division

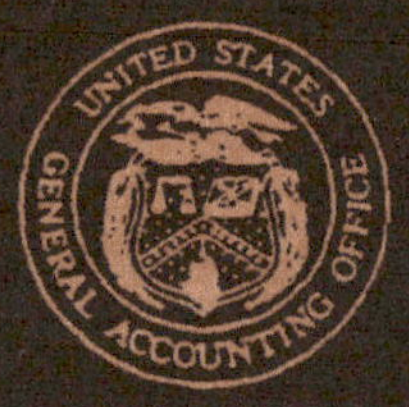

GAO/T-GGD-93-33

6911

REPORT BY THE

Comptroller General OF THE UNITED STATES

The Affirmative Action Programs In Three Bureaus Of The Department Of Justice Should Be Improved

As requested by the Subcommittee on Civil and Constitutional Rights, House Committee on the Judiciary, GAO evaluated the operation of the affirmative action program of the Department of Justice and each of its component organizations.

Some progress has been made toward improving the employment situation of women and minorities in Justice's Offices, Boards, and Divisions; Federal Prison System; and Law Enforcement Assistance Administration, but a disparity between women and men and minorities and nonminorities remains. Women and minorities are generally concentrated in nonprofessional occupations.

Improvements can be made to strengthen the bureaus' affirmative action program and increase the representation of women and minorities in professional jobs.

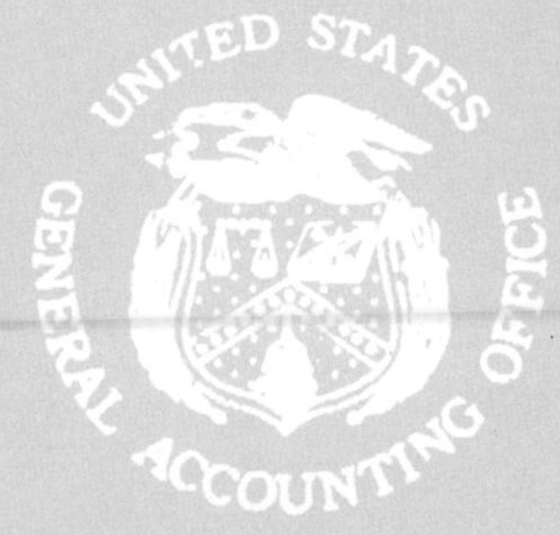

FPCD-78-53
JULY 5, 1978

BY THE COMPTROLLER GENERAL

Report To The Congress

OF THE UNITED STATES

9244

The Department Of Justice Should Improve Its Equal Employment Opportunity Programs

Greater efforts are needed to bring minorities and women into the Justice Department's work force. Representation of minorities and women at higher levels, in more responsible jobs, and in certain occupational groups remains low. Using a GAO-developed forecasting tool and Justice's statistics on General Schedule employees, it is anticipated that employment and advancement of minorities and women in the General Schedule ranks may not increase greatly over the next 5 years. GAO found a disparity in pay levels between white men and most women and minorities in certain occupational categories.

Management at all levels should exert more leadership and commitment to accomplishing equal employment opportunity objectives and be held accountable for achieving them.

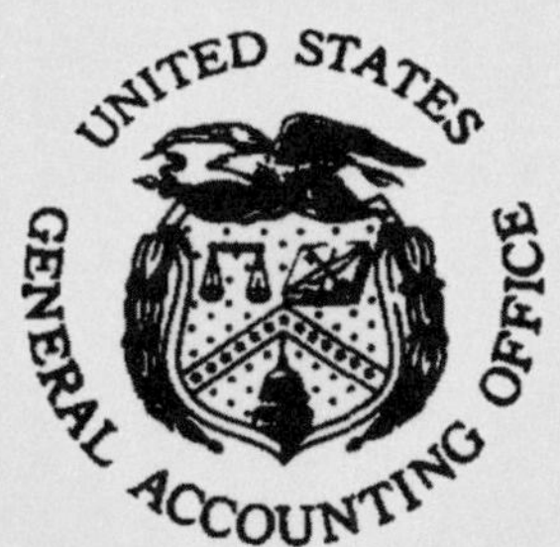

FPCD-78-79

FEBRUARY 23, 1979

BY THE U.S. GENERAL ACCOUNTING OFFICE

Report To The Honorable Shirley Chisholm House Of Representatives

The National Institute Of Education Should Further Increase Minority And Female Participation In Its Activities

The National Institute of Education has improved its equal employment opportunity profile during the last 2 years and is encouraging more minority- and female-oriented educational research and development with its sponsors.

The Institute's employment profile generally has a good representation of minorities and women. However, the representation of minorities and women in the work forces of Institute-funded organizations has not been good, and few institutions operated by minorities and women received Institute grants and contracts.

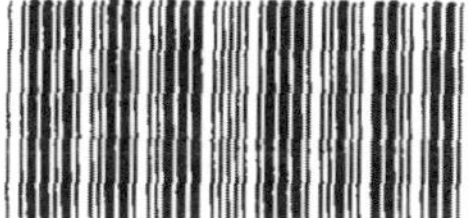

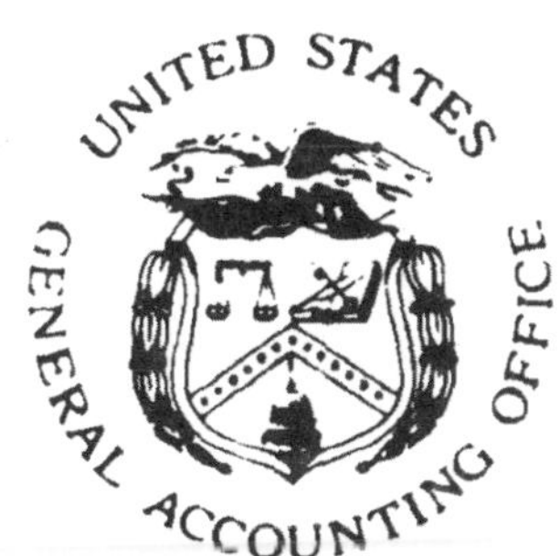

HRD-81-3

NOVEMBER 10, 1980

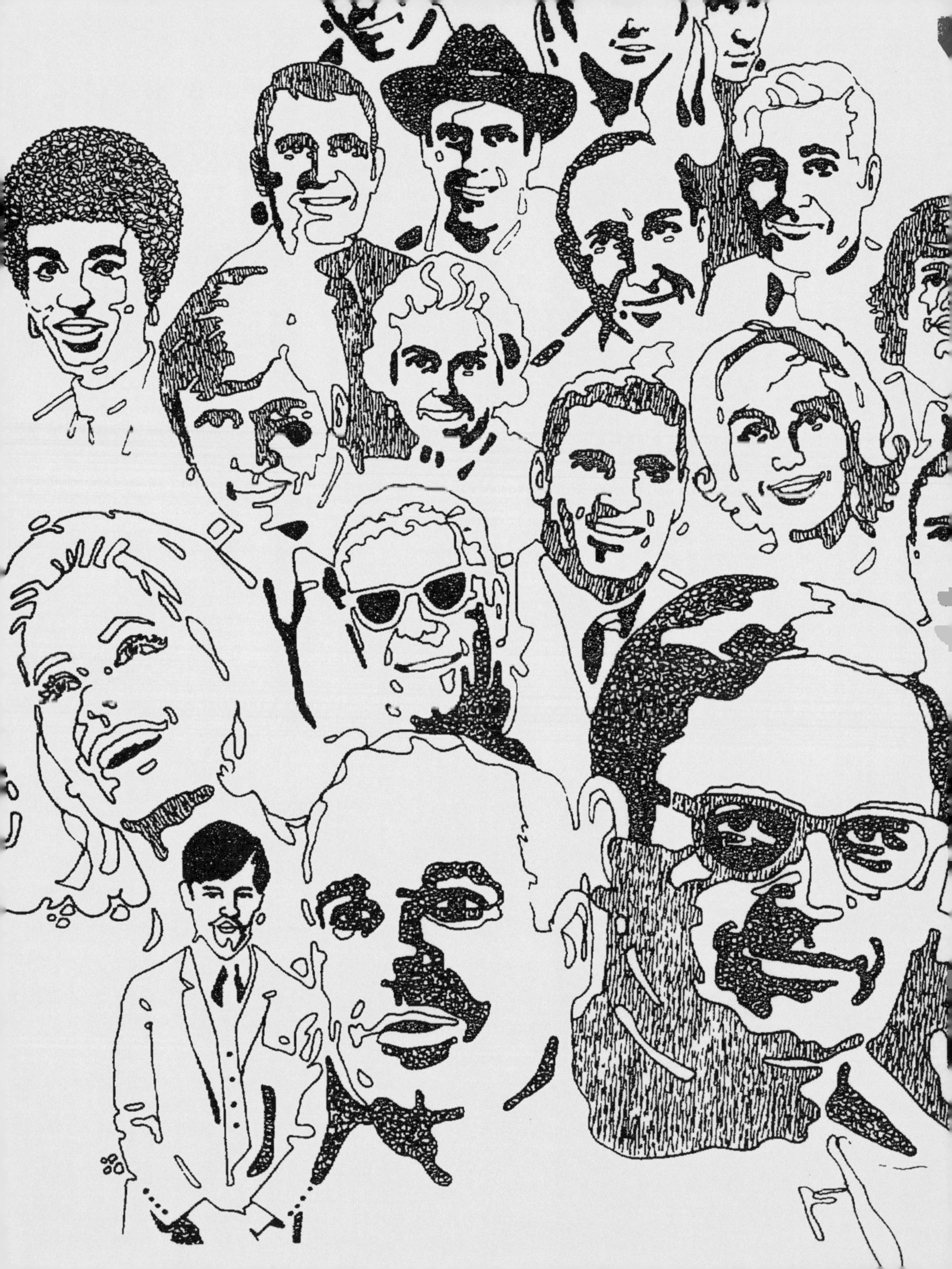

TER 1974

United States Government Accountability Office

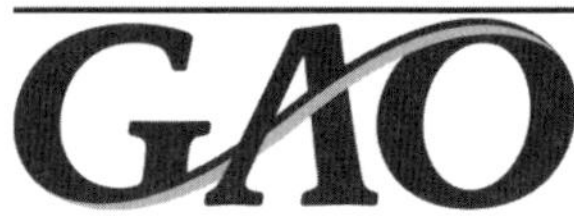

Testimony
Before the Committee on Financial Services, House of Representatives

For Release on Delivery
Expected at 10:00 a.m. ET
Thursday, June 20, 2019

BOARD DIVERSITY

Strategies to Increase Representation of Women and Minorities

Statement of Chelsa Gurkin, Acting Director, Education, Workforce, and Income Security

women in the workplace

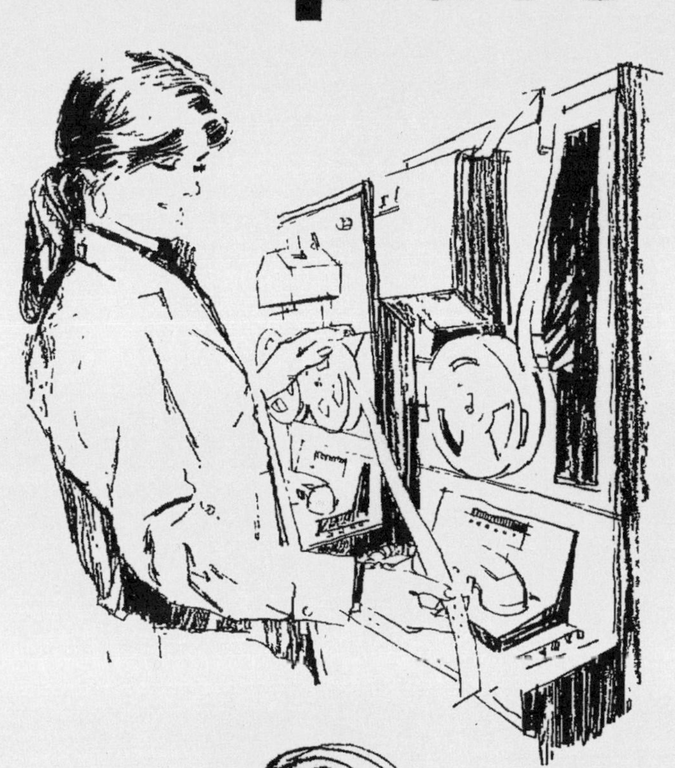

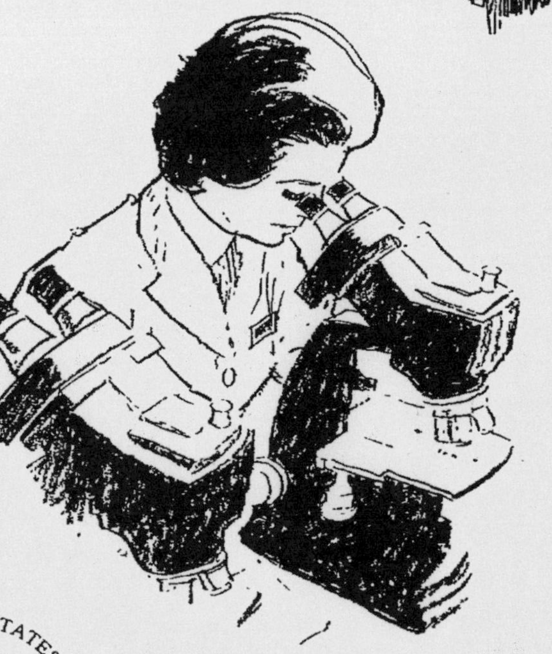

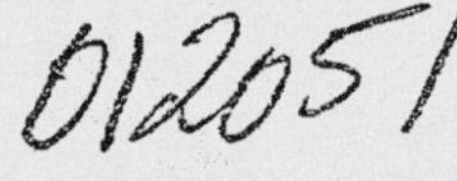

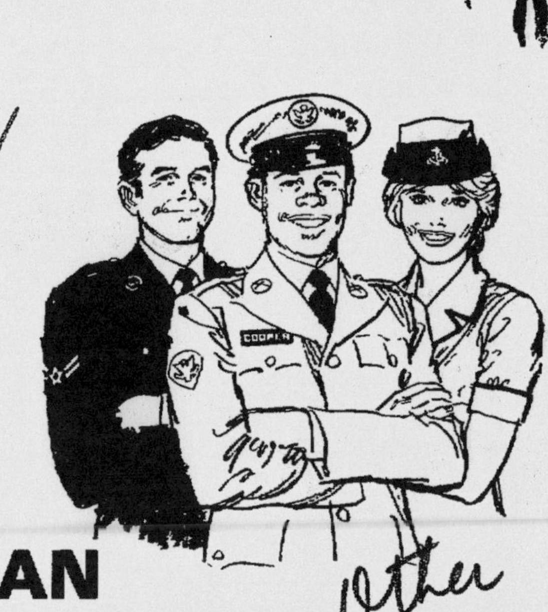

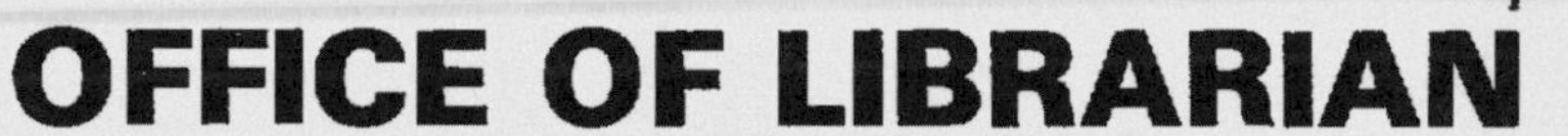

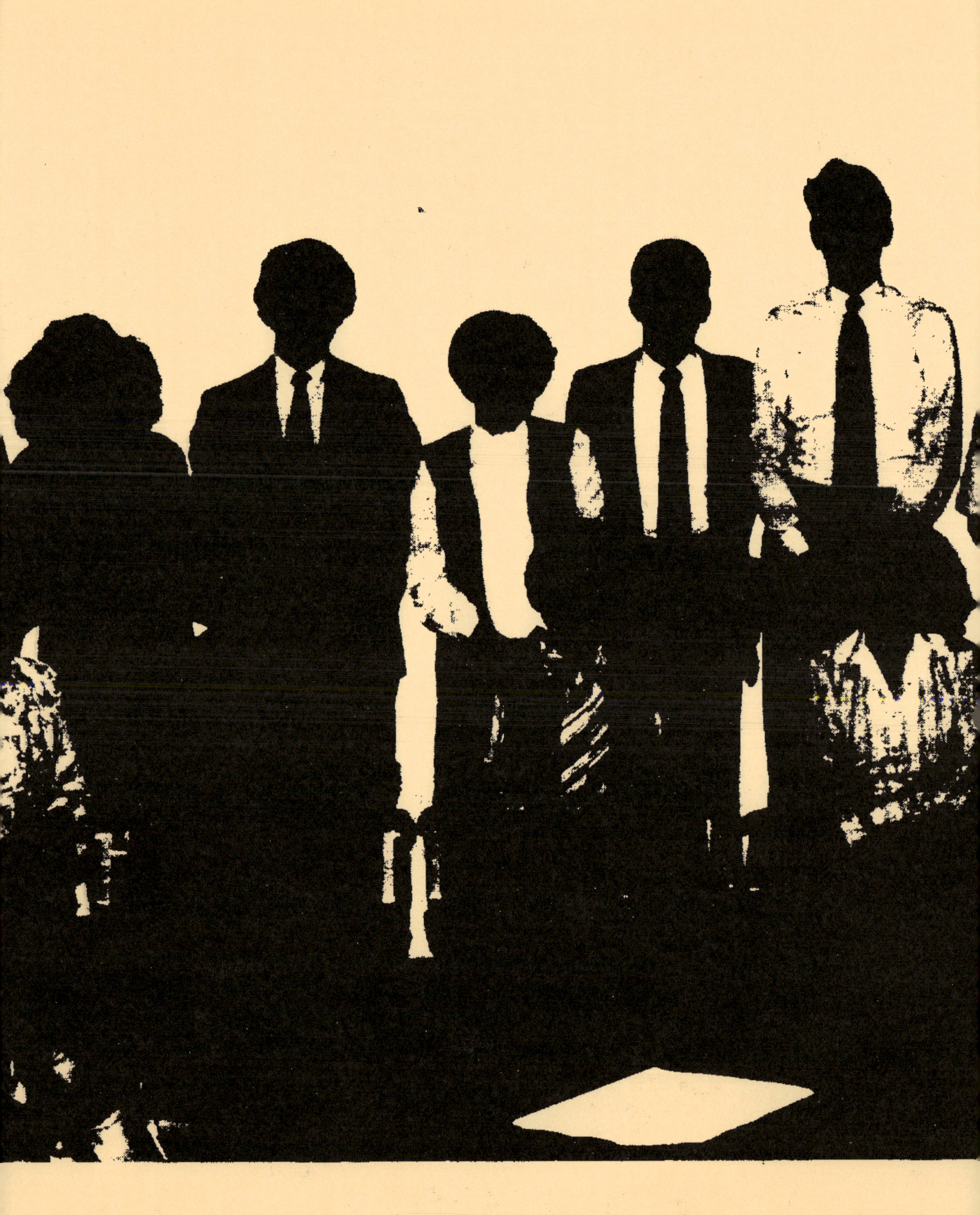

eral Accounting Office's Equal o provide a medium

United States General Accounting Office

GAO

To the Comptroller General

April 1986

Women's Advisory Council 1985 Annual Report

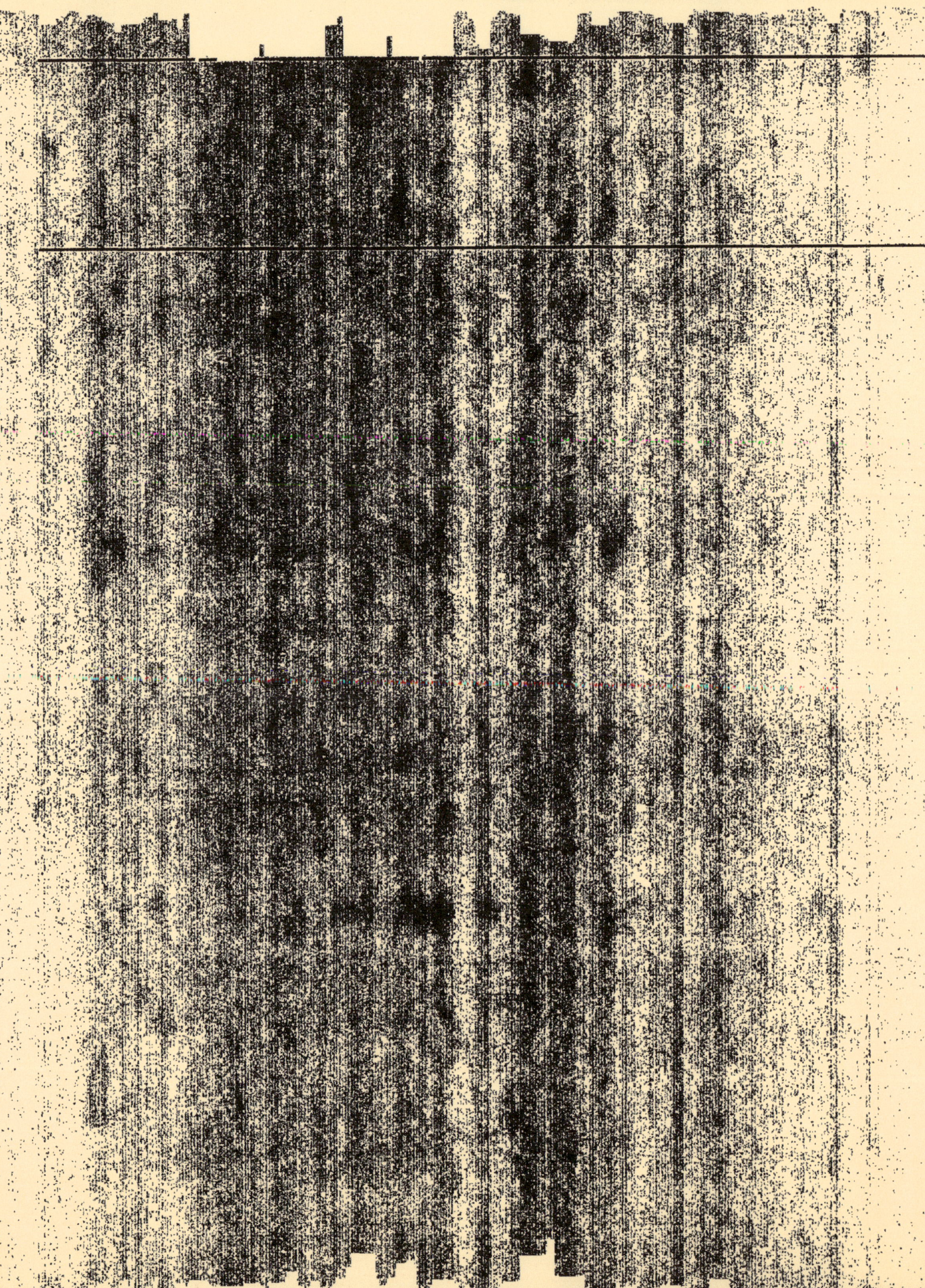

United States General Accounting Office

GAO

Report to the Chairman, Committee on Governmental Affairs, U.S. Senate

May 1991

FEDERAL AFFIRMATIVE ACTION

Better EEOC Guidance and Agency Analysis of Underrepresentation Needed

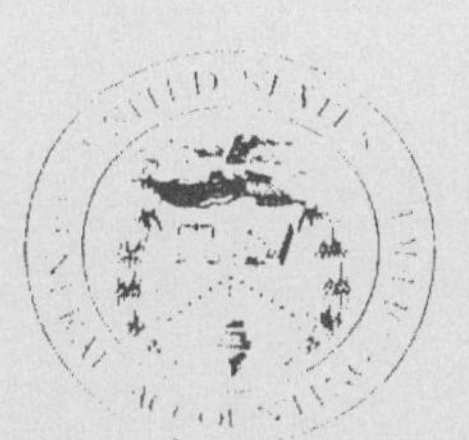

GAO/GGD-91-86

United States General Accounting Office

GAO

Report to the Chairman, Select Committee on Aging, House of Representatives

January 1989

SOCIAL SECURITY ADMINISTRATION

Employment of and Service to Hispanics

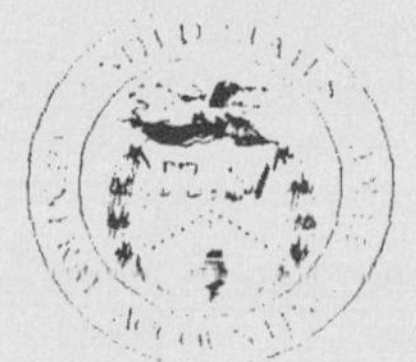

GAO/HRD-89-35

United States Government Accountability Office

GAO

Report to the Ranking Member, Committee on Financial Services, U.S. House of Representatives

April 2013

DIVERSITY MANAGEMENT

Trends and Practices in the Financial Services Industry and Agencies after the Recent Financial Crisis

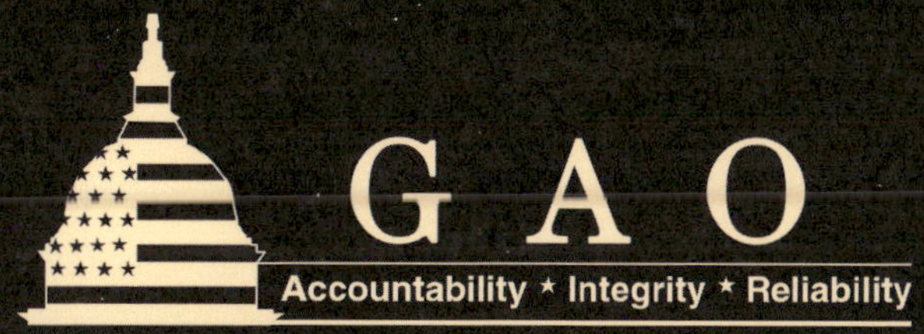

GAO-13-238

United States General Accounting Office

GAO

Report to the Chairman, Committee on Government Operations, House of Representatives

September 1990

EDA

Treatment of Blacks at the Economic Development Administration in the 1980s

GAO/HRD-90-148

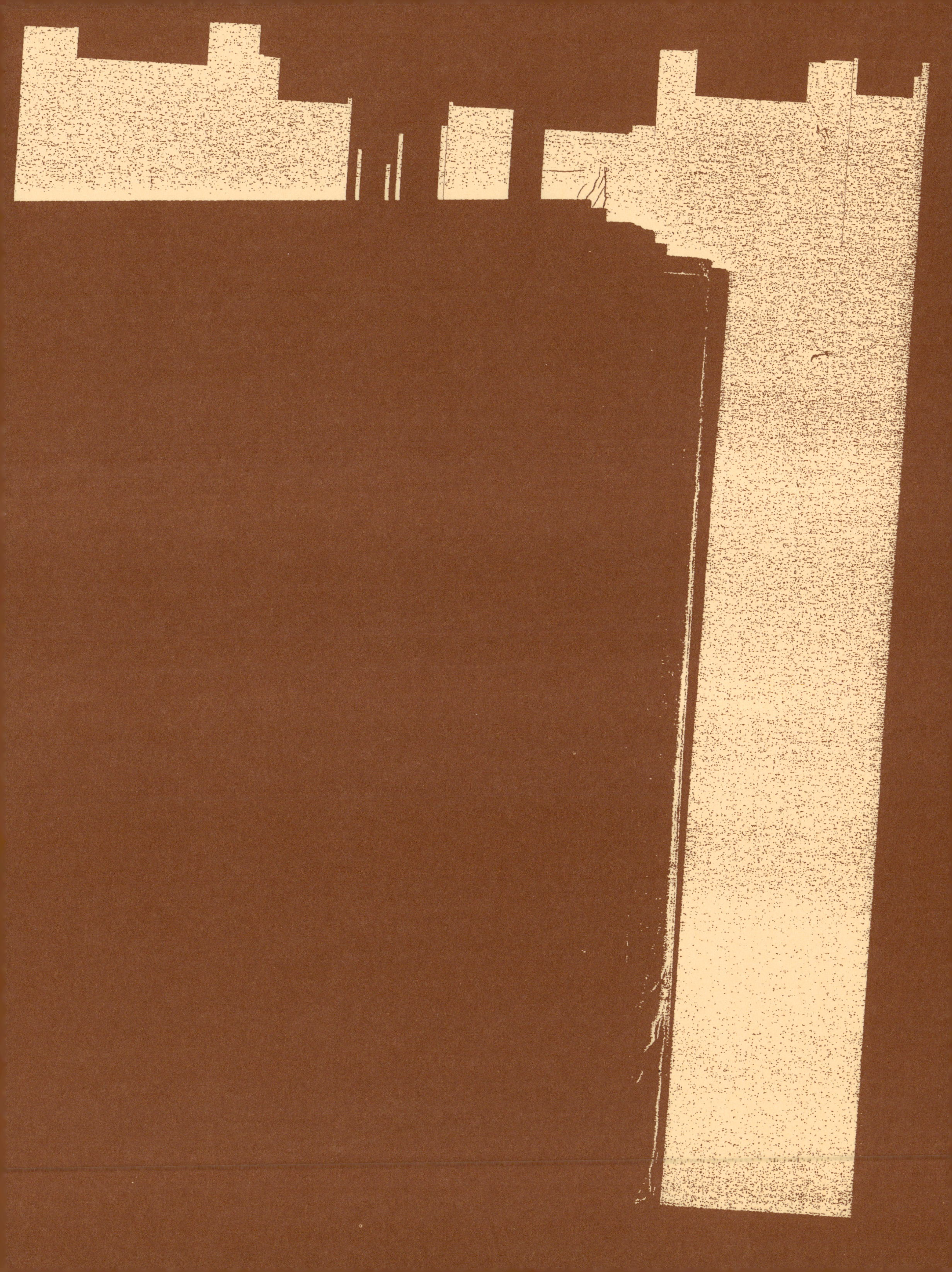

AN EQUAL OPPORTUNITY EMPLOYER

UNITED STATES
GENERAL ACCOUNTING OFFICE
WASHINGTON, D.C. 20548

OFFICIAL BUSINESS
PENALTY FOR PRIVATE USE,$300

POSTAGE AND FEES PAID
U. S. GENERAL ACCOUNTING OFFICE

THIRD CLASS

STUDY BY THE STAFF OF THE U.S.

General Accounting Office

A Compilation Of Federal Laws And Executive Orders For Nondiscrimination And Equal Opportunity Programs

This staff study identifies and provides information about Federal laws and Executive orders which deal with nondiscrimination and equal opportunity programs.

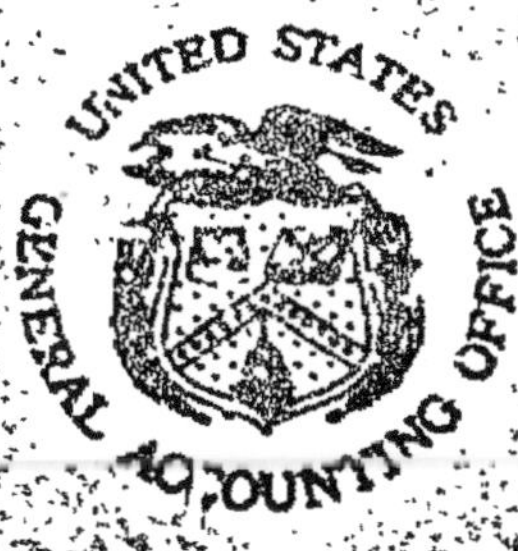

HRD-78-138
AUGUST 2, 1978

United States
General Accounting Office
Washington, D.C. 20548

Official Business
Penalty for Private Use $300

First-Class Mail
Postage & Fees Paid
GAO
Permit No. G100

095090

095091

25

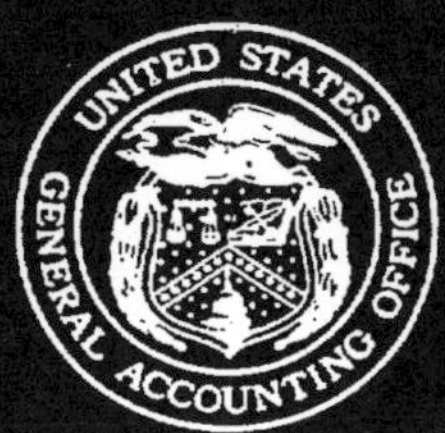

MANUAL FOR
GENERAL GOVERNMENT MATTERS
FEDERAL APPROPRIATIONS

UNITED STATES
GENERAL ACCOUNTING OFFICE
OFFICE OF GENERAL COUNSEL

706230

United States General Accounting Office

GAO

Report to the Honorable Dana Rohrabacher, House of Representatives

December 1995

DEPARTMENT OF EDUCATION

Efforts by the Office for Civil Rights to Resolve Asian-American Complaints

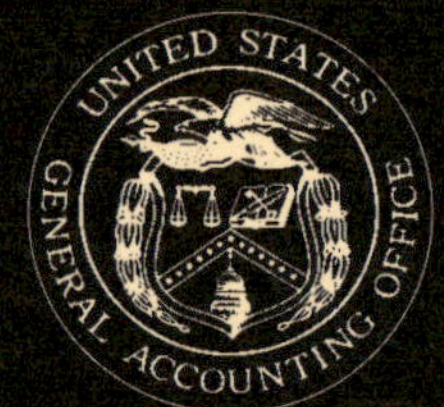

GAO/HEHS-96-23

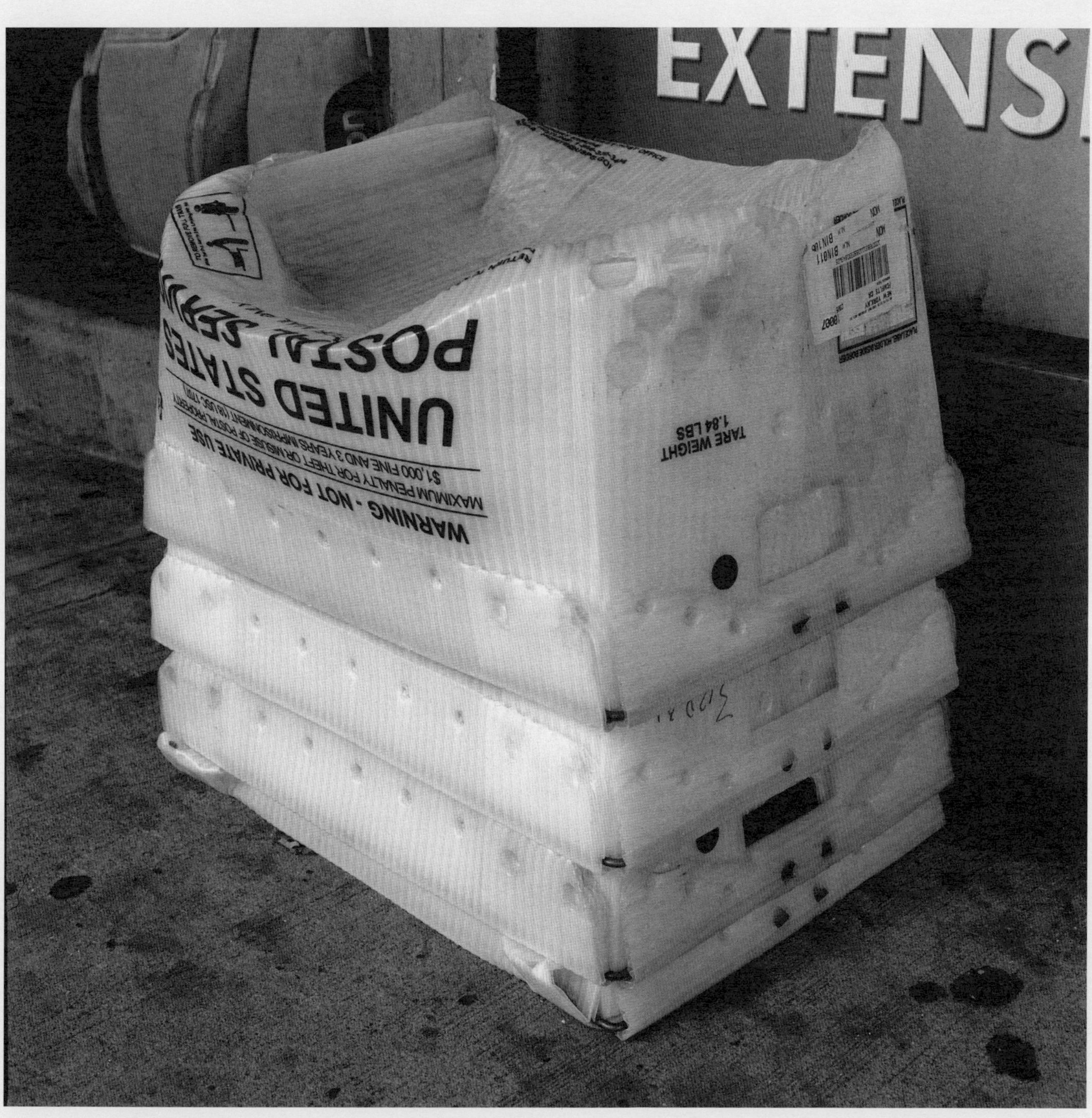
EXTENS
WARNING - NOT FOR PRIVATE USE
MAXIMUM PENALTY FOR THEFT OR MISUSE OF POSTAL PROPERTY
$1,000 FINE AND 3 YEARS IMPRISONMENT (18 USC 1707)
UNITED STATES
TARE WEIGHT
1.84 LBS

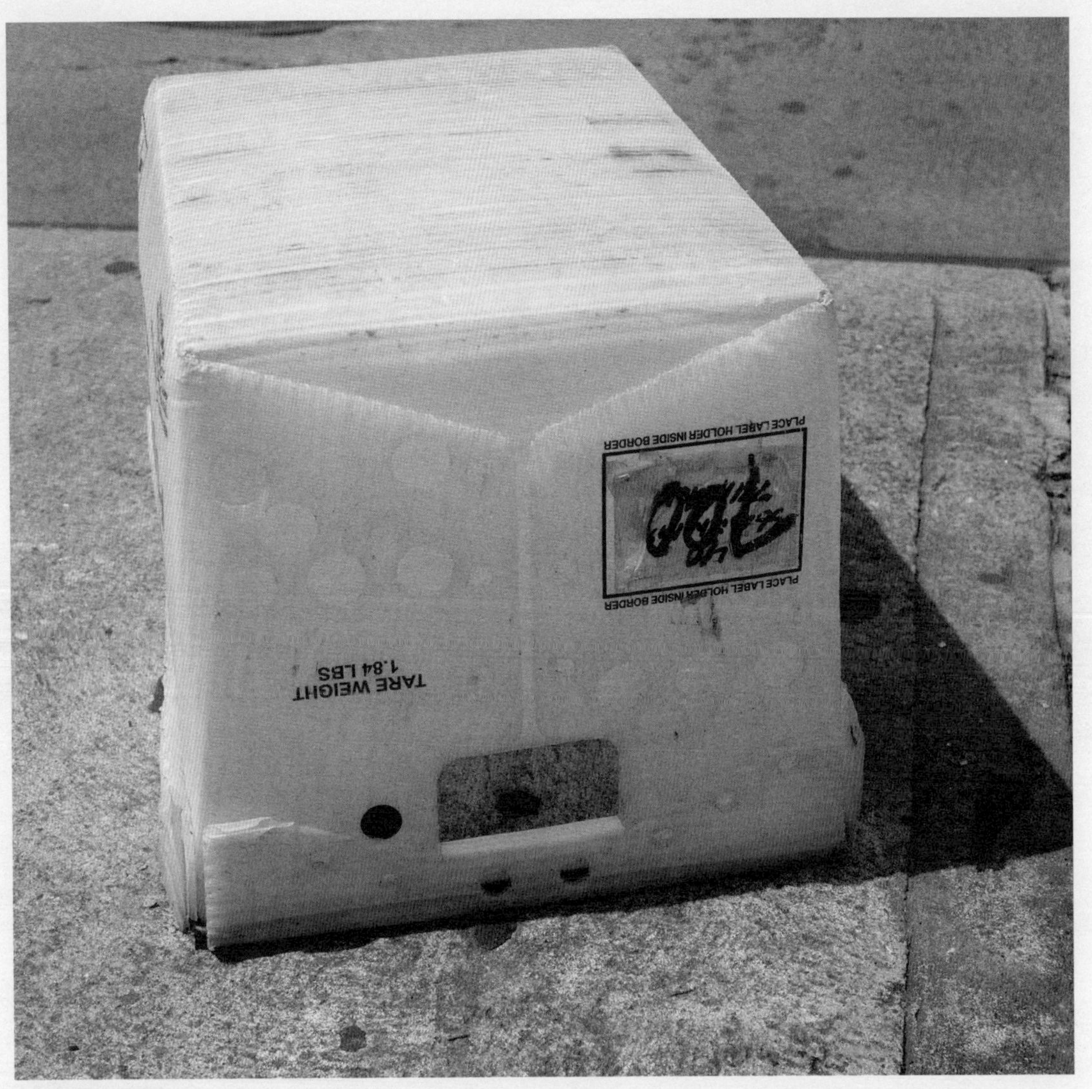
PLACE LABEL HOLDER INSIDE BORDER
PLACE LABEL HOLDER INSIDE BORDER
TARE WEIGHT
1.84 LBS

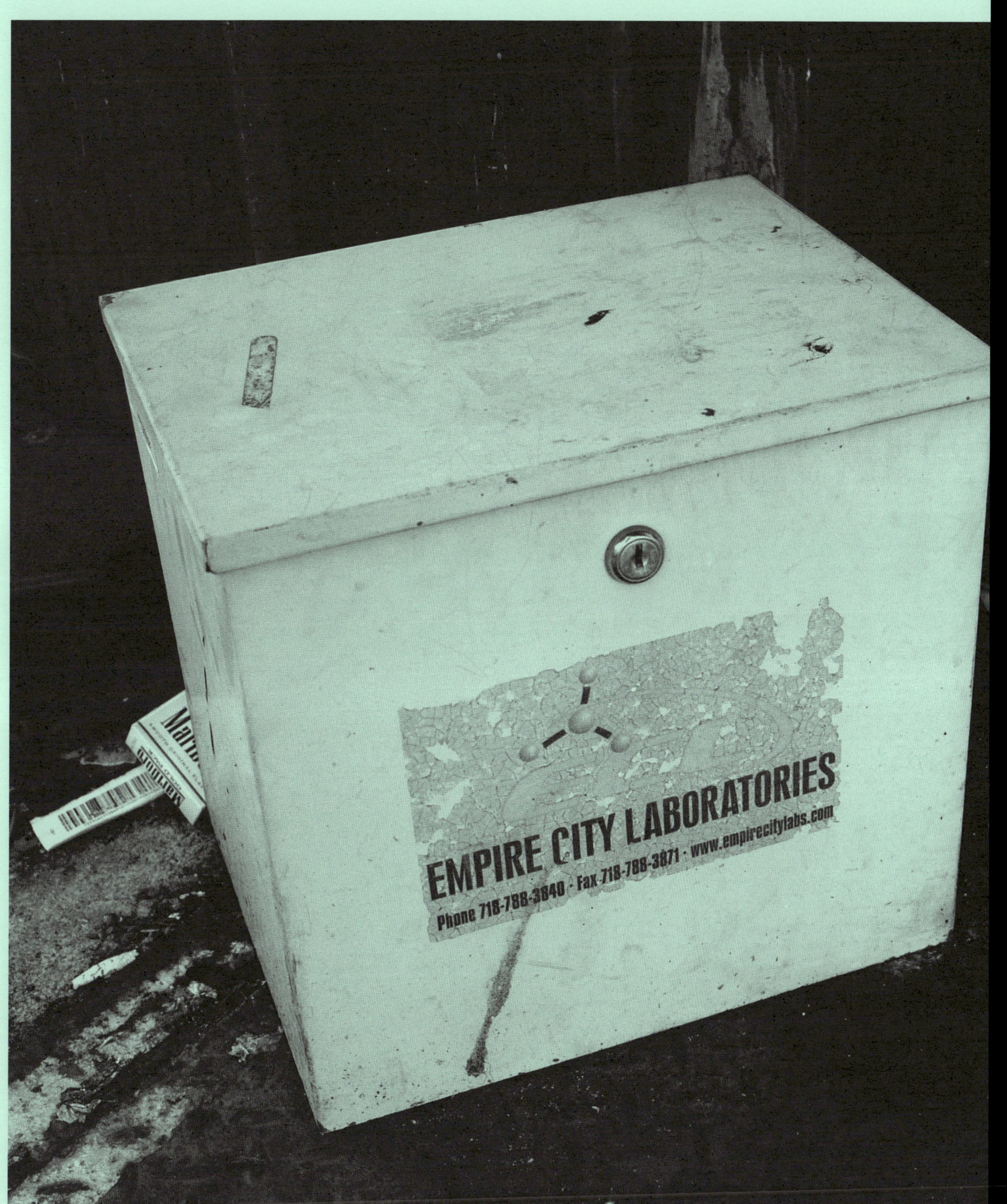
EMPIRE CITY LABORATORIES
Phone 718-788-3840 · Fax 718-788-3871 · www.empirecitylabs.com

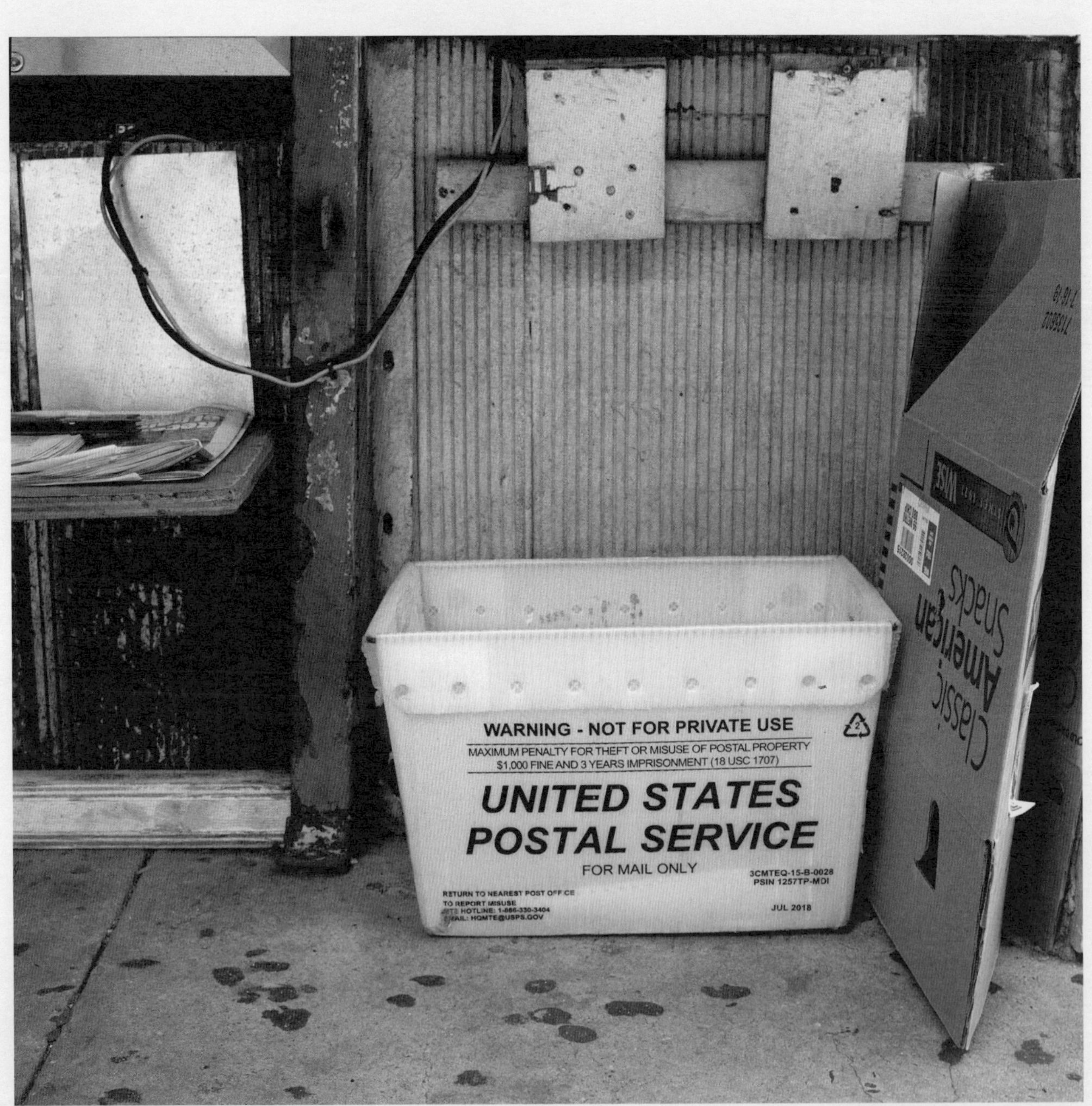
WARNING - NOT FOR PRIVATE USE
MAXIMUM PENALTY FOR THEFT OR MISUSE OF POSTAL PROPERTY
$1,000 FINE AND 3 YEARS IMPRISONMENT (18 USC 1707)
UNITED STATES
POSTAL SERVICE
FOR MAIL ONLY
3CMTEQ-15-B-0028
PSIN 1257TP-MDI
JUL 2018
Classic
American
Snacks

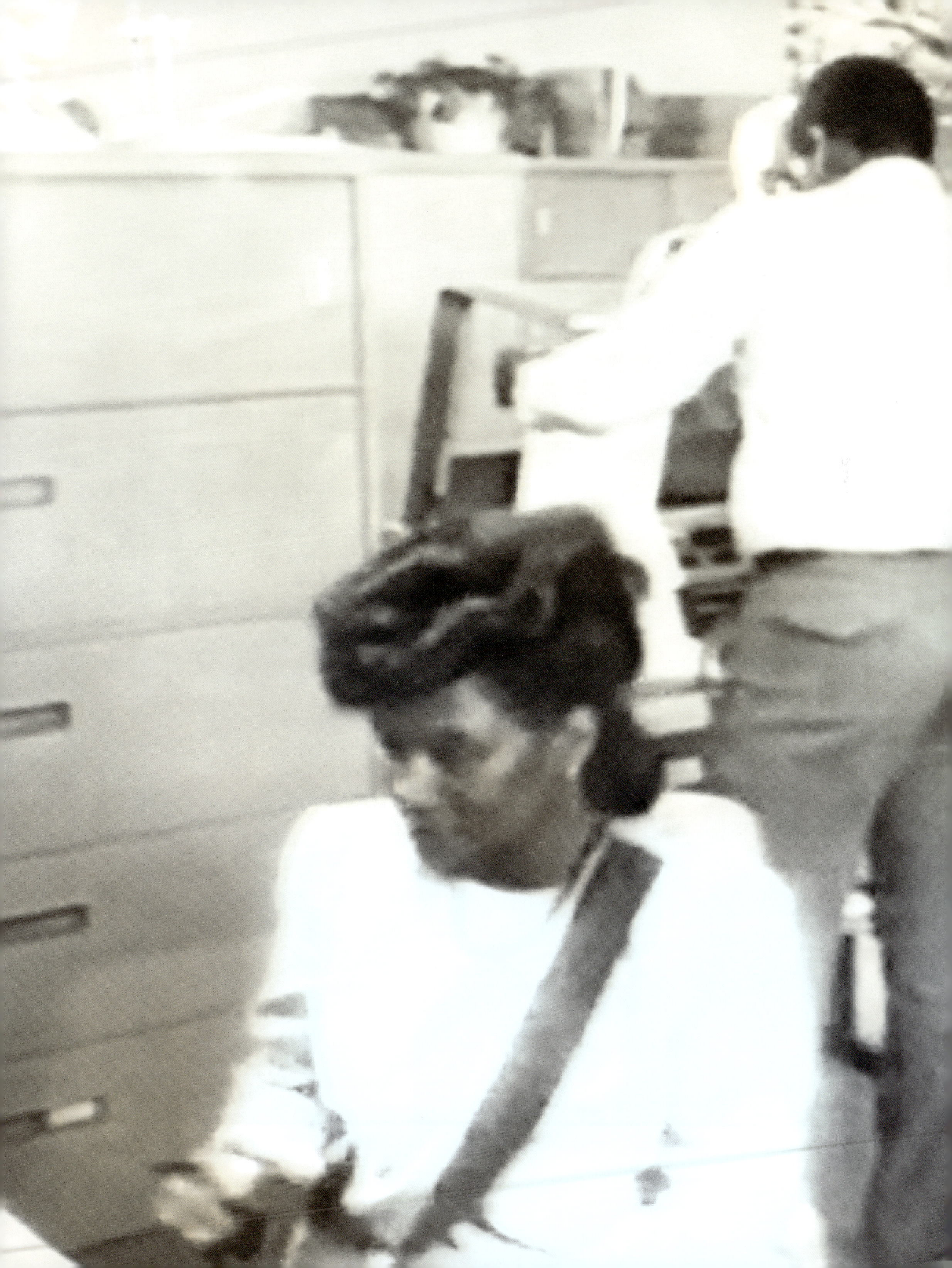

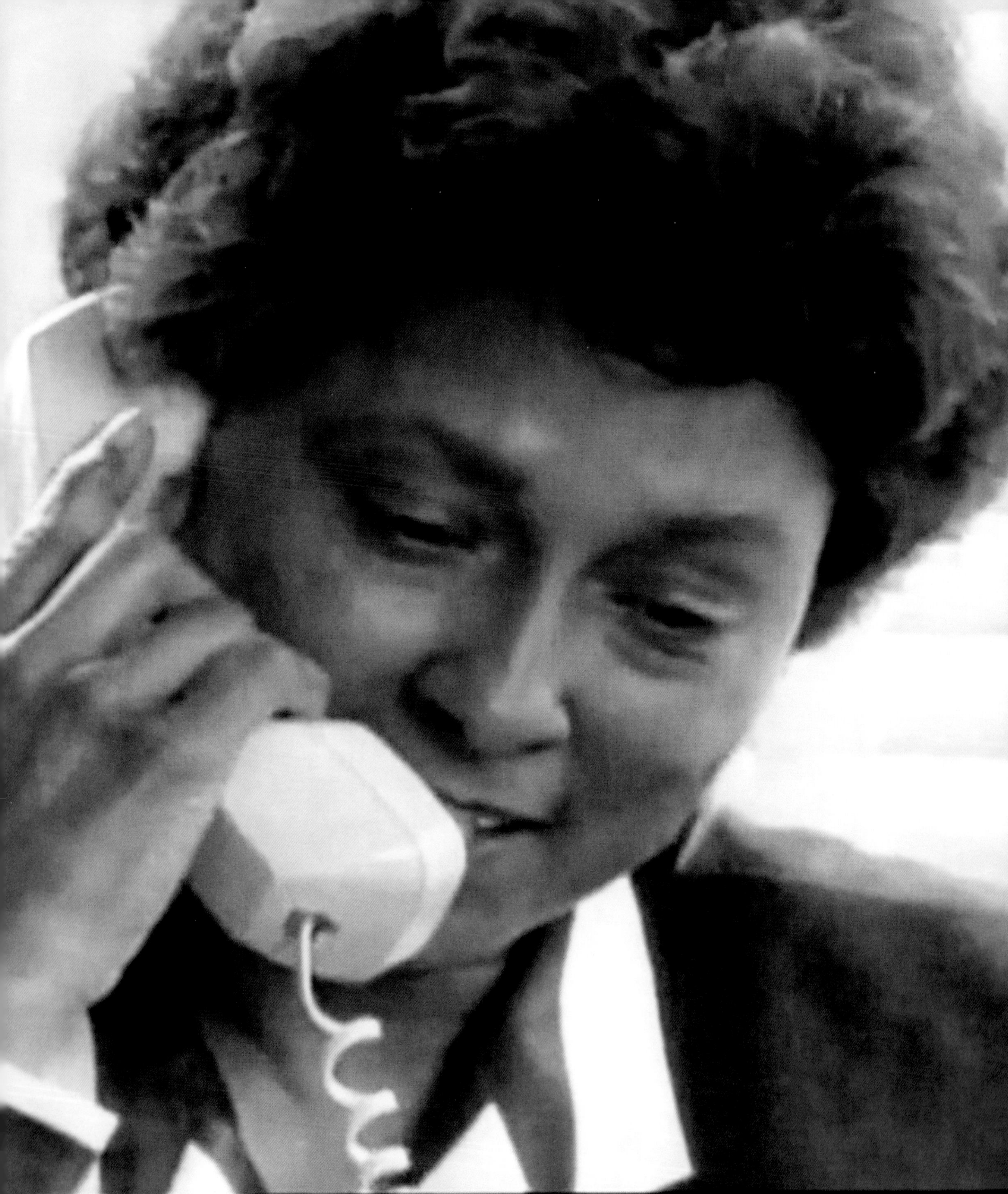

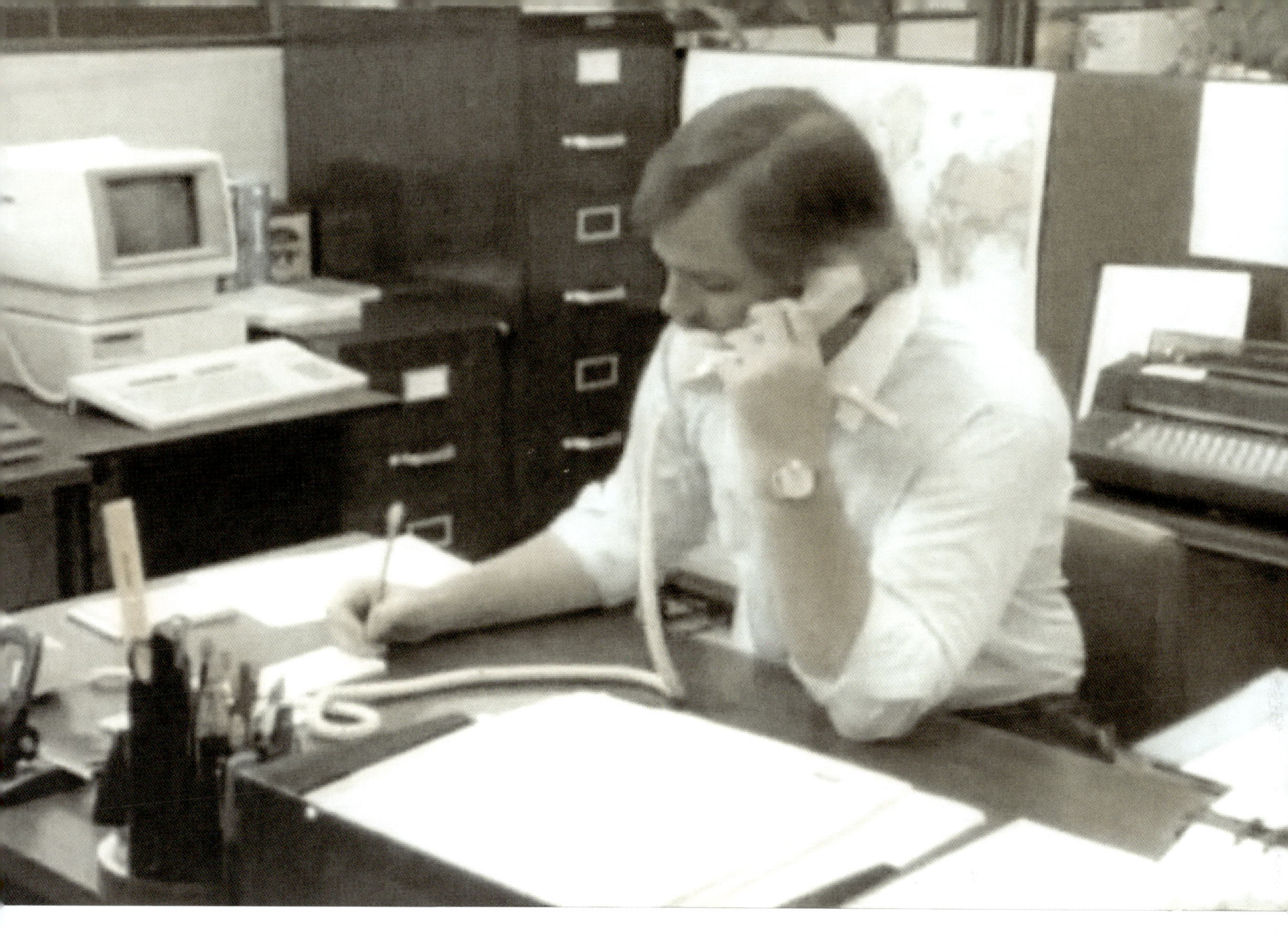

Organizations that have a competitive edge are those that make the best use of the richness of their diverse human resources.

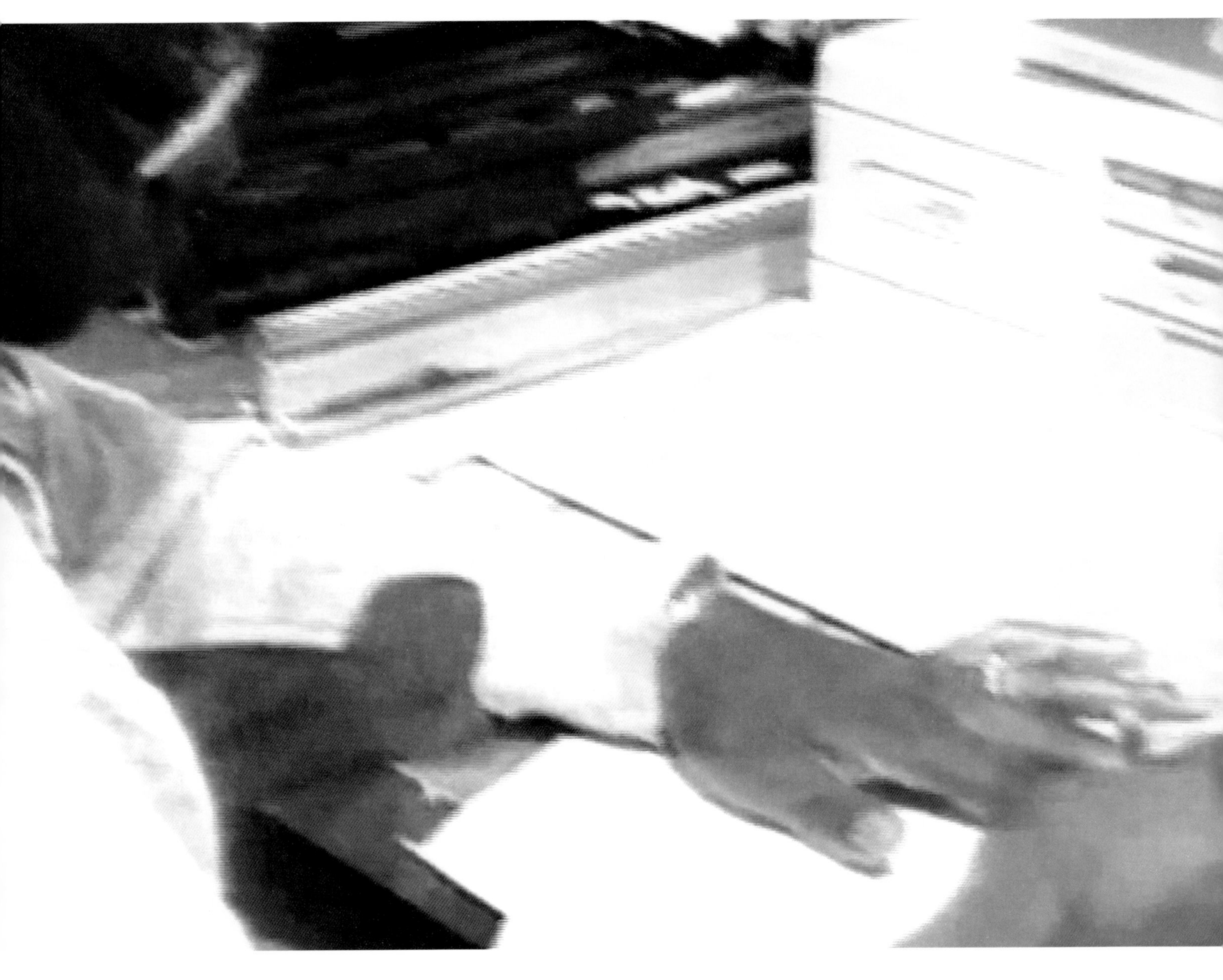

We encourage people to understand what the goal is and the goal of valuing differences is productivity. Valuing differences is about productivity.

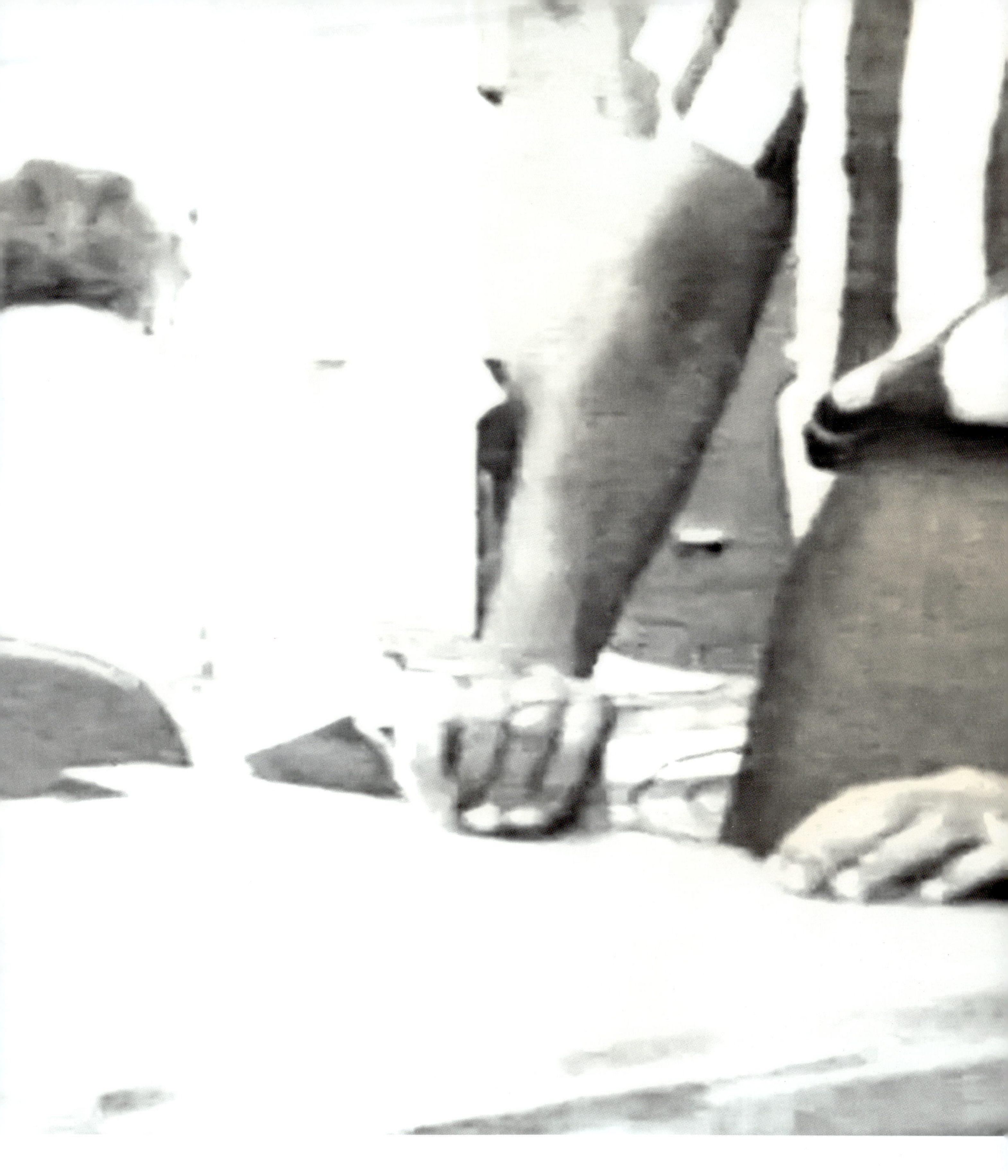

I am convinced that performance will pay off.

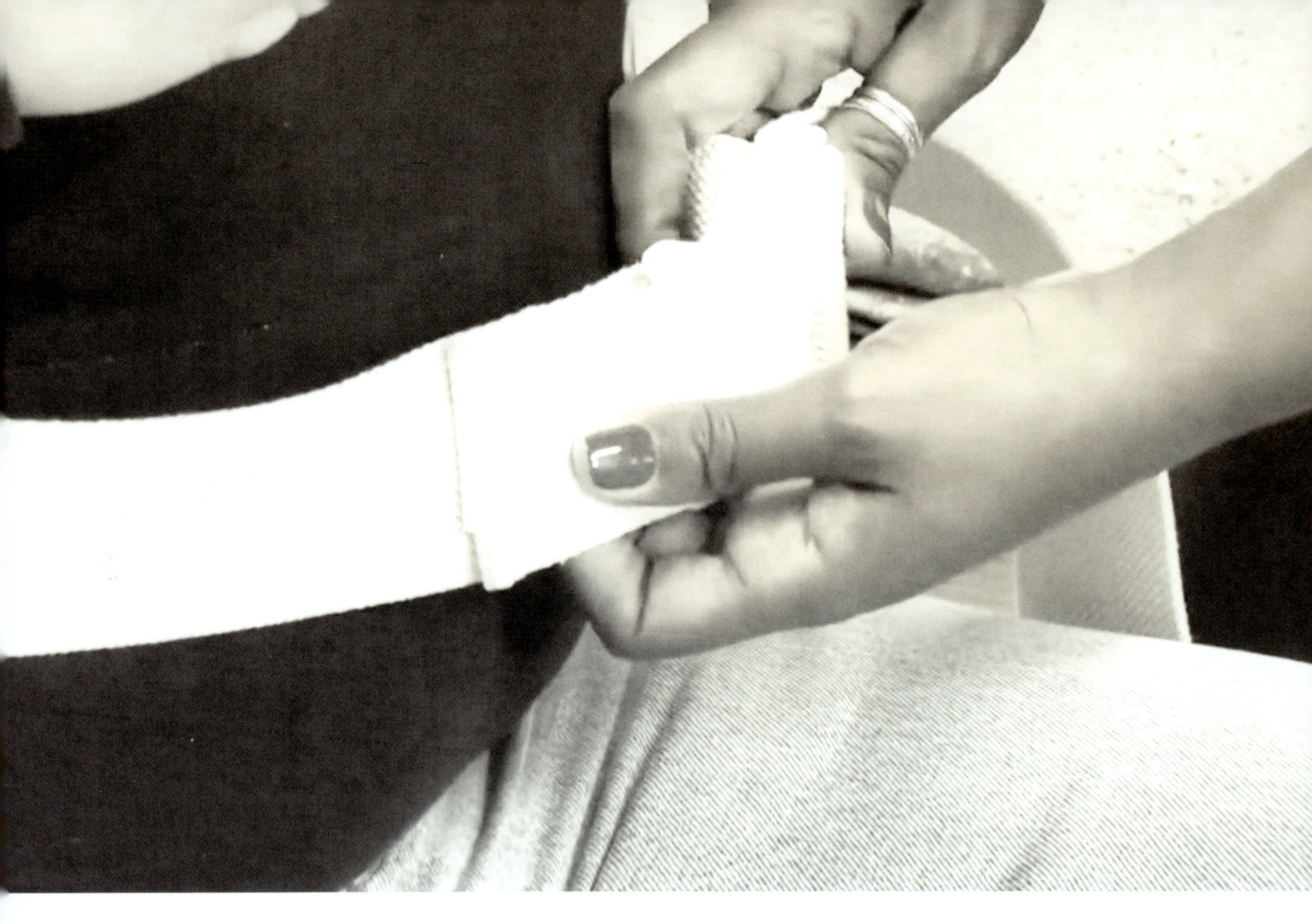

Valuing diversity is a journey.

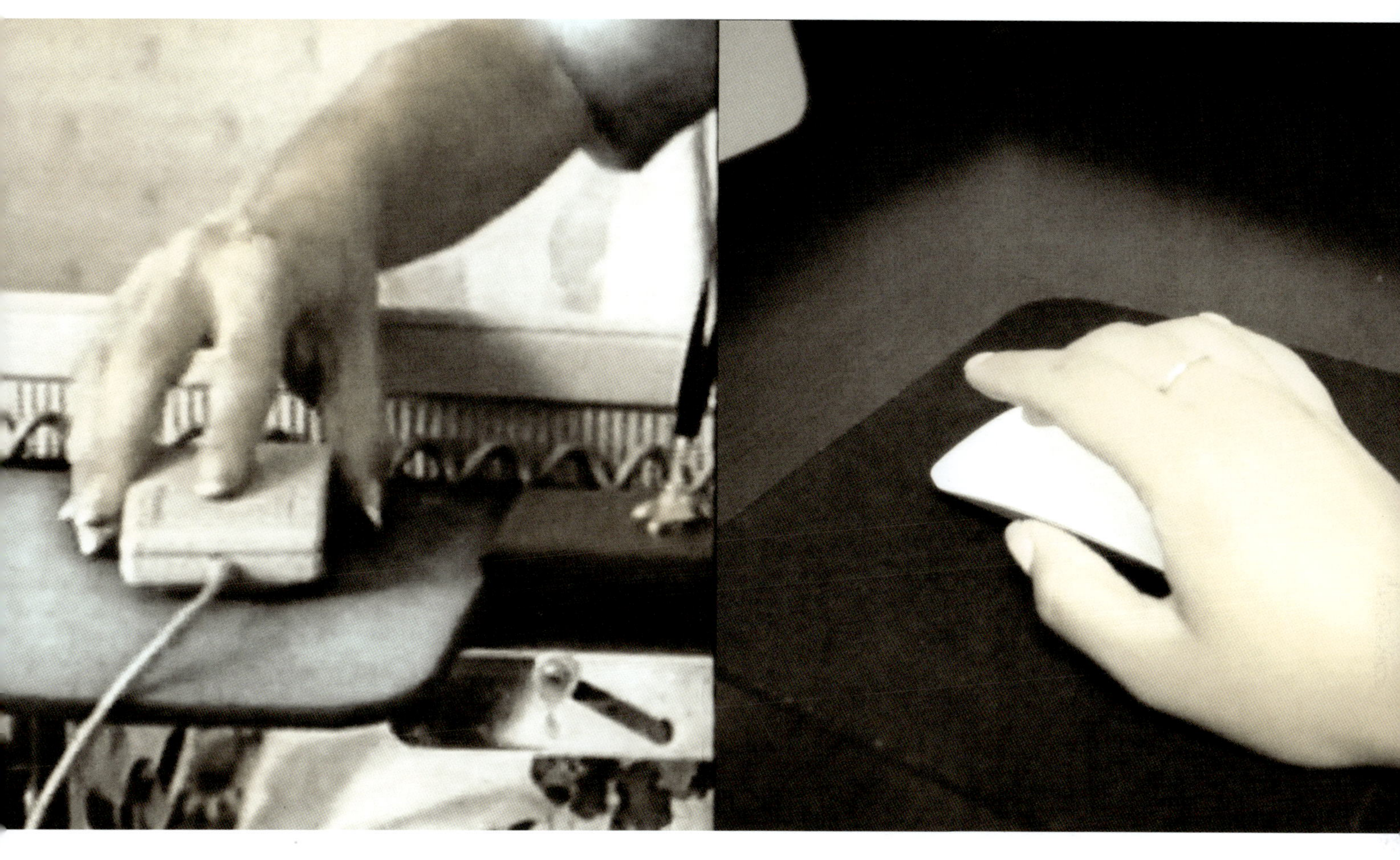

Recently we had a black engineer working with the two senior people in the company who helped us with a sense of understanding. I spent a good deal of time privately talking about how I related with the minority community.

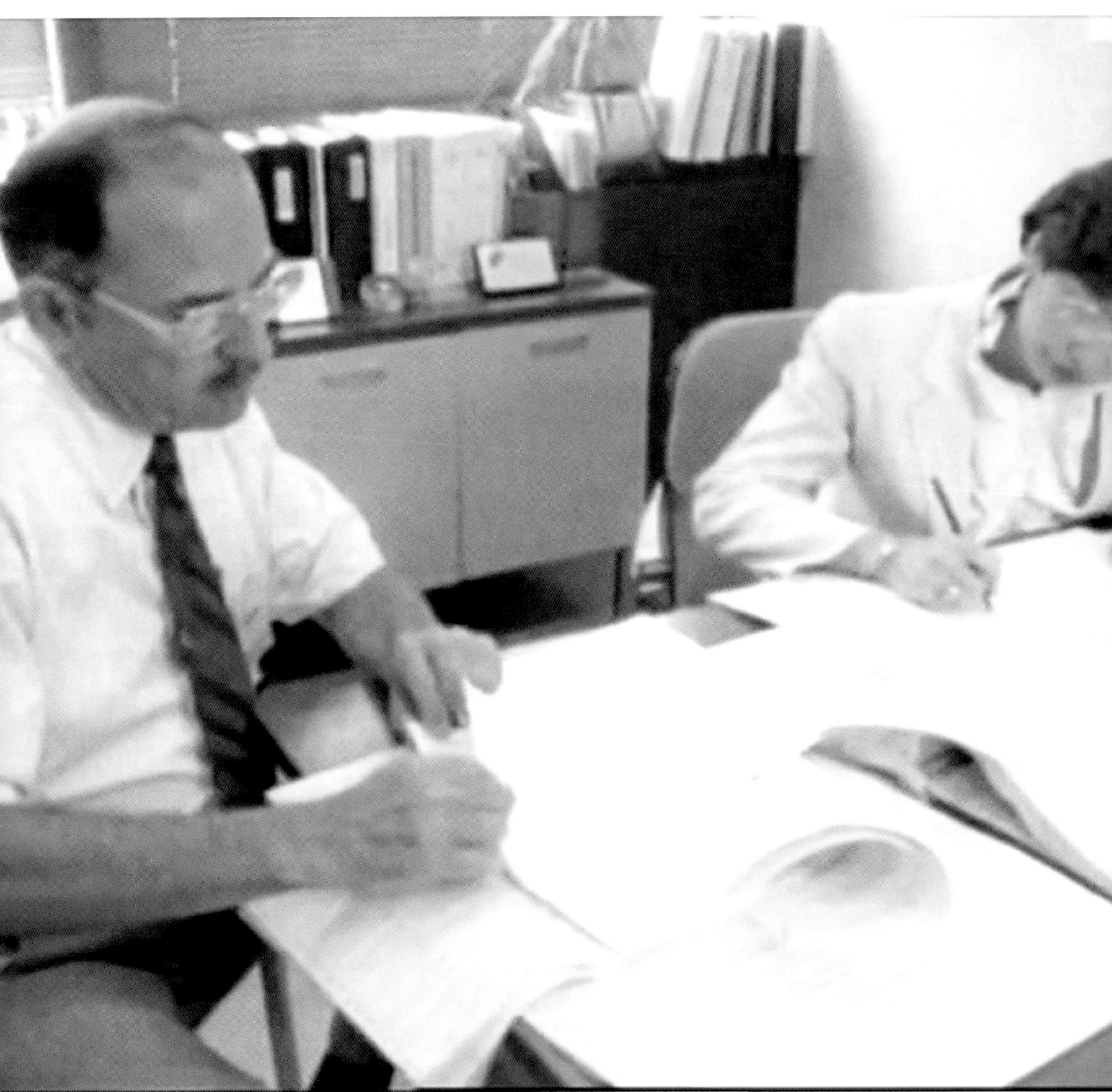

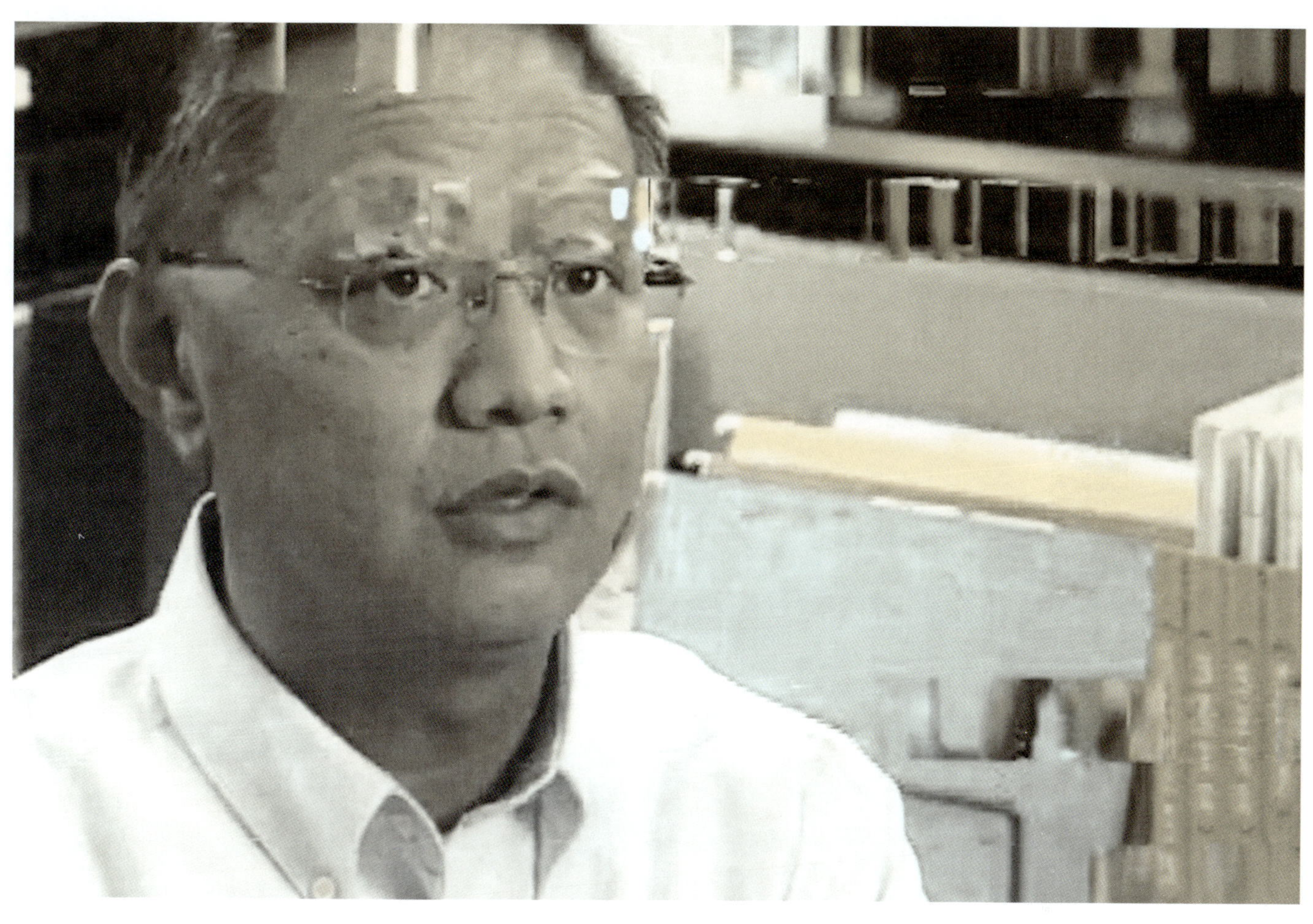

As a supervisor I am responsible for managing resources and those are equipment, materials and people.

"WALKING

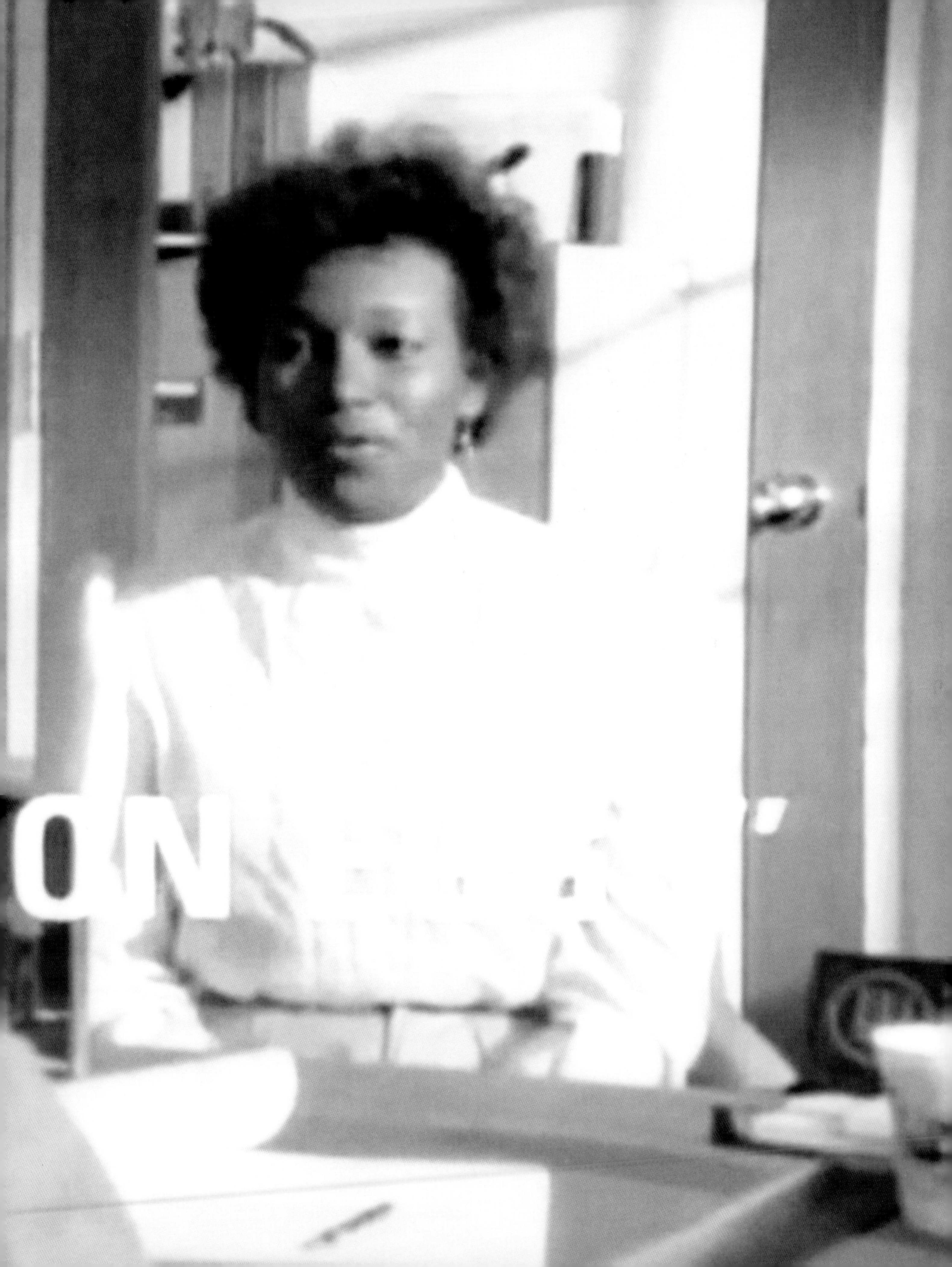
ON

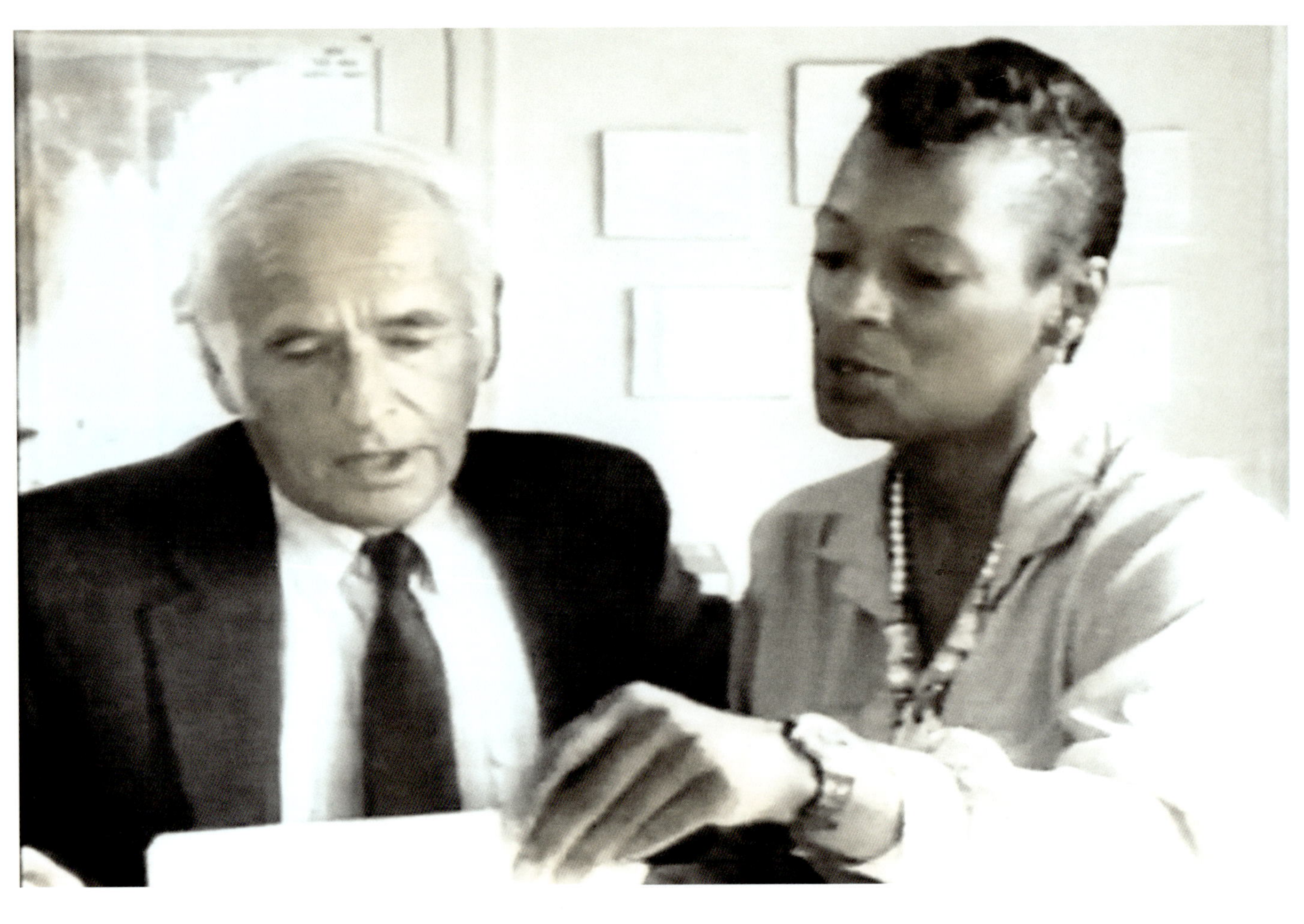

Work is a major portion of our lives.

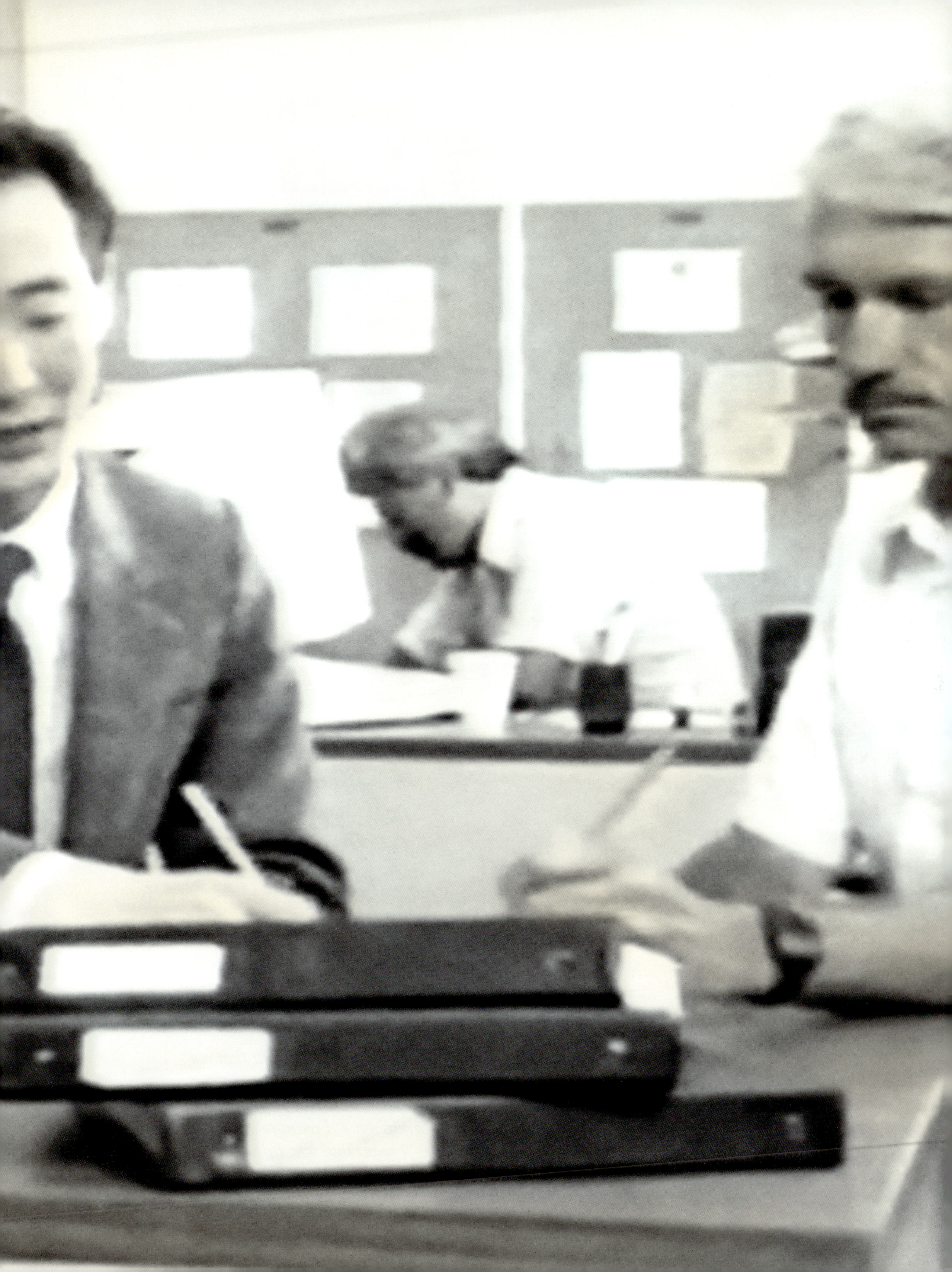

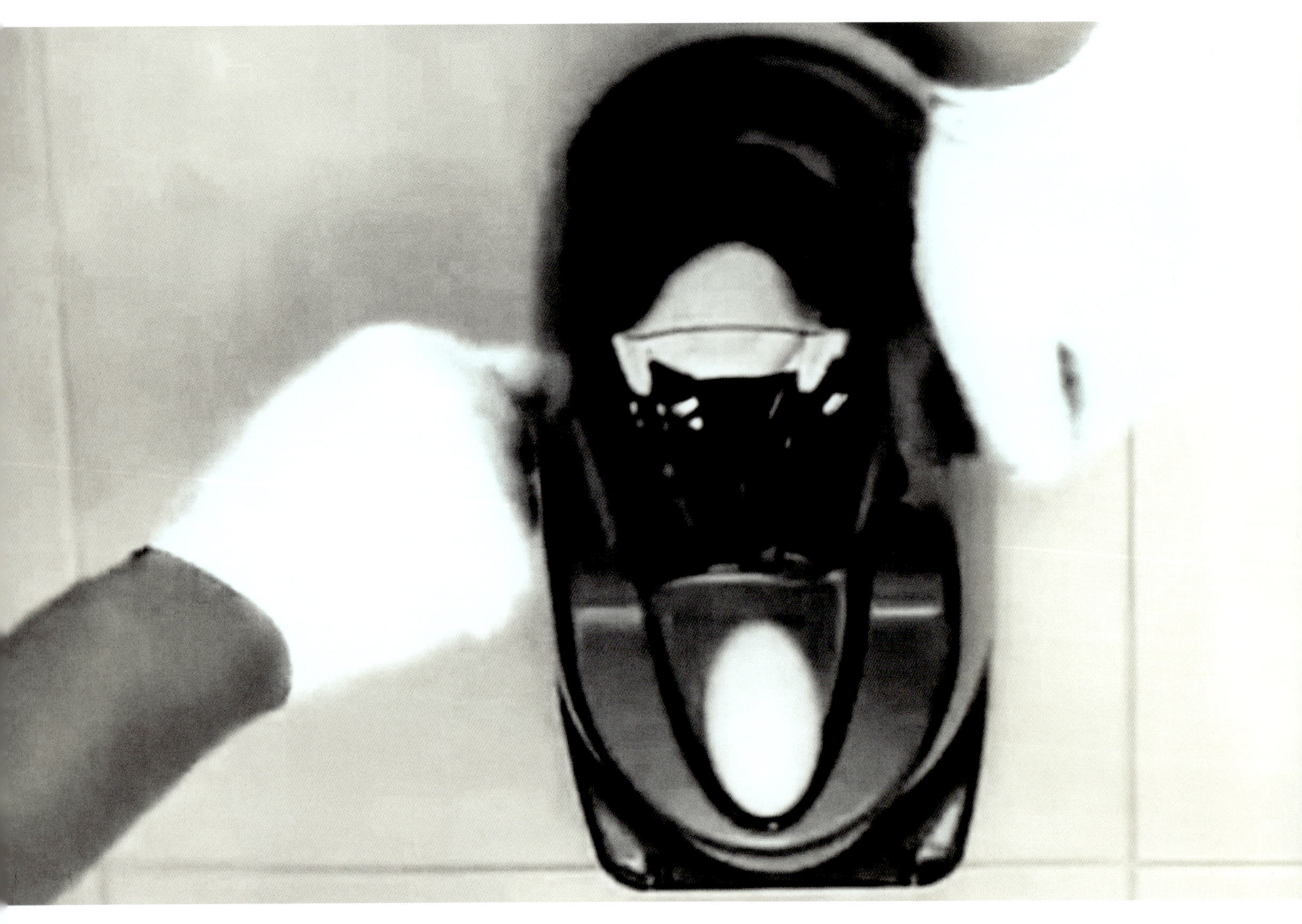

In our corporate culture we like aggression. It is very important that we have aggressive, driving people. We will have a white male banging on the table saying, "I want that schedule done today" and everyone will say, "Wow he is good, he is a leader, he gets things done. I want to be on his team." Same situation with a black male. "I want that schedule done today" and everyone in the room is quiet. He is seen as militant, and violent.

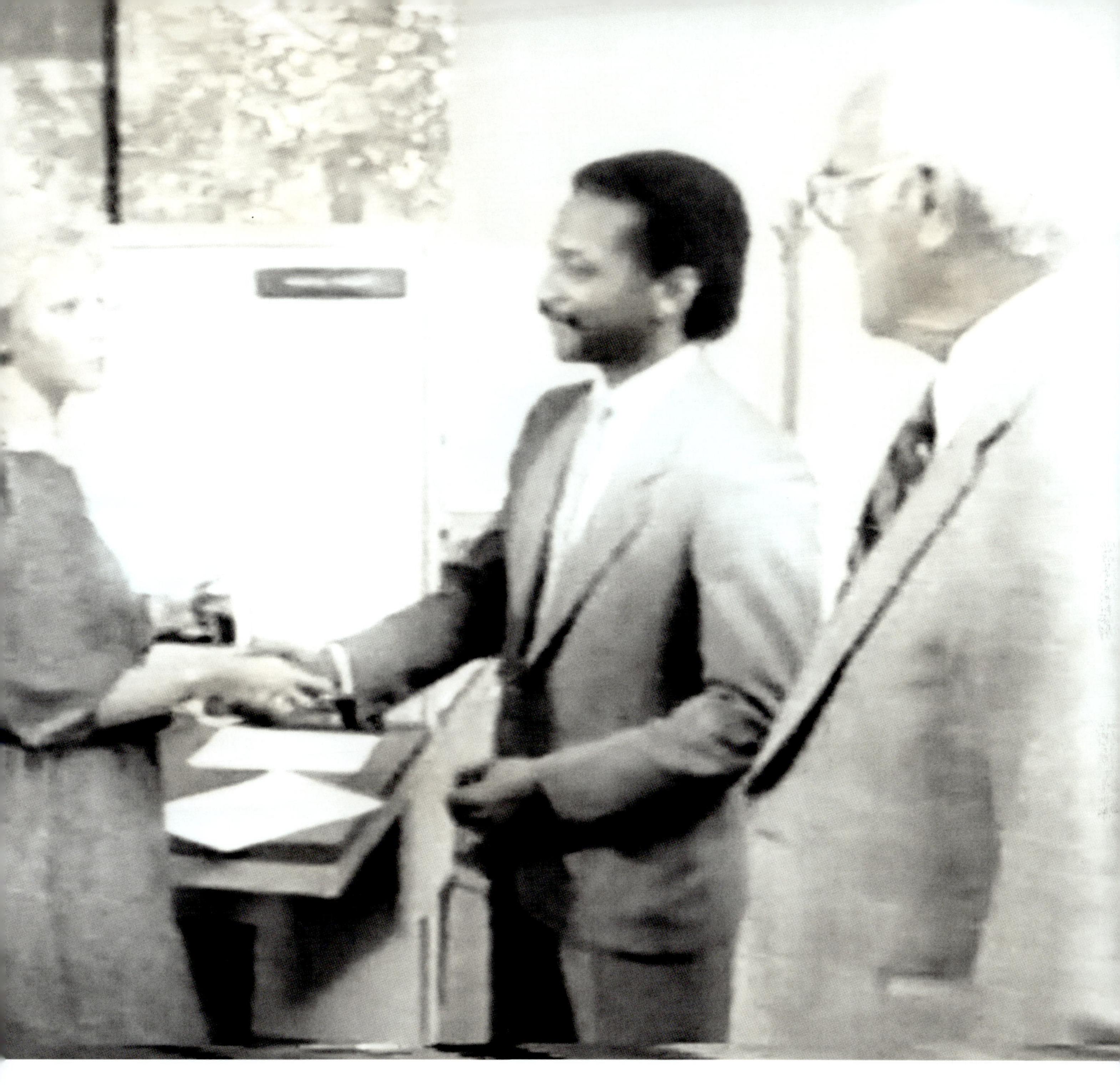

Eventually you will not produce for the corporation what it wants from you. Bottom line, dollar.

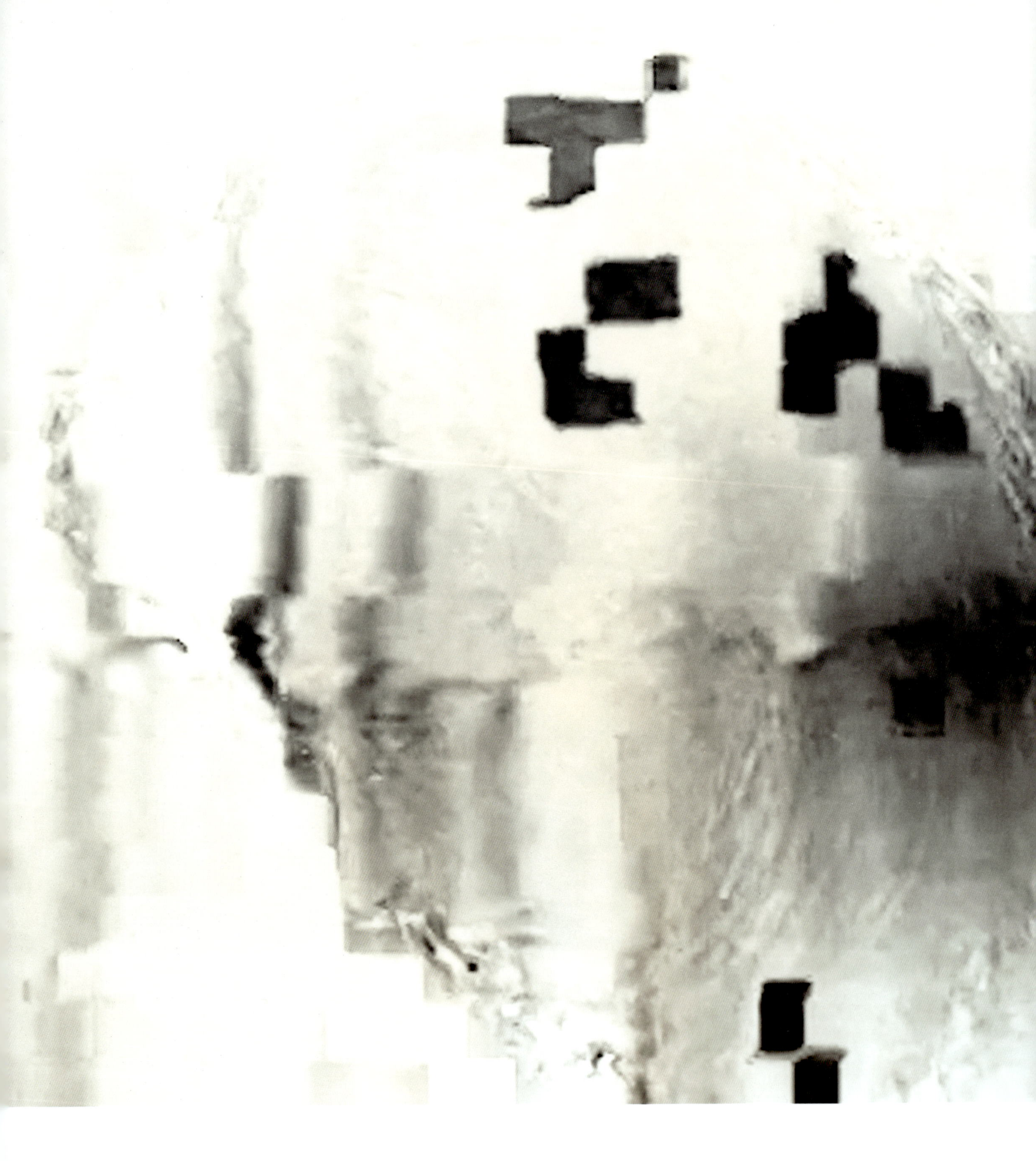

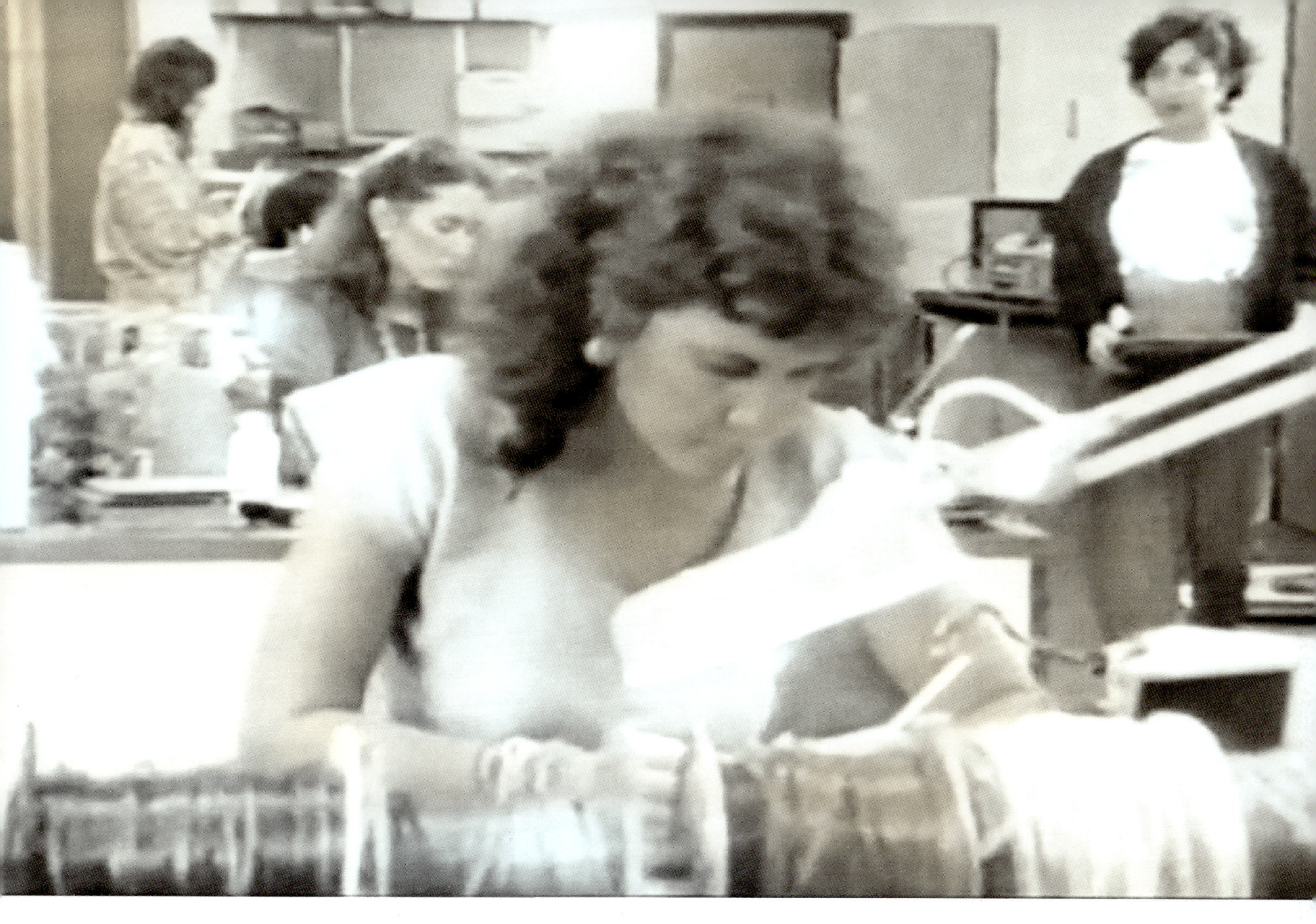

They both tend to walk on eggshells. The white male is reluctant to give them an honest assessment of their performance because they are not quite sure how the individual will react.

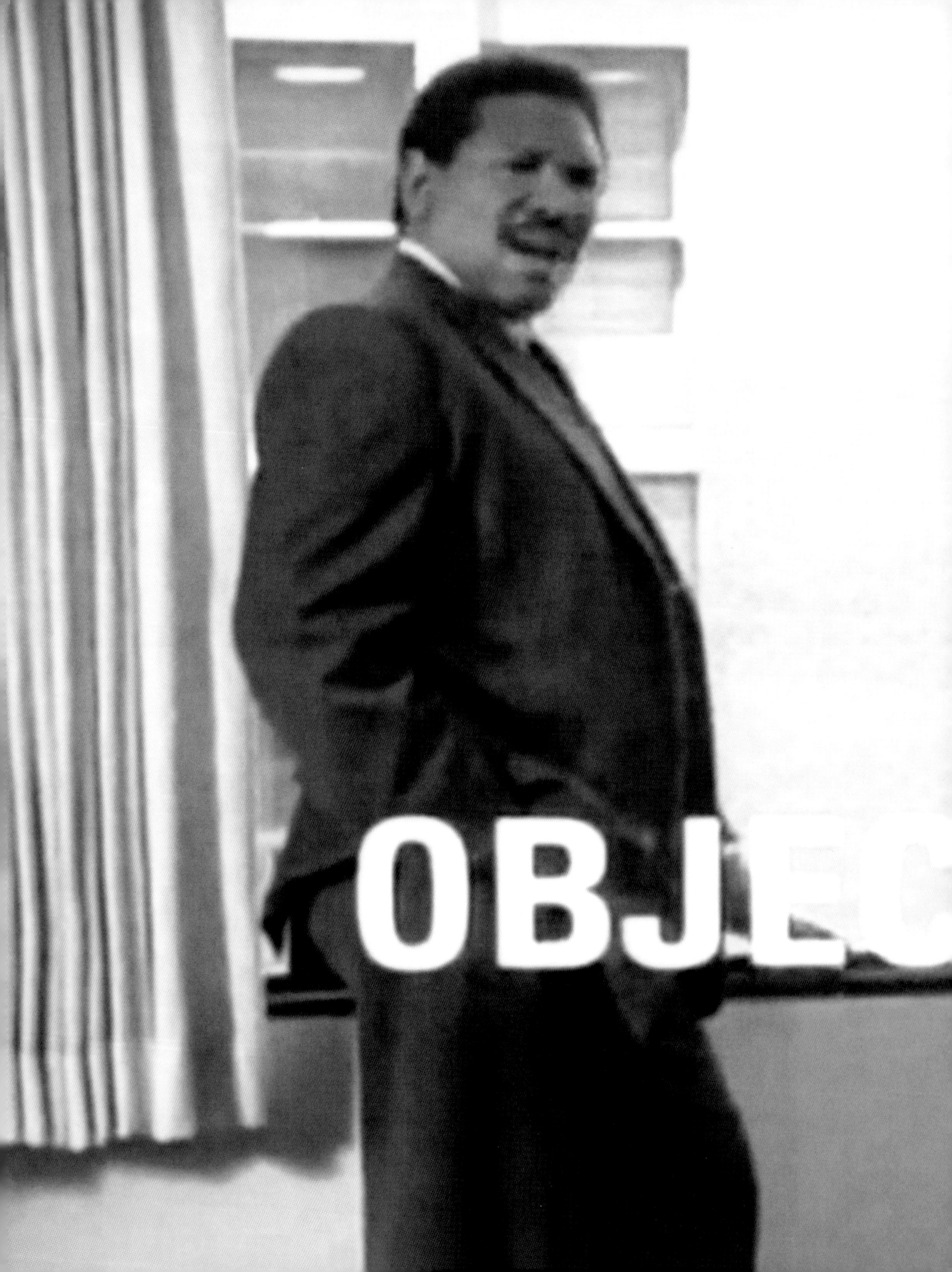

OBJEC

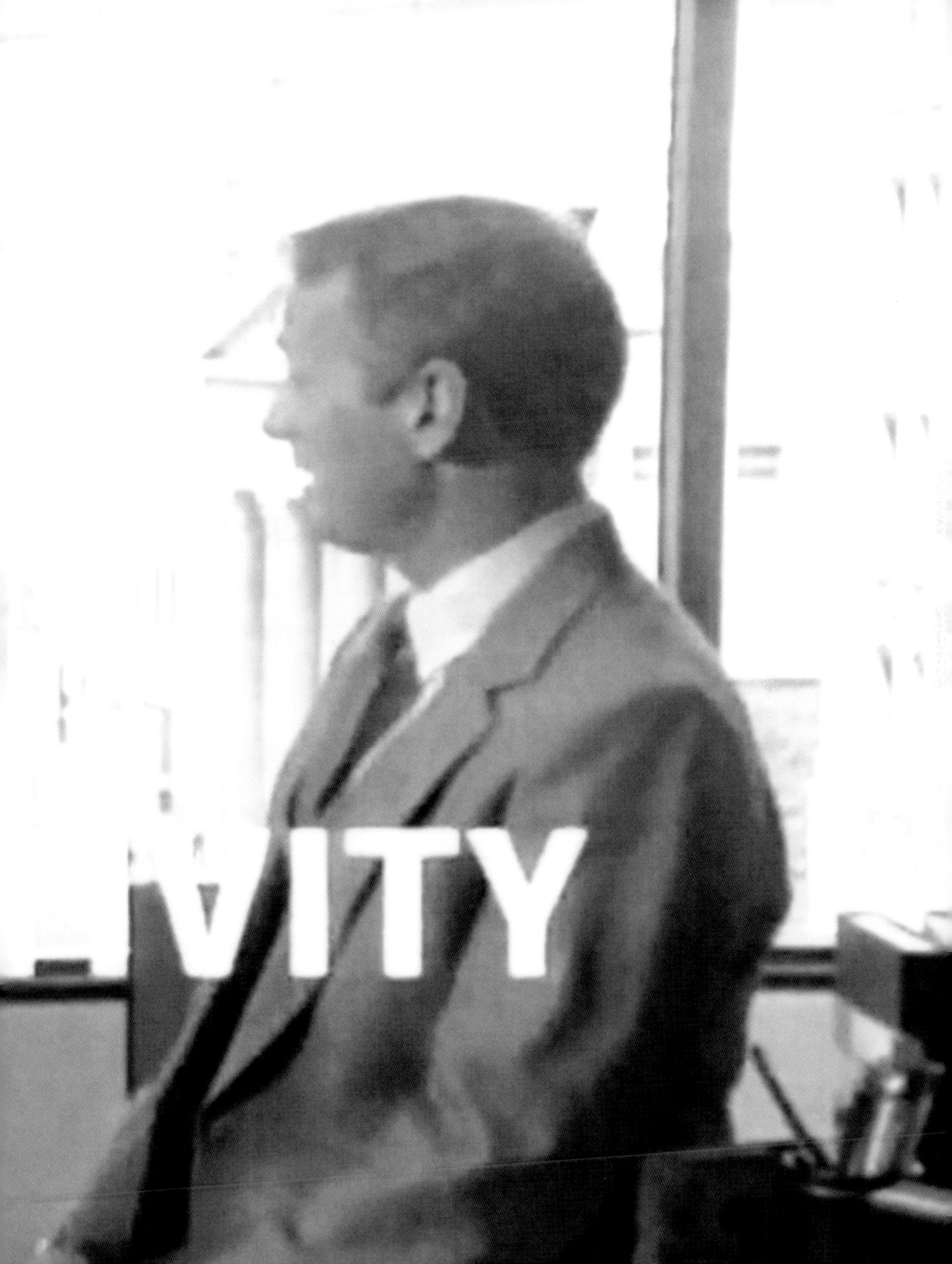
VITY

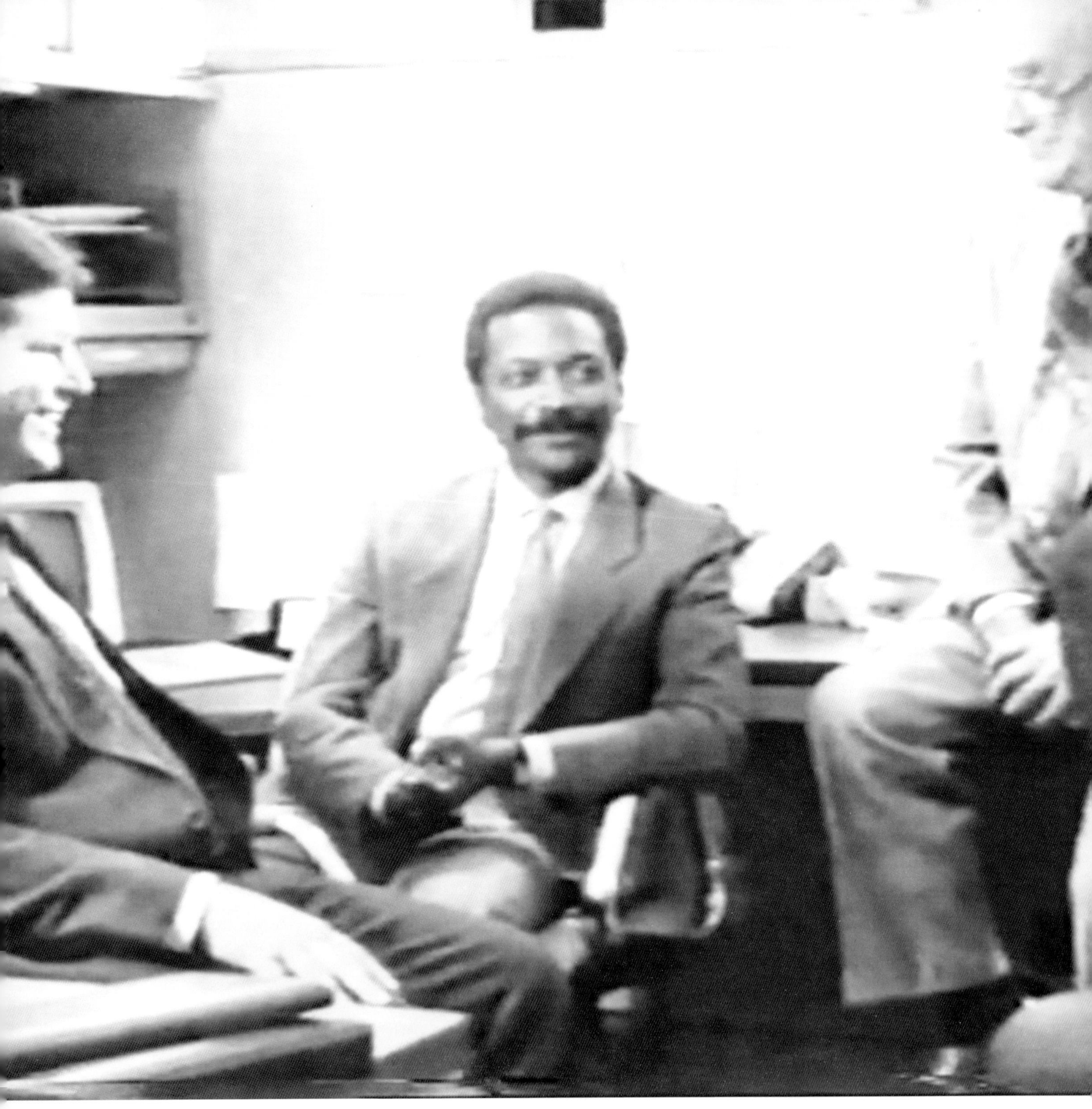

What I need to do is learn more about my cultural training and the bicultural part of me comes out. This is how I have to perform in corporate life.

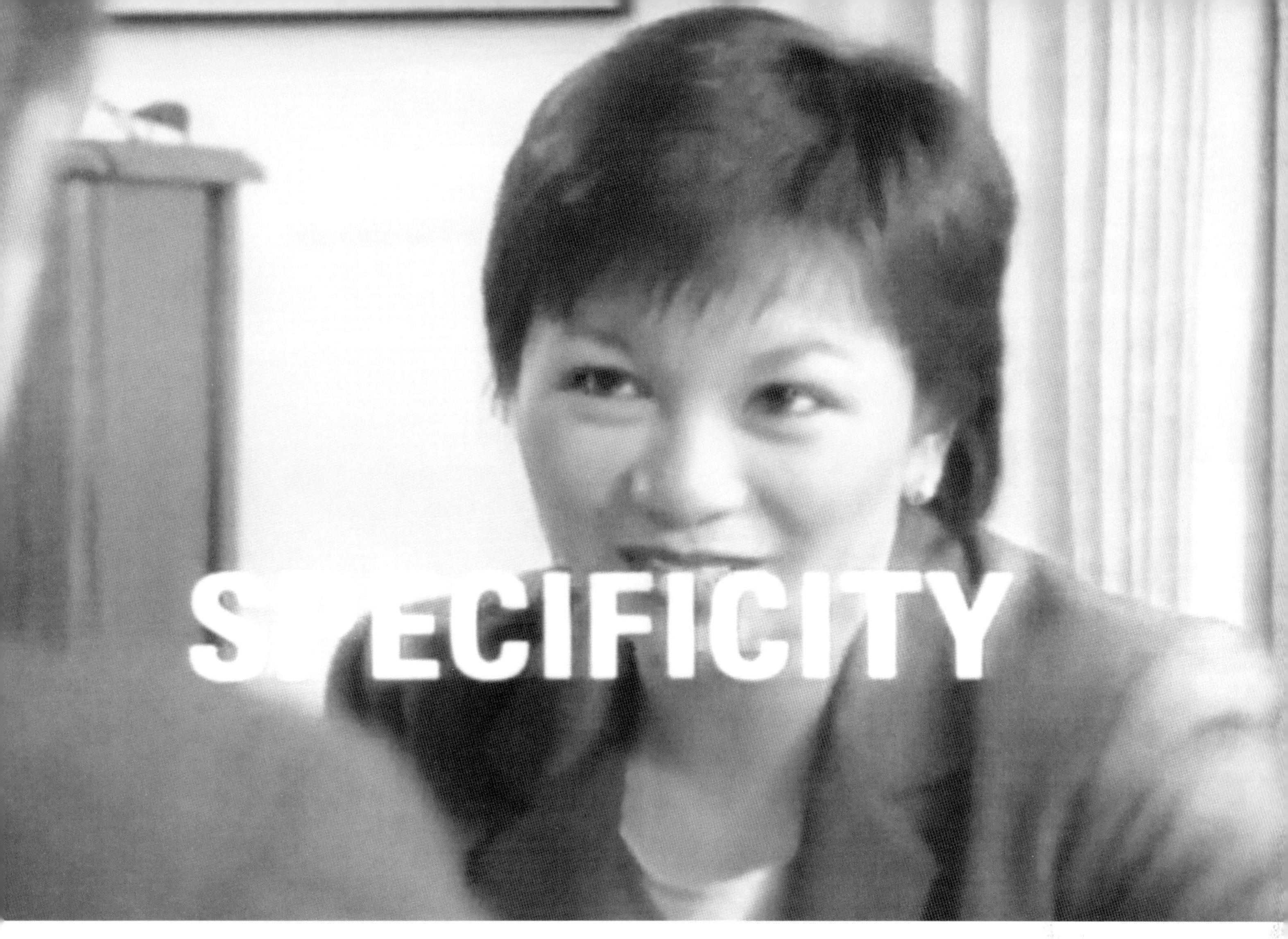

I observed how the white males interacted with each other. I observed how some of them were more successful than others. I took notes on what they said and how they said things. How they wore conservative suits, white shirts, burgundy ties, and suspenders. I had to really observe their interactions and what made them successful. I observed who they had lunch with. Who they played tennis with. Who they went to coffee with.

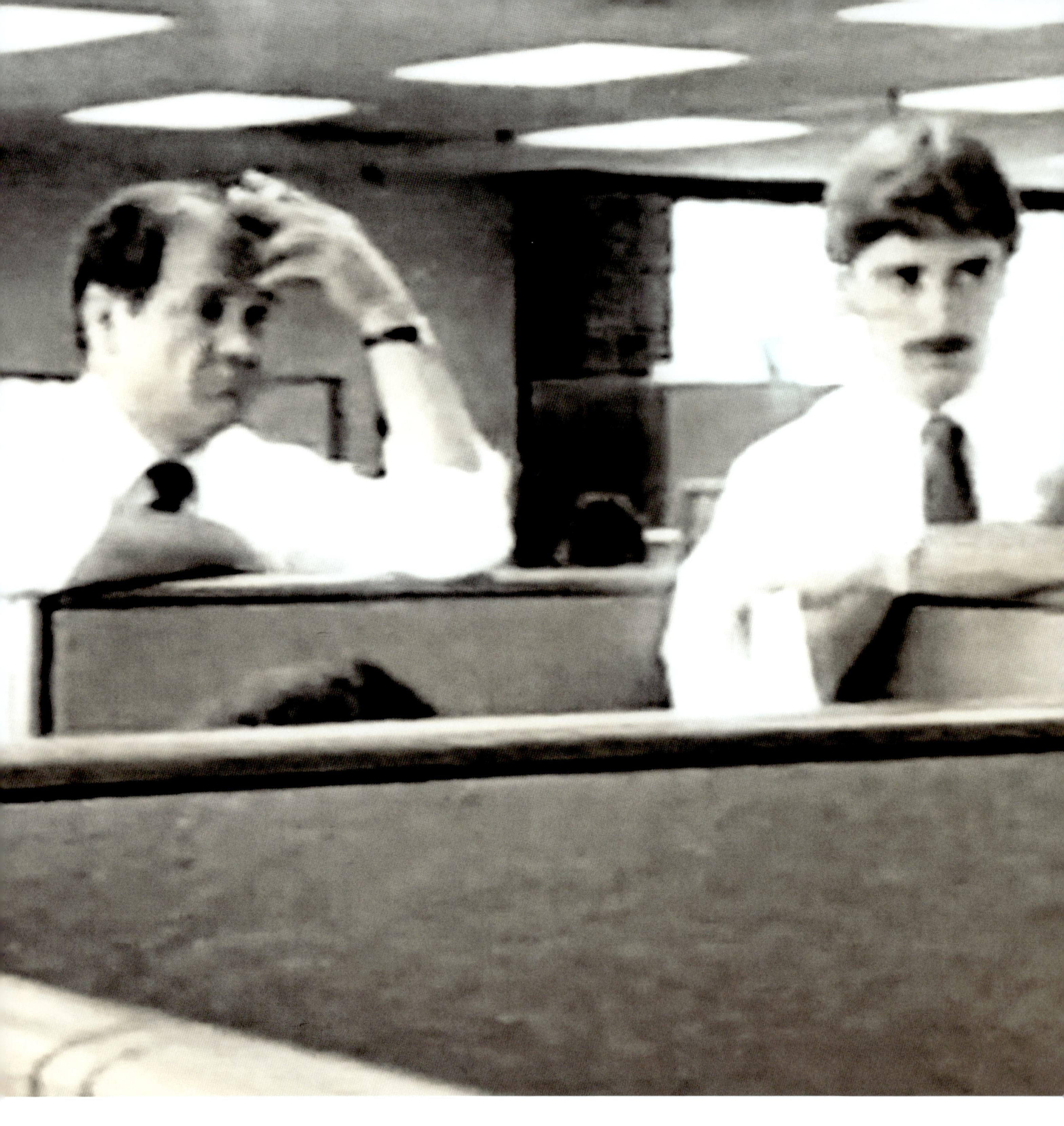

Organizations become part of our lives and membership can be extended in small ways.

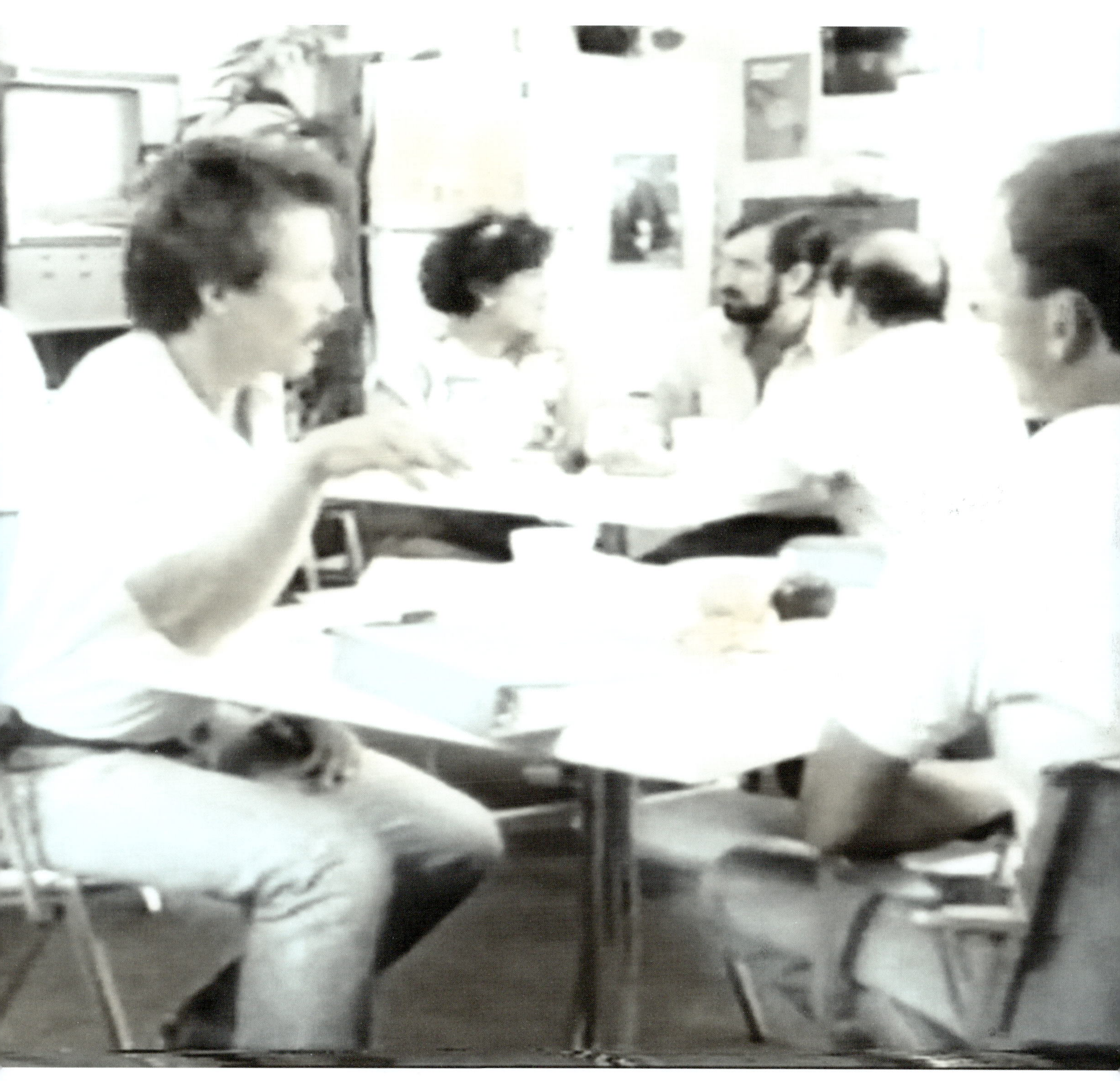

A common complaint in all kinds of organizations is that minorities cluster and this makes other people suspicious and uncomfortable. White men and women do not think of themselves as clustering although they too seek out others like themselves.

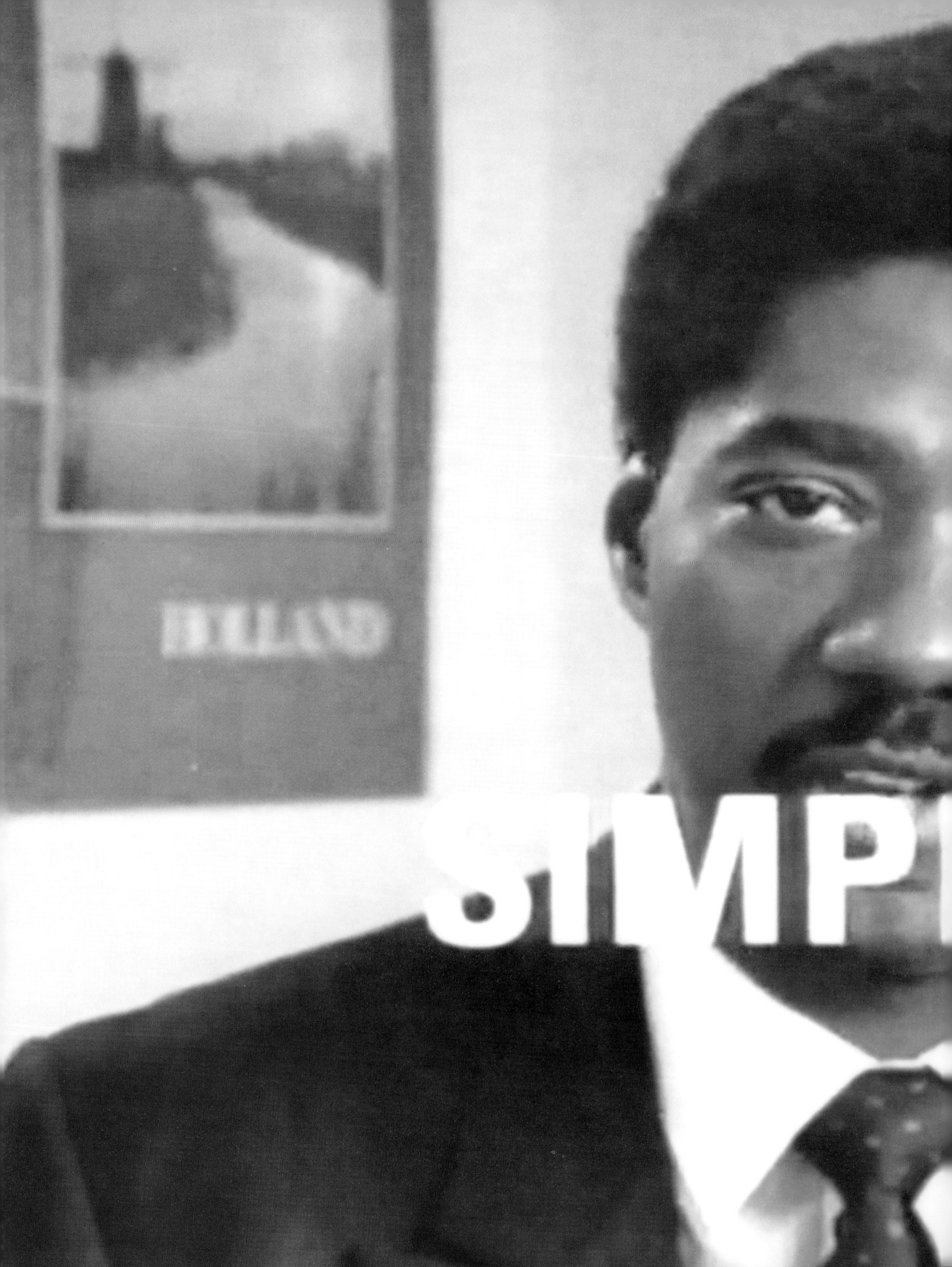
HOLLAND
SIMP

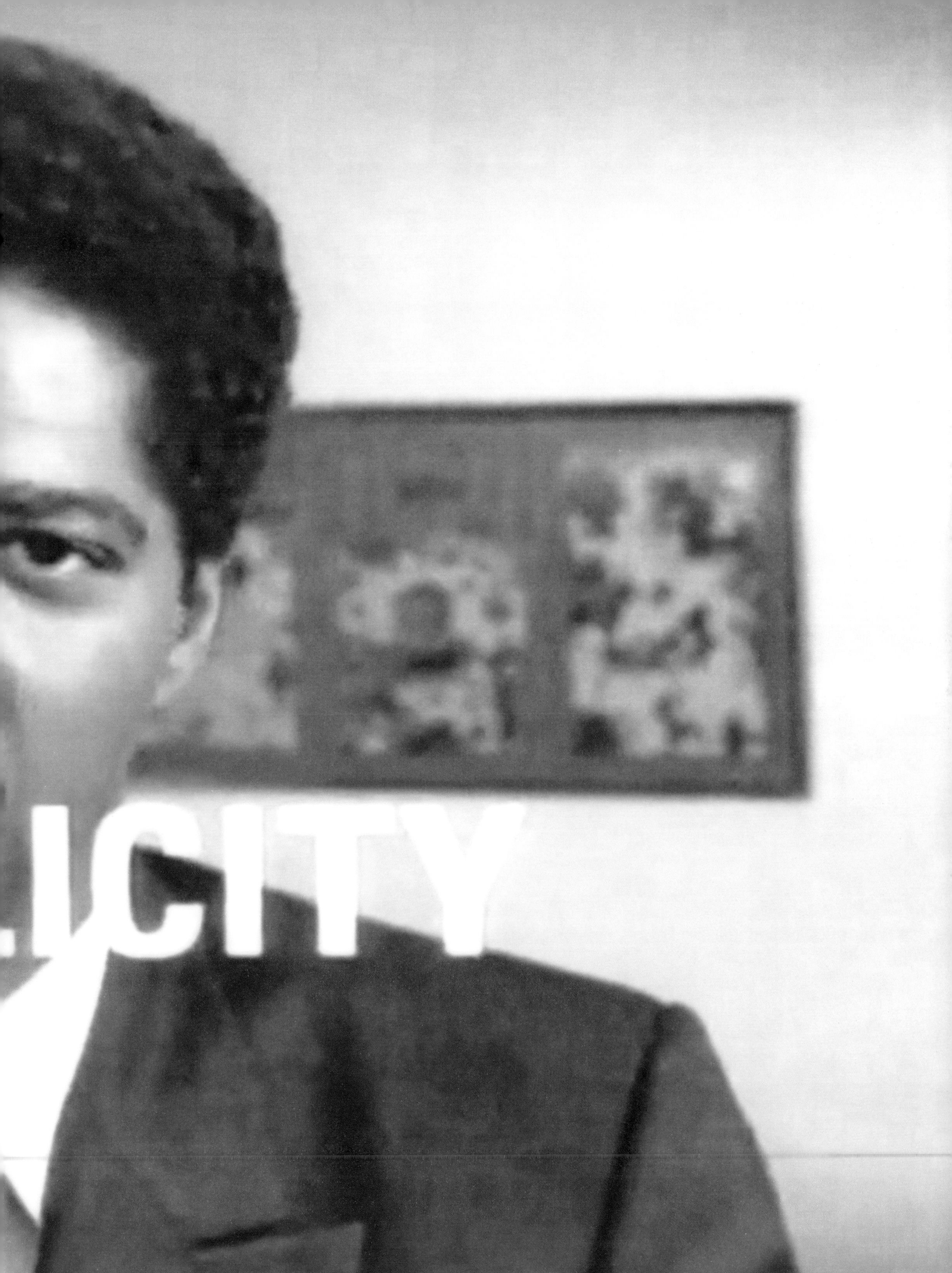
ICITY

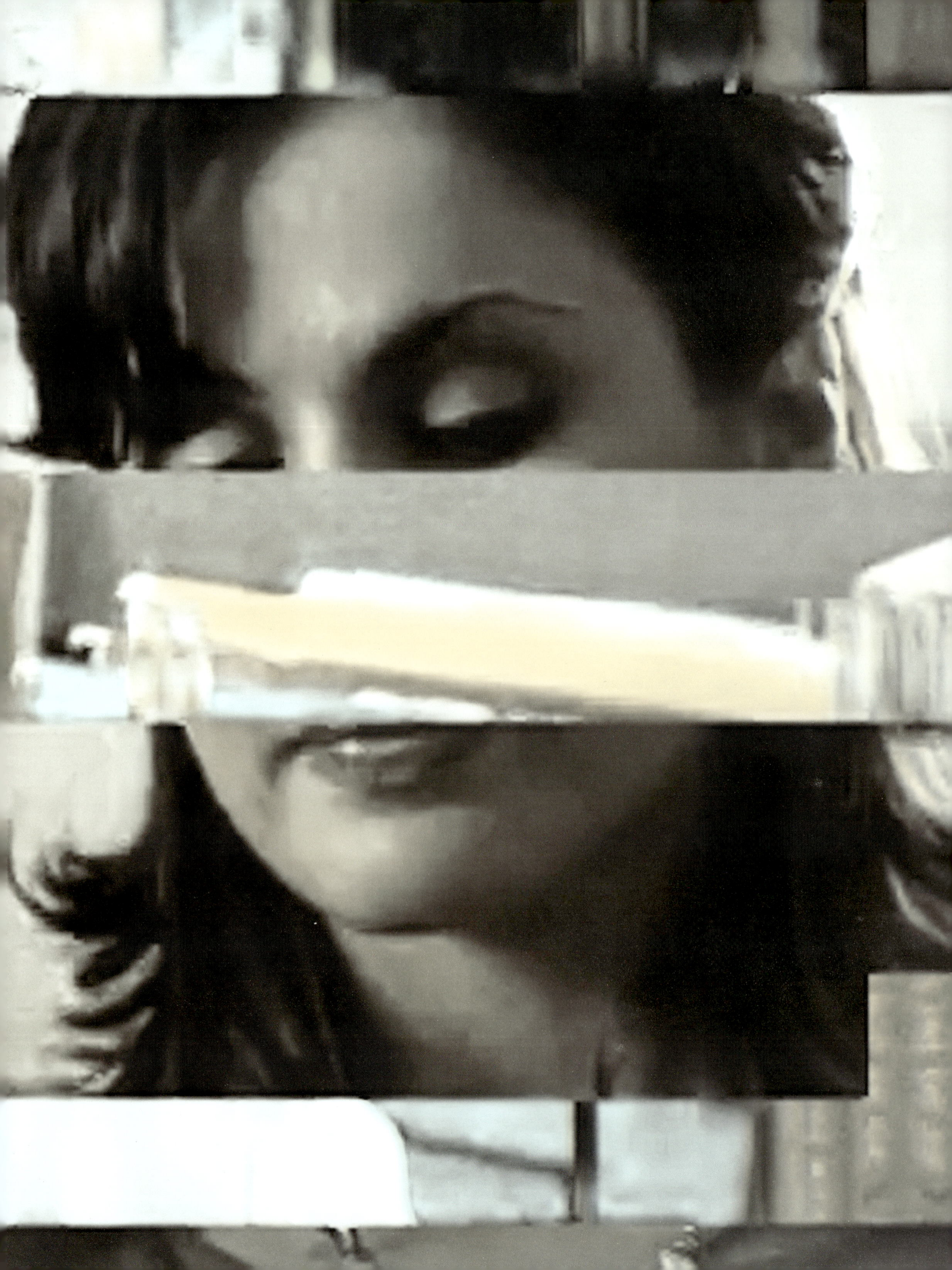

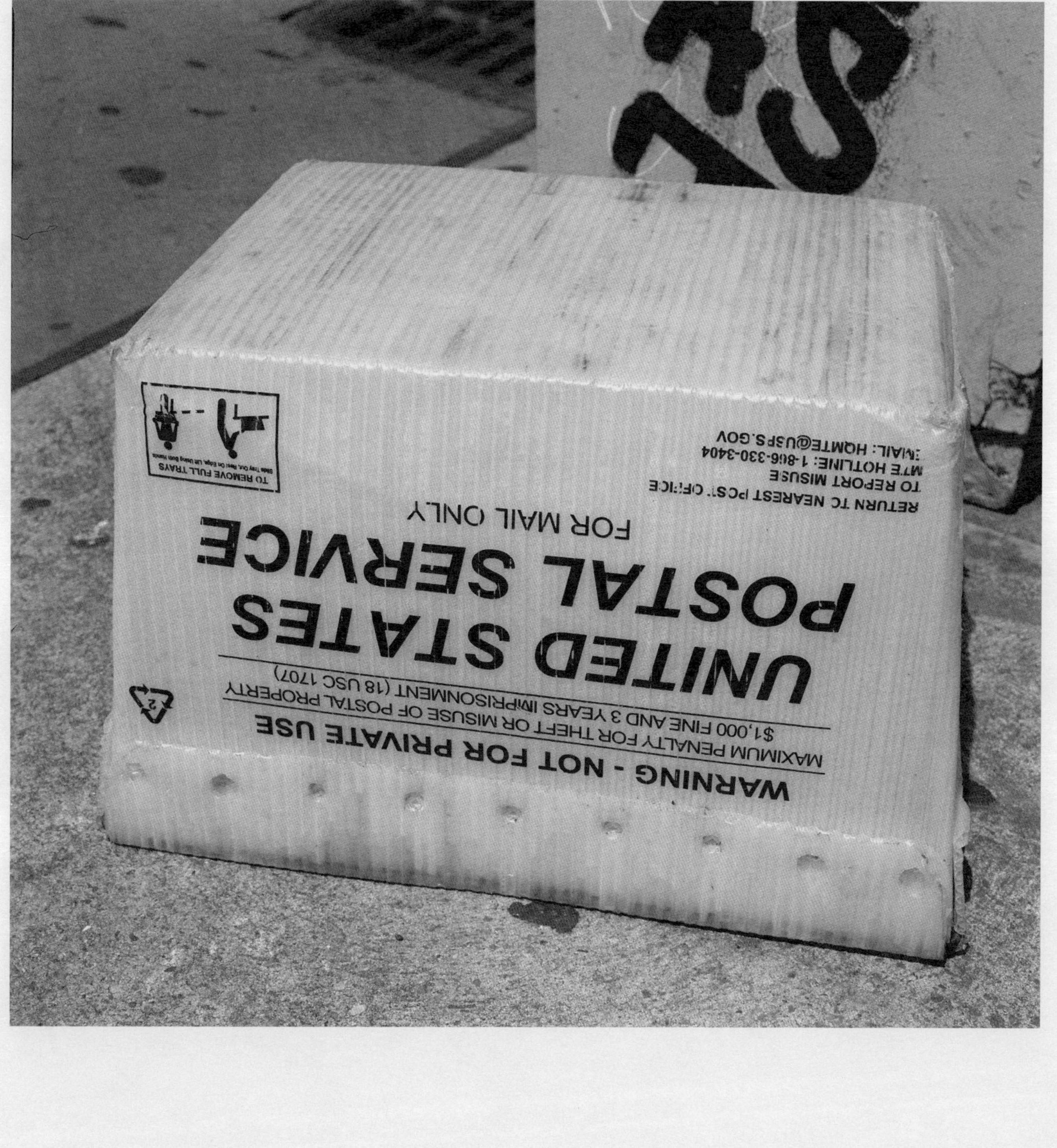
WARNING - NOT FOR PRIVATE USE
MAXIMUM PENALTY FOR THEFT OR MISUSE OF POSTAL PROPERTY
$1,000 FINE AND 3 YEARS IMPRISONMENT (18 USC 1707)
UNITED STATES
POSTAL SERVICE
FOR MAIL ONLY
RETURN TO NEAREST POST OFFICE
TO REPORT MISUSE
MTE HOTLINE: 1-866-330-3404
MAIL: HQMTE@USPS.GOV
TO REMOVE FULL TRAYS

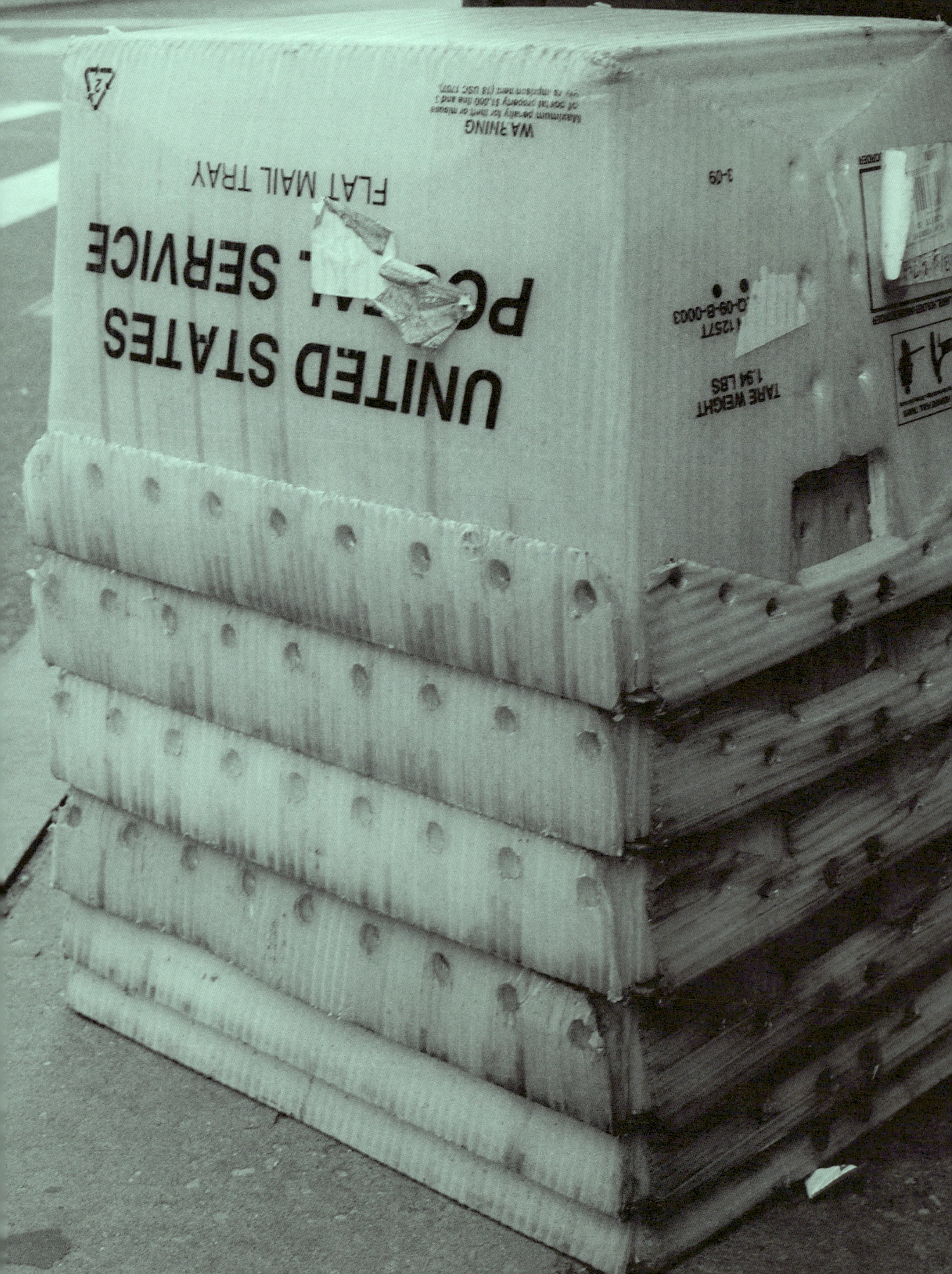
WARNING
FLAT MAIL TRAY
UNITED STATES
SERVICE
3-09
TARE WEIGHT
1.94 LBS

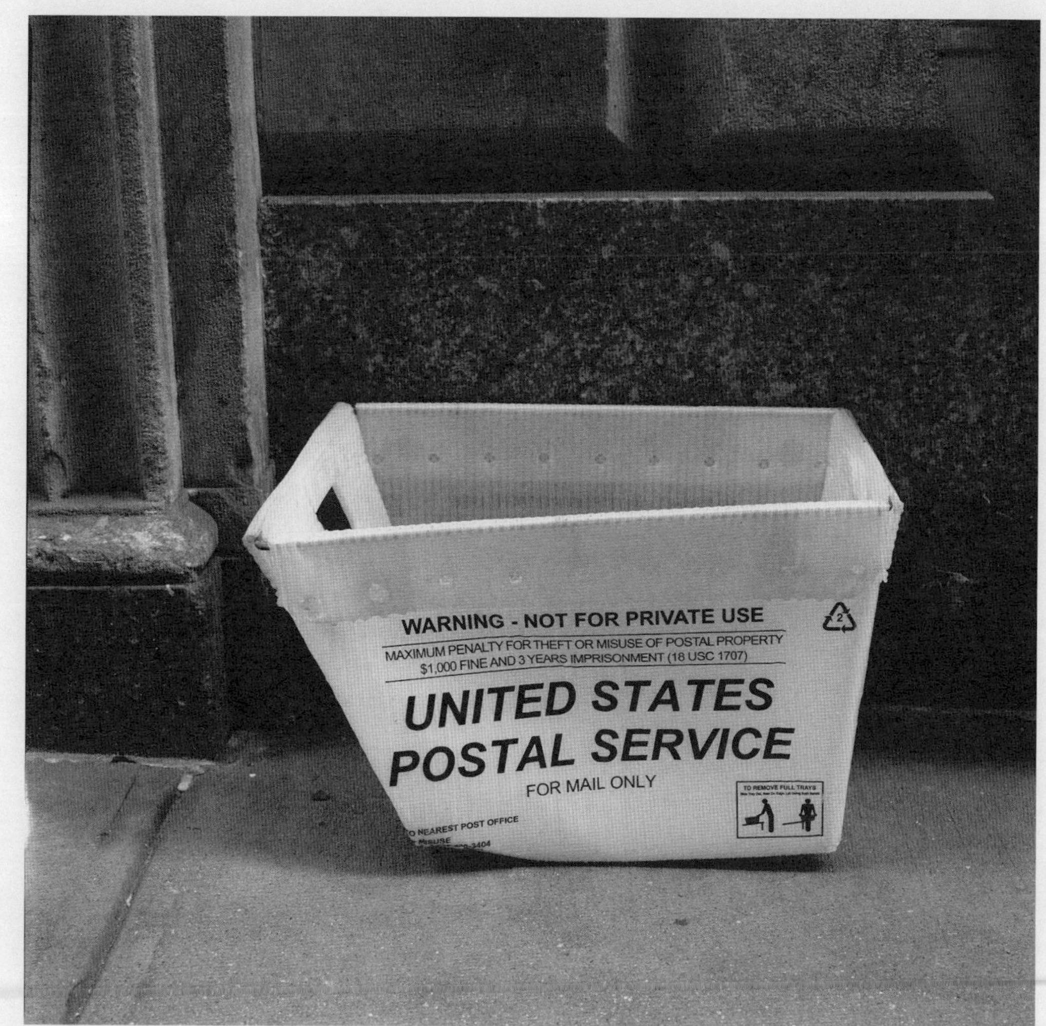
WARNING - NOT FOR PRIVATE USE
MAXIMUM PENALTY FOR THEFT OR MISUSE OF POSTAL PROPERTY
$1,000 FINE AND 3 YEARS IMPRISONMENT (18 USC 1707)
UNITED STATES
POSTAL SERVICE
FOR MAIL ONLY
TO REMOVE FULL TRAYS

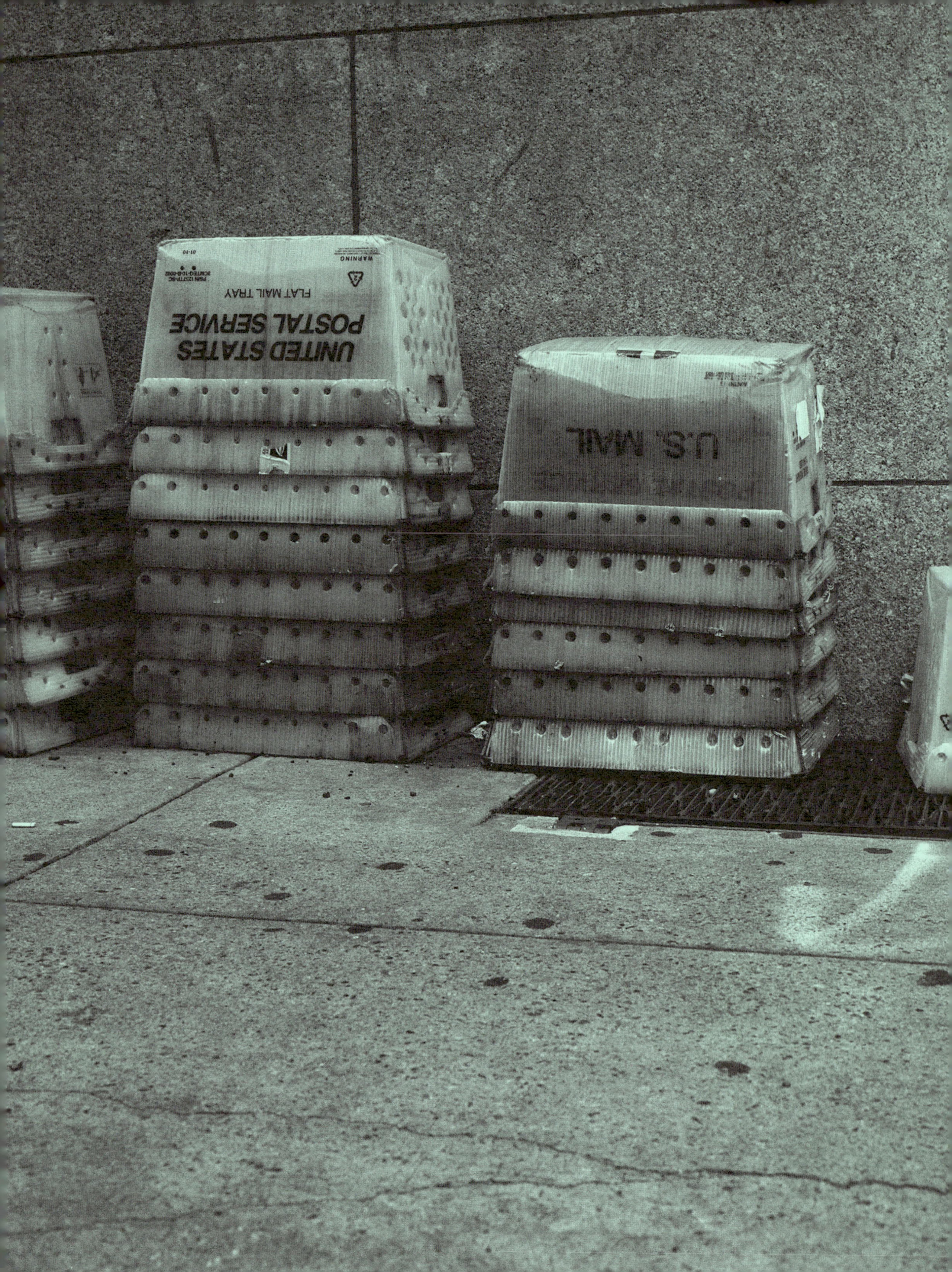
UNITED STATES
POSTAL SERVICE
FLAT MAIL TRAY
U.S. MAIL

VALUING DIFFERENCES IS ABOUT PRODUCTIVITY

Modular architecture is architecture stripped down to function. It can be replaced at any time without affecting a system. Its form can change at any moment. It can be readily redistributed, and smaller units of modular architecture fit neatly in open floor plans. Its general appeal and aesthetic qualities fit the moment, generation or fad that it occupies. Its function is not about longevity, but the value it can immediately give to the user.

The parts and materials that create modular architecture are purposefully malleable, readily attainable, and reduced to the most minimal terms. Its production is quick and lifespan dictated by the end user. Its instructions and tutorials for installation are also interchangeable, versatile, and equipped for either the single installer learning from boxed pre-packaged instructions or the trade-specific union worker. Anyone can install and manipulate onsite. No longer is the question of authorship or narrative of the architect in mind: the material is solely about its use, monetary value, production and convenience factors.

On the assembly line, production and cheap labor is what matters. Are the parts all produced to specification? Were the parts made with resources that are expendable and at cost? Do colors match? Can they interlock and be put together with as few means and tools as possible? Also, how much space does the material or form take up on a display shelf at the store?

Its geometry appears inherently basic. In the US materials are measured on the imperial system, and nominal units of 2 and 4 reign supreme. These standards are used not only for their divisibility, but also to ensure that the unit or structure can pass through many nations, systems and economies with ease and interchangeability. This architecture is registered and guided by standards administered by large bureaucratic organizations like the American Standards Institute (ASI) and the International Standards Organization (ISO).[1]

A TYPICAL PLAN PROVIDES MULTIPLE PLATFORMS OF 20th CENTURY DEMOCRACY

The manufacturing and construction trades were the most visible forms of employment in the United States after WWII.[2] From the pipes laid and ceilings built to the air conditioning ducts and electrical work outfitted in office spaces, a large percentage of workers were situated in a plethora of industries to create new American infrastructure. Interlocking parts made on the assembly line made it possible to streamline and train workers quickly within the construction trade.

Modular architecture registers towards the unplanned form and something waiting to take shape. An open floor plan houses modularity with the unplanned seamlessly. Open floor plans became the architectural design layout and footprint of many new building fabrication techniques. The space could be outfitted for a particular industry with modular construction parts and furniture, or refined for the downsizing of the number of office workers. The open office concept intentionally left floor plans "flexible" and without partitioned buildouts to attend to the demands of the market. Open floor space configurations continued to be the standard for office developments post WWII and into the 21st century.

HOLES: OUR PRIMARY GOAL IS TO BE SUCCESSFUL

Rem Koolhaas in his 1993 essay "Typical Plan" associated open floor plans to multiple platforms of 20th century democracy — an architecture that accumulates adjacent to speculative financial endeavors.[3] In practice these plans excluded

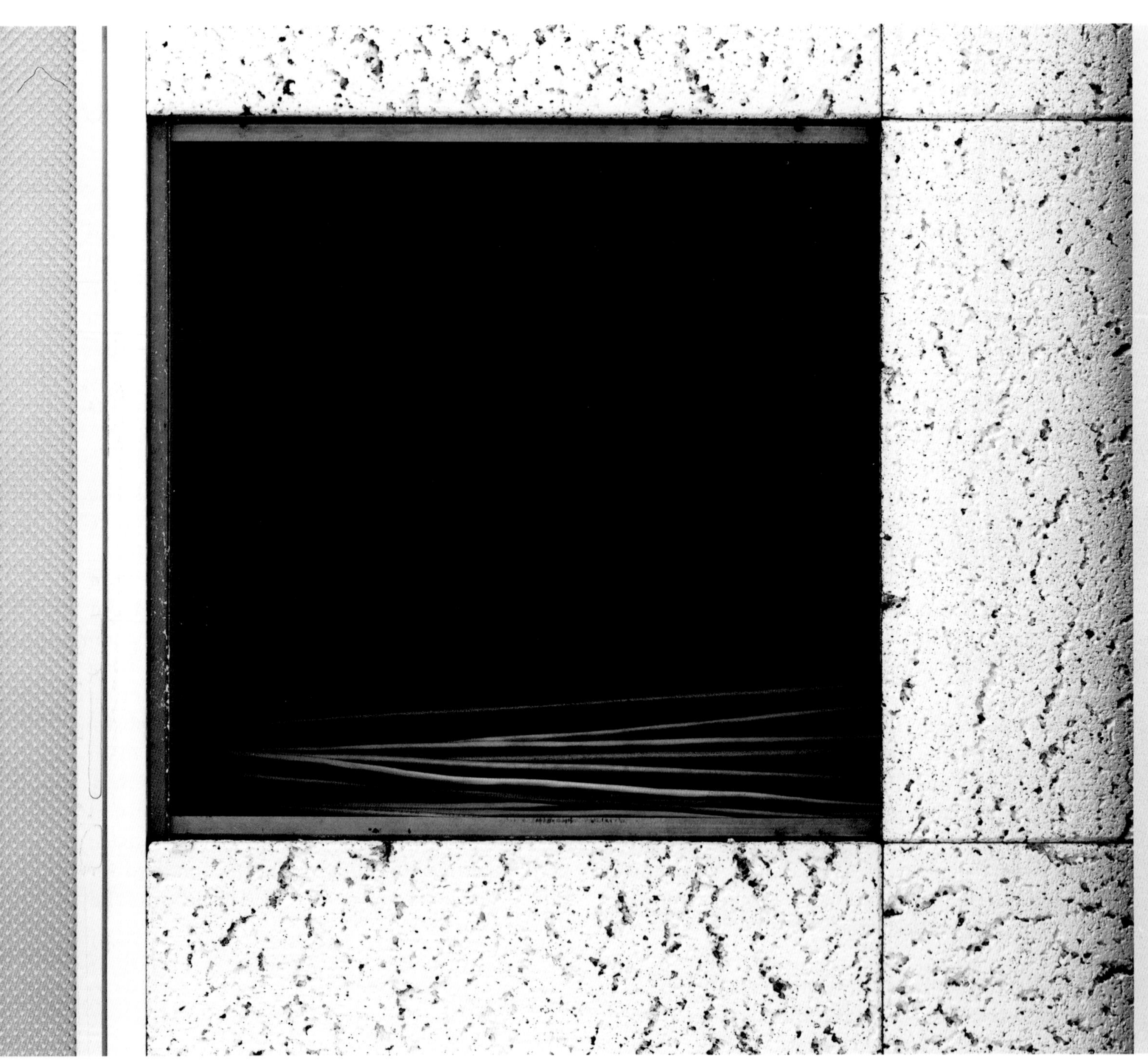

rather than included and these endeavors overlooked the inconsistent ways in which capitalism, contracts and policy can impact workers of color. The modular office spaces built by workers in city centers are an example of the transferring of material construction and factory labor to the immaterial production and compliance structures found in bureaucratic and financial office spaces. This architecture is based on finance, efficiency and the convergence of neoliberal labor policies with late 20th century civil rights policies.[4]

The efforts made by the government in the late 60s and early 70s to readily integrate some but not all job sectors of the economy are telling of the limitations and self-contradiction towards "democratization" presented by these open and modular architecture plans. Affirmative Action under Title VII in the Civil Rights Act of 1964, put into effect forceful anti-discrimination laws in support of equal access to education and employment for racial, gender and ethnic minorities in the United States.[5] Specifically, Black trade workers during the 1970s gained access to employment in government construction projects through affirmative action job training programs, as well as their own community activism. Although Black workers build this corporate and government infrastructure, they are left out as the majority end users of these spaces.

In Mike Kelley's 1991 "Proposal for the Decoration of an Island of Conference Rooms (with Copy Room) for an Advertising Agency Designed by Frank Gehry," the artist blows through this modular construction. In it, Kelley proposes opening up the ceiling to reveal exclusively the metal frames that hold the ceiling afloat, and cutting through walls to make visible private spaces and reveal the hierarchy of the workplace. From the enlarged faxed images of inside jokes painted on office walls ("IF ASSHOLES COULD FLY THIS PLACE WOULD BE AN AIRPORT;" "THE FLOGGINGS WILL CONTINUE UNTIL MORALE IMPROVES;" "NO JOB IS FINISHED UNTIL THE PAPERWORK GETS DONE"), screwing with the architecture here is identified exclusively as a class and status problem.[6] The characters drawn in the cartoons wielding power for the joke (a larger than life baby, an astute person wearing a suit) are black and white line drawings of male-gendered figures. Racial difference is made intangible in these painted reproductions of faxed images and text. Kelley's project was fabricated in 1992 for the exhibition *Helter Skelter: L.A. Art in the 1990s* at the Museum of Contemporary Art, Los Angeles, and the exhibition *This Brush for Hire: Norm Laich & Many Other Artists* at the ICA LA in 2018.

WHEN YOU LEARN TO BE BICULTURAL YOU CAN SUCCEED IN THE ORGANIZATION

The "Peach Book"— a document published by the US Government Accounting Office in 1975— was where contractors could find the construction and building codes for fire safety, HVAC considerations, material build-out for partitioned walls, lighting, electrical standards and accessibility. This modular approach to architecture and building layouts identified cost saving and efficiency measures with the office worker in mind, from a building's temperature rate/consistency and substrate water absorption rate, to the resilience and solidity of flooring and surface materials.

Herman Miller, the brand synonymous with the modern contemporary office, piloted a series of efficiency experiments in US government-built and operated buildings — one at Senator Hatfield's office in Oregon in 1973, as well as an experiment at the Michigan Department of Social Services Office in 1975–76. Herman Miller proposed efficiency measures for the internal workings of the offices by outfitting them with interior modular systems (cubicle workstations) that distributed particular job functions, foot traffic, and material concerns (such as lighting and cooling) more uniformly. Modular materials such as carpet tiles were deemed an appropriate floor covering that offered easy replacement of discrete areas of damage or stain and the potential to exchange tiles in high traffic areas to equalize wear patterns.[7] The measures suggested in these reports were similar if not identical to the material and performance specifications found in the Peach Book.

These specifications referencing building compliance became central to whether or not management or a business would receive a government contract.[8] The measures figured both in the architecture building standards and in the US government's efforts to integrate new workers into the labor sector through forms of affirmative action in the bid process. The bid process incorporated standards for manufacturing techniques, human resource management, real estate and financial investment practices, and anti-discrimination compliance.

IT IS ABSOLUTELY CLEAR THAT WE HAVE TO MANAGE DIVERSITY

The use of standards and efficiency measures like the Peach Book and the burgeoning subgenre of consultant work employed by Herman Miller are no strangers to the labor market. A labor market, based on work in construction and fabrication assembly developed generationally with the implementation of civil rights policy in the United States. Given historical patterns of discrimination, much of this policy in the 1970s was initially aimed at implementing equitable hiring of racial and ethnic minorities in federal government contracts for major infrastructure projects. By the 1990s, private corporations in various sectors of the economy began hiring their own consultants and specialists to recast actual equal employment opportunity and affirmative action laws as diversity initiatives that had little to do with legal requirements and were politically distinct from Affirmative Action.[9] By co-opting the language and many of the practices of the diversity ideology made popular by these consultants, corporations could avoid additional mandatory affirmative action requirements.[10] In these diversity initiatives, racial and ethnic differences are never made entirely clear, like how the details of a black and white faxed image are obscured or left out. A more flexible, modular, malleable and abstract use of the term "diversity" became the norm.

Managers began distinguishing diversity from affirmative action by emphasizing business goals, efficiency, and maintaining a competitive global edge.[11] Much of this language focused on statistical data taken from the US Department of Labor's projections of what the US workforce would look like in 2000; the need to contend for uncertain deregulated market demands; and to deal with a projected shrinking white male working population. The language found in diversity training tutorials mirrors the ethos and language of efficiency and productivity found in working manuals and sale specification guides of retailers like Herman Miller.[12]

> "Companies experimenting with new ways of organizing themselves to improve productivity, responsiveness, and competitiveness find that traditional office layouts can cramp their style."

> "Although flattened corporate hierarchies and increased corporate real estate costs have conspired to eliminate big, status symbol offices, people still look to office accoutrements for clues about roles and functions within organizations."

> "In an increasingly competitive business climate, organizations need to use every means available to differentiate themselves in the market and communicate their unique qualities to customers and employees."

"Companies competing for knowledgeable and experienced professionals and technicians find that a stimulating office environment can improve their ability to recruit and retain these 'gold-collar' workers."

Ethospace brochure, Herman Miller, 1986 [13]

Issued by the manufacturer when a new product launched, these full color sales brochures reveal the infrastructural components and general specifications of the office systems. They directly link economic and social benefits of the product to the client. Insisting on efficiency, notational systems, and productivity as a means of saving money has consequences that abstract not only space and material in real time, but also the workers who occupy and build these workspaces — specifically racial and ethnic minority workers who benefit from actual laws that seek to address past racial injustice. Through a convergence of interests in the economy, higher returns on profit, cheaper labor, cost savings and speculative contractual language, modular architecture maps onto the raced body in adverse ways.

MOST OF US ARE IN BUSINESS TO OFFER A PRODUCT OR SERVICE

Some thirty years since Koolhaas' 1993 essay, open floor plans, modular architecture, and the co-working lease model have become quotidian. Co-working ventures operate on a global scale with the intent of providing a short-term hub for future capital, real estate, and infrastructure.[14]

The modular yet generic sensibilities of an open floor plan that allow for different types of labor to occur on the same floor coincides with the type of body/worker invited to rent flexible co-working spaces. The WeWork building sublease franchise for example, with its trendy high-end interior design, contemporary fabric and color choices for furniture, wallpaper and plants, all of which are designed to be reminiscent of domestic spaces, brands itself and functions as a space for the young, global, entrepreneurial, "multicultural" and "diverse" able-bodied worker.[15]

A business model for these leased spaces conflates enterprise ventures with demographics to help shape the aesthetics of these contemporary open floor plans. Other co-working operators appeal to specific subcultures, even more narrowly defining flex space markets: spaces exclusively for cannabis entrepreneurs, creative art workers, or women-only spaces.[16]

Efficiency is now rendered visible in these spaces through the free and open transaction of varied businesses collaborating and exchanging services side-by-side. Free of commonplace cubicle partitions that cut through sight lines and traditional lease structures that require tenants to abide by customary terms, small business ventures and satellite offices that avoid the lingering and watchful eye of human resource compliance measures (like Affirmative Action or the Affordable Care Act), and the conversion of workers from 1040 (wage earners) to 1099 (contract workers) thrive in these plans.[17] In the 21st century, open floor plans and the modular architecture housed in it function as aesthetics that homogenize and "manage the diversity"[18] of office workers.

Endnotes:

1. Easterling, Keller. *Extrastatecraft: The Power of Infrastructure Space* (London: Verso, 2016), 170-173.

2. Golland, David Hamilton. *Constructing Affirmative Action: The Struggle for Equal Employment Opportunity* (The University Press of Kentucky, 2011), 9-15.

3. Koolhaas, Rem. "Typical Plan," *S,M,L,XL* (New York: The Monacelli Press, 1995).

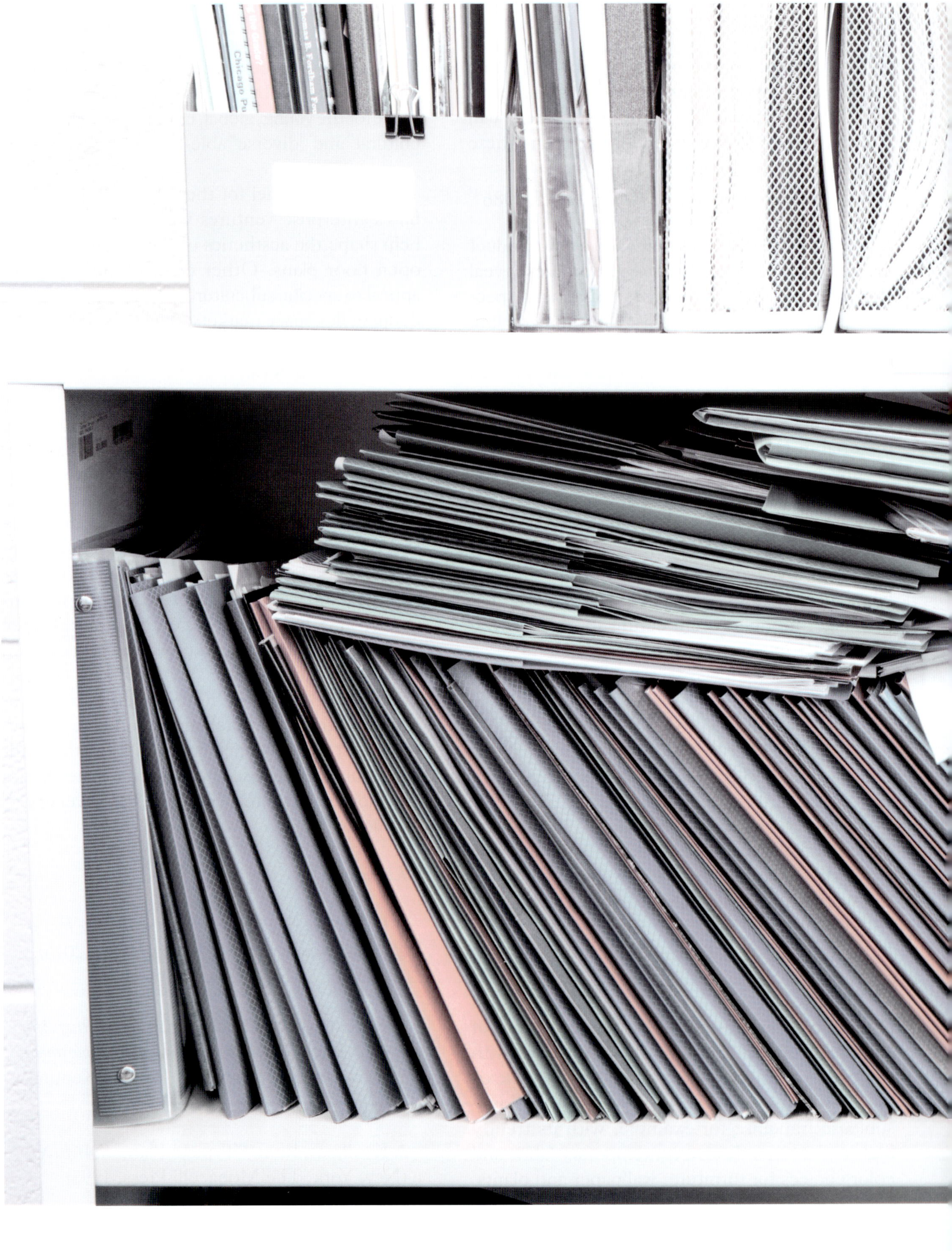

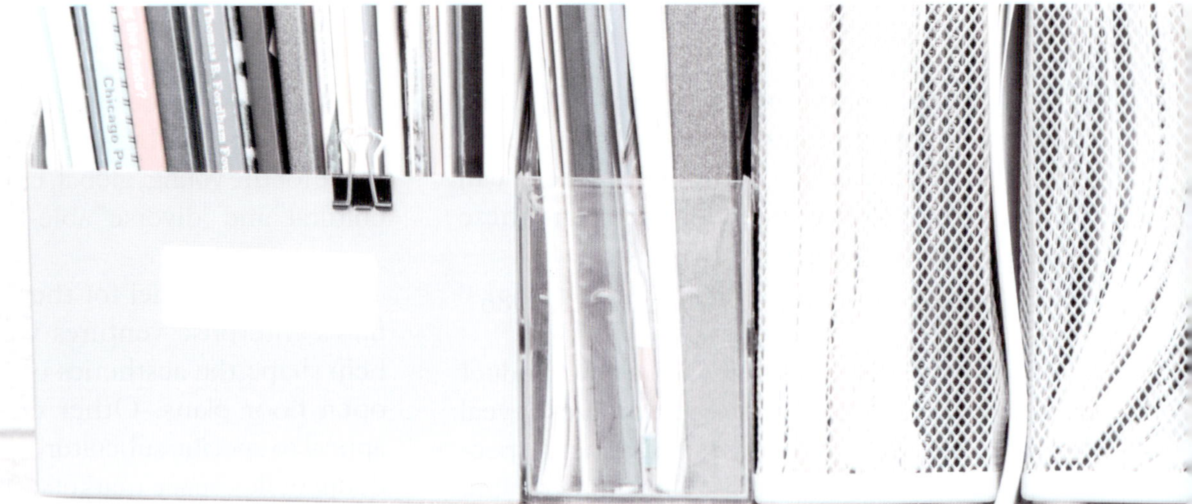

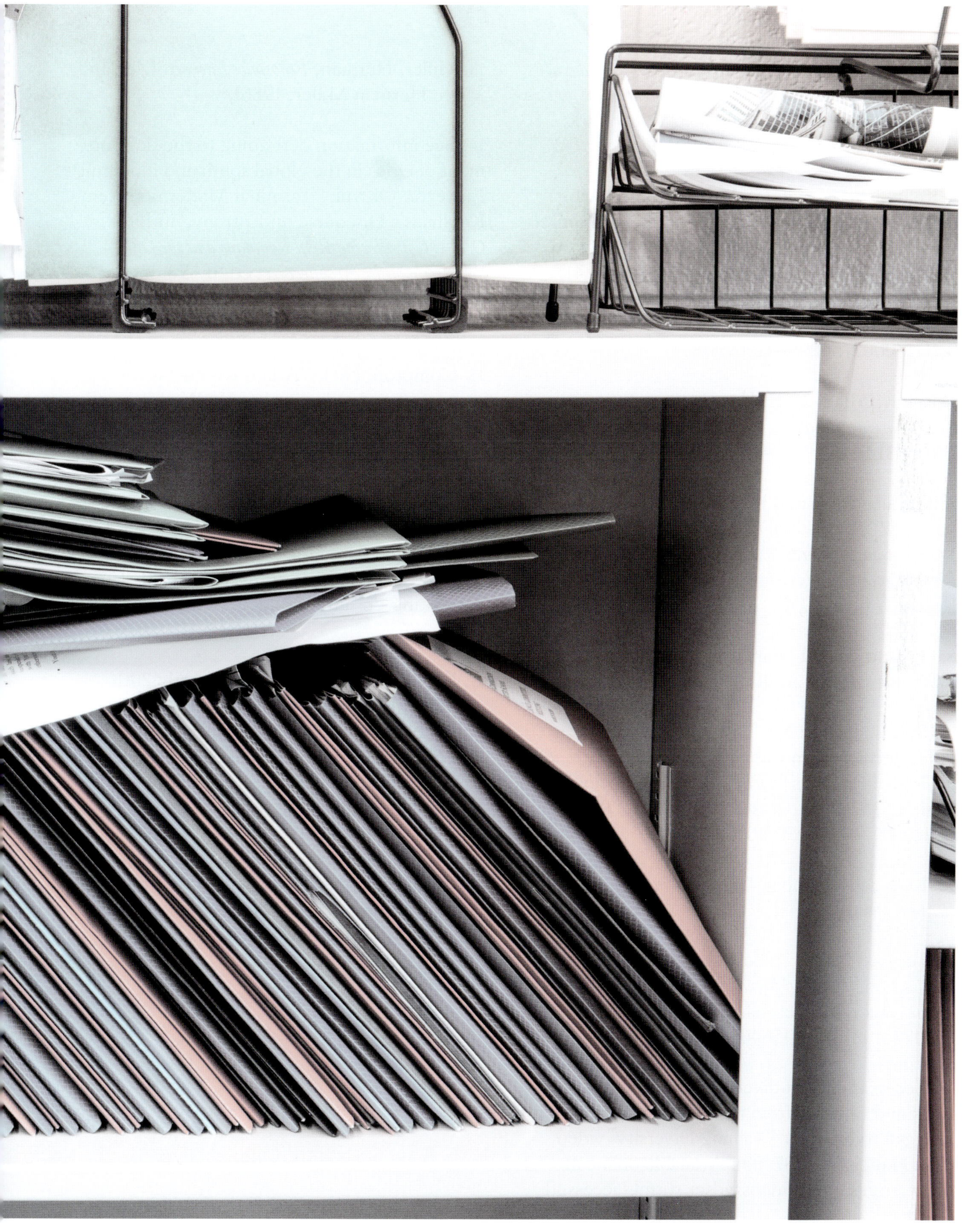

4. Spencer, Douglas. *The Architecture of Neoliberalism: How Contemporary Architecture Became an Instrument of Control and Compliance* (New York: Bloomsbury Academic, 2018), 94-109.

5. Kelly, Erin, and Frank Dobbin. "How Affirmative Action Became Diversity Management: Employer Response to Antidiscrimination Law, 1961-1996." *The American Behavioral Scientist* 41, no. 7 (04, 1998): 960-84. Accessed January 15, 2019. https://doi-org.libproxy.newschool.edu/10.1177/0002764298041007008.

6. Kelley, Mike. *Minor Histories: Statements, Conversations, Proposals* (Cambridge, Mass: MIT, 2004), 312-315.

7. Nuttall, Chris, and Propst, Robert. *The Integrated Office Facility: New Design Criteria and Specifications Required to Achieve Integrated Facility Performance* (Ann Arbor, Mich: Herman Miller Research Corp., 1979), 30.

8. Golland, David Hamilton. *Constructing Affirmative Action*, 36-40.

9. Collins, Sharon M. "Diversity in the Post Affirmative Action Labor Market: a Proxy for Racial Progress?" *Critical Sociology* 37, no. 5 (2011): 521-540. Accessed January 30, 2019. doi:10.1177/0896920510380076.

10. Kelly, and Dobbin. *"How Affirmative Action Became,"* 960-984.

11. Torres, Gerald. "Neoliberalism and affirmative action." *Cultural Dynamics* 27, no. 1 (2015): 43-62. Accessed February 5, 2019. doi: 10.1177/0921374014564654.

12. See examples of diversity training consultant work and tutorials from the 1990s in Copeland Griggs Productions' "Valuing Diversity" video (San Francisco: 1987–90). Available online at www.griggs.com/videos/vdser.shtml (accessed 2019).

13. Miller, Herman, *Ethospace Interiors* (Zeeland, Mich: Herman Miller, 1986).

14. See information pertaining to the development of cities in the global south and modernity: Enwezor, Okwui. "Terminal Modernity: Rem Koolhaas's Discourse on Entropy," in *What is OMA: Considering Rem Koolhaas and the Office for Metropolitan Architecture*, ed. by Véronique Patteeuw (Rotterdam: NAi Publishers, 2003), 116.

15. Compton, Nick. "Adam Kimmel is recharged and redirected as WeWork's creative chief." https://www.wallpaper.com/lifestyle/wework-adam-kimmel-interview (accessed November 30, 2019).

16. Margolies, Jane. November 19, 2019. "They Don't Call Them Hot Desk for Nothing." https://www.nytimes.com/2019/11/20/style/coworking-design.html (accessed November 30, 2019).

17. For literature about 19th and early 20th century workspaces in skyscrapers and the practice of perception and racial recognition see: Brown, Adrienne R. *The Black Skyscraper: Architecture and the Perception of Race*. Johns Hopkins Paperback ed., Johns Hopkins University Press, 2019.

18. This concept is developed by R. Roosevelt Thomas, who in 1983 founded the American Institute for Managing Diversity.

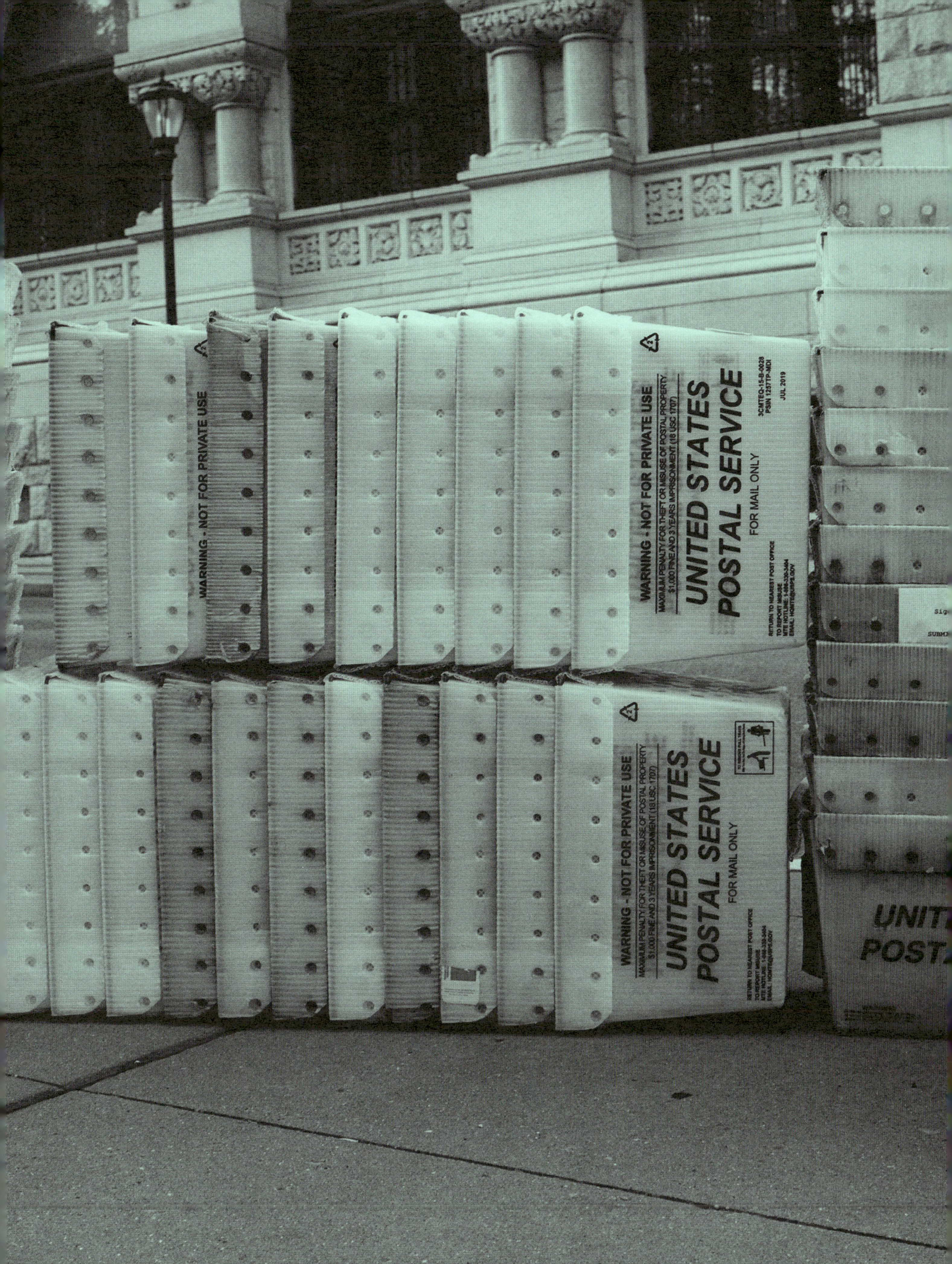
WARNING - NOT FOR PRIVATE USE
UNITED STATES
POSTAL SERVICE
FOR MAIL ONLY
WARNING - NOT FOR PRIVATE USE
WARNING - NOT FOR PRIVATE USE
UNITED STATES
POSTAL SERVICE
FOR MAIL ONLY

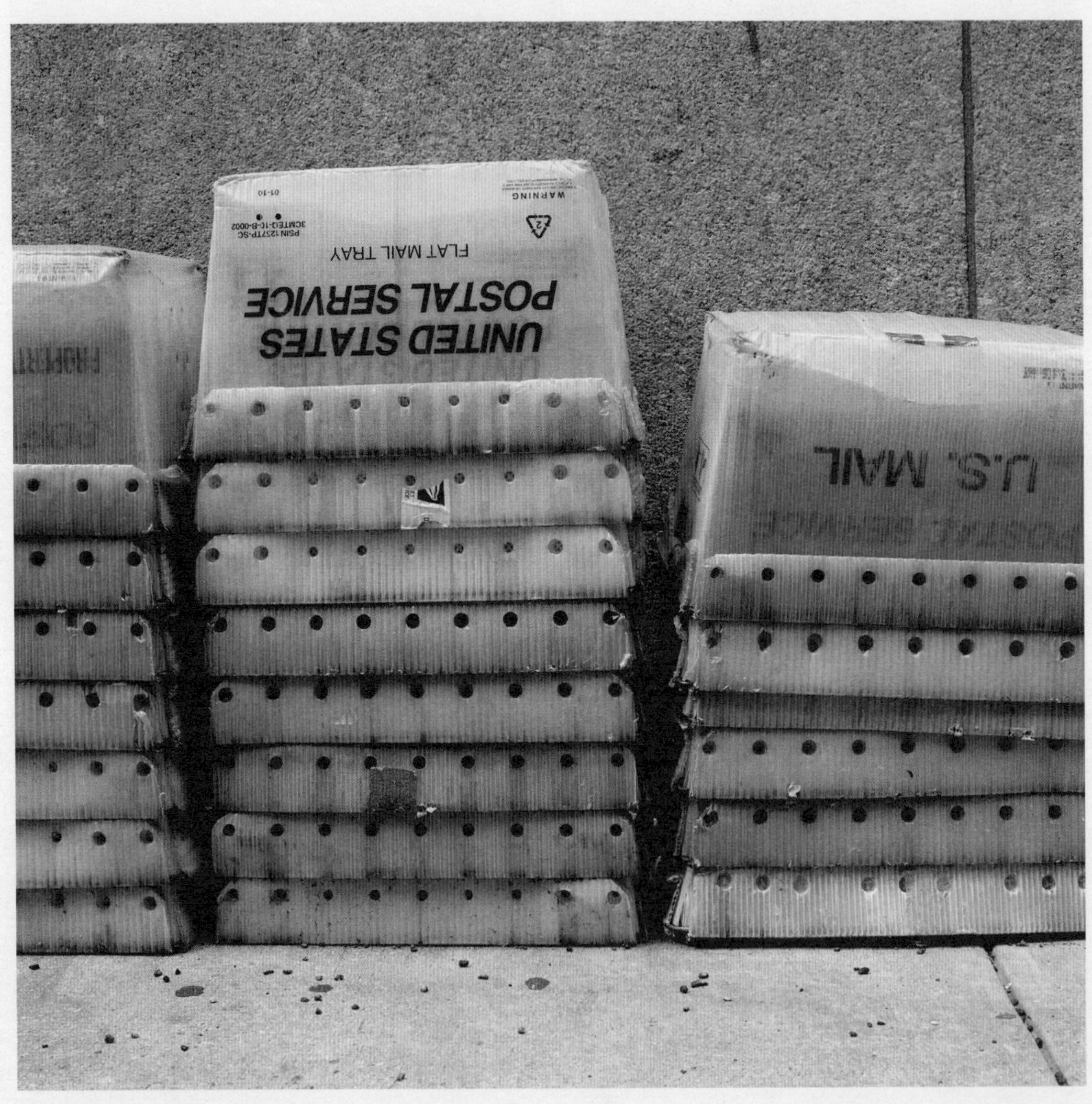
UNITED STATES
POSTAL SERVICE
FLAT MAIL TRAY
WARNING
U.S. MAIL

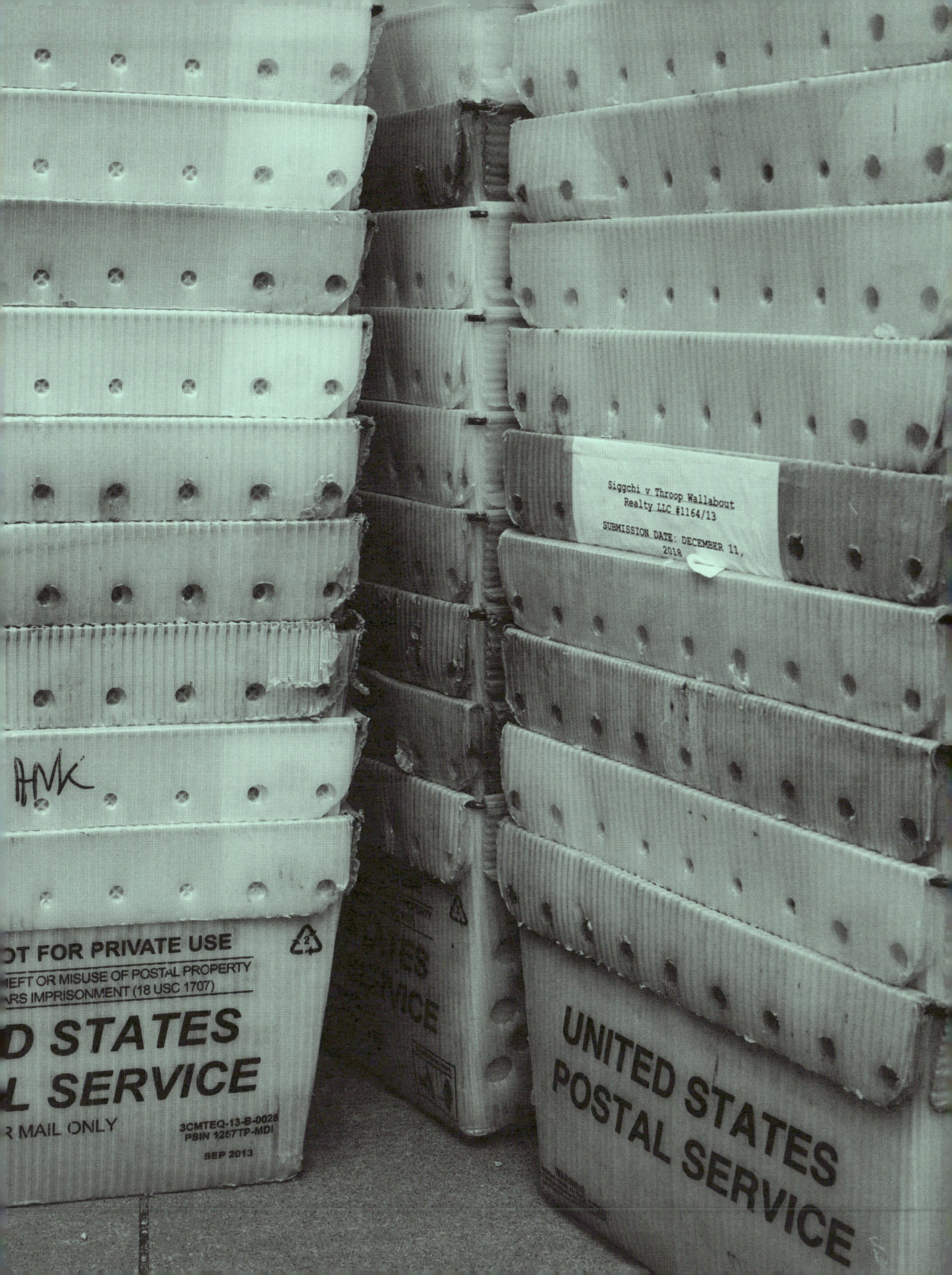

Siggchi v Throop Wallabout
Realty LLC #1164/13
SUBMISSION DATE: DECEMBER 11,
2018
OT FOR PRIVATE USE
HEFT OR MISUSE OF POSTAL PROPERTY
ARS IMPRISONMENT (18 USC 1707)
D STATES
L SERVICE
R MAIL ONLY
3CMTEQ-13-B-0028
PSIN 1257TP-MDI
SEP 2013
UNITED STATES
POSTAL SERVICE

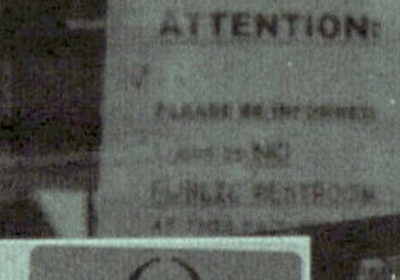
BIOHAZARD

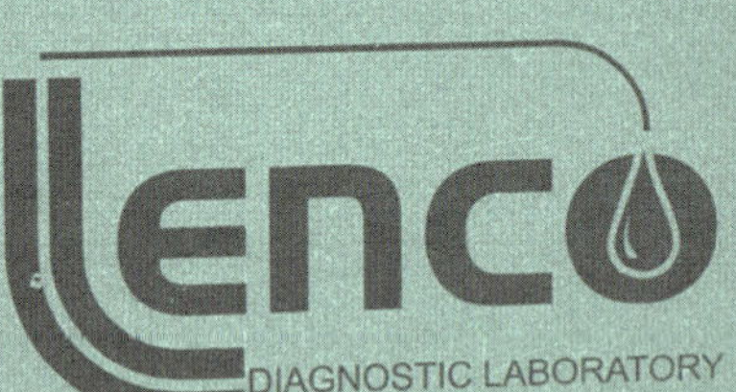
Lenco
DIAGNOSTIC LABORATORY

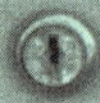

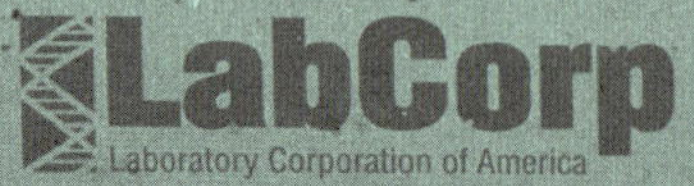
LabCorp
Laboratory Corporation of America

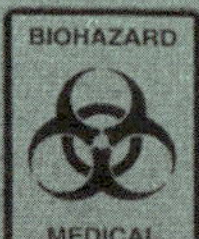
BIOHAZARD
MEDICAL SPECIMENS

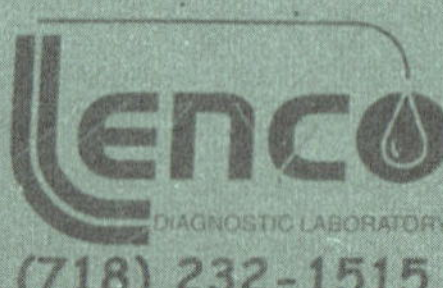
Lenco
DIAGNOSTIC LABORATORY
(718) 232-1515

An Interview with Jessica Vaughn
by Magdalyn Asimakis

MA: You've been working on a new project lately that expands your investigation into how material and physical structures can and do shape our reading of space and labor—and you do that through sculpture, video, and text. Though this is the first time you're looking at corporate spaces in your work, it's not the first time you're examining institutional space and institutional infrastructure.

JV: Right. My previous works brought together a series of objects procured from different manufacturing corporations that provide seating for the Chicago Transit Authority. "After Willis (rubbed, used and moved)" was made from used, stained, and worn seat inserts from the Chicago Transit Authority trains. Additionally, there were sculptures made from discarded, leftover upholstery and scraps from the manufacturers' assembly lines. These works, named after the manufacturers' color swatches, were arranged on the floor. This series focused on materials taken directly from the production of assembly—or the corporate setting—and from the infrastructure that they served: city infrastructure and public transit.

MA: In your new work, compliance comes up as something both physical and conceptual. The word compliance, in this context, originates in physics—this idea of a flexible material that supports production. So, when thinking about this characteristic in corporate or institutional spaces where, in this case, diversity training was required to comply with government standards for equal opportunity workplaces, it becomes a loaded term in that the businesses must comply, but the organizational hegemony is sometimes unaltered. So, I was wondering how you think about this incompatibility.

JV: Sure. I do see compliance operating as both a physical and conceptual term. With the train seats from my previous works, for example, international standardization dictated the particular measurements of the seats, along with configurations from the American Standards Institute. The standards are based, for example, on the limits of machinery, typical body mass, safety measures, and economics. Also, written laws and policy figure as measures of compliance—executive orders, civil rights policy, the law in concrete ways, and sometimes in indirect ways—register compliance in spaces of labor and on their workers.

The beginnings of affirmative action in the United States, first initiated under the US federal government contracts in the 60s, were aimed at implementing equitable hiring of racial and ethnic minorities, given historical patterns of discrimination, specifically towards African Americans. When training under the guise of diversity management is, as you suggest, implemented to replace Affirmative Action or elements of equal employment opportunity measures—actual law—it obfuscates the original means of address. Diversity becomes a concern exclusively for soft policing or correction of isolated incidents—a hope, in a way, that the market will correct past grievances and discrimination, rather than the state. In this case, compliance removes difference, in an attempt to make the worker and goods accessible for production and consumption. In a sense, measures to address diversity become the invisible language of global bureaucratic and corporate structures.

MA: And, building on that, you and I speak a lot about diversity rhetoric and the use of optics and metrics to prove diversity in an organization, or more accurately to prove the compliance with diversity goals. Inclusion is vital, but due to the use of corporate processes in places such as art museums, the success of diversity initiatives are up to metric optics, mainly strategically gathered metrics that translate well into board lingo. And taking a historicist approach to this data can also give the impression that the progress is more comprehensive than it is in reality. So, we are essentially taking contemporary ideas and dropping them into archaic infrastructures.

JV: Yeah, I do think that there's a way in which cultural institutions sometimes miss the mark on moving beyond treating their programming as advertisement or a product directed at specific viewer demographics. Especially when the actual structure of the institutions stay the same. For example, small, wealthy board memberships that dictate not only funding structures, but also—to a degree—curatorial framing based on trends in the art market. When these institutions rely specifically on data, metrics, and attendance numbers, it allows their programming and curatorial decisions to function without commentary or critique. It is kind of like, if the data says so, it must be right. When the primary concerns for an institution's programming are based upon this matrix—a color-blind, one-size-fits-all approach, with the feeling of actually counting for everyone—the institution has, in practice, only accounted for those who chose to identify. From my perspective as an artist, sometimes you work with curatorial departments that have little knowledge of work by artists of color. Not just lacking knowledge of the historical lineage, or contemporary cousins that influence the work, but not even having the language to be in conversation with an artist. When the language cannot be accounted for by the institution, you are left with museums and galleries exhibiting work by artists of color through the lens of either an intense pedagogical framework—as literal advertisements for their public programs—or through figurative representations mediated by the current political news cycle. This really leaves no room for critical interpretation that considers where the artist's work sits in the world or the multitudes the work may derive from. We are not afforded that luxury unless the artworks can be explicitly read through the figure. Magdalyn, as a curator, how do you make decisions about inclusion, and what does that mean to you?

MA: It's something that I think about a lot, and not just in my practice but also in terms of infrastructural strategies like what you're exploring in your work. I'm interested in what you said about the relationship between artists of color and curatorial and marketing departments. And my criticality around diversity metrics comes from my time working in institutional contexts where infrastructures can basically translate identifications into checked boxes, or where single individuals can become responsible for representing entire communities, and that's a lot of weight, which is what you were saying, as well. Translation is so important in a calcified bureaucracy. There's a desire for mastery, which museums strive for and is rooted in the colonial mindset. But it also becomes this kind of neoliberalization of inclusion, which is why I ask you about hegemony. I'm always curious about the tension between old structure and contemporary work, which you understand from a different perspective than me. I try to ask how can you engage in praxis from beginning to end rather than just in representation. There's no one answer, but for me it's ongoing dialogues with artists, listening to what they're trying to do, reading, and always thinking about intersectional anticapitalist ethics and approaches to process. These can be applied in any context, as a modest way of pressing back on a colonial and neoliberal arts infrastructure, instead of putting a lot of energy into making sure that practice translates to the way that we have all already been conditioned to see things.

JV: I like what you're saying, especially when thinking about inclusion. I also think of inclusion as a process that is ongoing, that doesn't rest, that isn't stagnant. It's about challenging representation and bringing individuals together to create a set of circumstances that will consider a diverse set of ideas and experiences for present and future projects. I think about how Andrea Fraser's book *2016 in Museums, Money, and Politics* does just that. Her listing of funding to American art institutions not only shows the intersection of money and politics over time, but also in the present and future. It acts almost as a guidebook to how artists can call attention to those institutional practices that don't serve the art, artist, or politics of equitable inclusion.

MA: It's really incredible how Fraser reveals the underpinnings of why things are structured the way they are in museums, and really importantly how that converses with American politics. Part of your new work includes footage from 1990s and 2000s diversity training videos, with transcripts of the text superimposed. How do you see these older videos in relation to contemporary institutional approaches to diversity, and not necessarily just in corporate spaces but perhaps also academia or art museums?

JV: There's still this flattening of differences that occurs in institutional spaces. A sort of "colorblindness," or lack of acknowledgement that problematic structures toward racial and ethnic equity exist because of historical patterns of racial discrimination in this country. I think that calls for racial and cultural equity have in more recent years come full circle to address concerns for civil rights gains from a moral perspective, but still, there is a tendency by many art institutions to address racial equity primarily and only out of market and economic concerns. Educational programming is seen as a conduit to bridge the market concerns of diversity within institutions. The US federal government historically had a hand in bridging educational and economic institutions together. The GI Bill post-World War II was used as a means of preventing a slowdown of the economy. Government labor policy that directly bargained with unions in technical and trade schooling, specifically for the inclusion of Black workers during the Second Great Migration and after the passing of the Civil Rights Act of 1964, is another example of stabilizing civic economic concerns through job training and education. In my forthcoming work in video sculpture and installation, I see institutional diversity training as an extension of such education driven by market concerns.

The training videos of HR employees mediate the financial and legal concerns of management through best practices and education. And, in this case specifically, inclusion and diversity. An older work by Allan Sekula, "School Is a Factory," is a great piece that directly extracts the relationship between schools and the economy. Not necessarily hitting on these ideas of diversity and racial inclusion, but still really pinpointing the link between schooling and economics.

MA: Your newer work uses materials and architecture found in different sites of labor. For example, cubicles, drop ceiling, and shelving. Can you speak to the spatial aspects of your new work's installation?

JV: Sure. I wanted to consider different architecture components that make up contemporary office work environments. The sculptures use acoustic tiles and fluorescent lights to create drop ceilings and cubicle walls that segregate workspace. With this work, I wanted to consider the space of the floor and the dead space of the ceiling. The use of a drop ceiling is an extension of a grid, just one that happens to be turned upwards. I wanted to mess with the logic of the grid and the structures imposed both by architects and city planners, to the extension of a city plan used by urban developers who divide neighborhoods targeted for economic development—or not—with mapped-out and gridded spaces. The materials I choose to work with fit the realm of modular architecture, something that is flexible and typical, architecture that corrects itself for the market. I have been looking at architecture that encompasses the large open floor plans built and aestheticized through typical plan build-outs coined by Rem Koolhaas in his "Typical Plan" essay from 1993 about office architecture, and smaller personal units of furniture produced and sold by IKEA, Herman Miller, or Steelcase. This material mimics and embodies the aspirational notion of being a fit for everyone. So, I would like to think that some of my concerns around conversations about race and how workers are figured or not, made visible or not, are elaborated upon through this hyper-market-driven material in architectural space.

MA: Is this something you're hoping that visitors feel as they're walking through?

JV: Yeah, I hope there's a sense of something being modular, or of these grid formations that we somehow take as being normative or inherently inflexible. The idea is that visitors are able to walk through the space and get a different sense of situating themselves through what is considered typical architecture.

MA: And in terms of the materiality of your work, and how it relates to labor, much of your practice includes discarded or surplus materials, architectural fragments, and essentially remnants of people's labor and presence. How does that connect with this new work?

JV: I think that there is an interesting way in which objects that have circulated through spaces have a matter-of-factness about themselves. These are the things that over time are reoriented, augmented, shared with others, and in indirect and sometimes very subtle ways show the process of how something is constructed, made, and exhausted. My sense of what I like to make comes from understanding materials that I've used and my experiences in different work environments. There's something about using decommissioned materials taken from the state and bureaucratic resources that calls attention to process, and specifically an overworked body, a system that is sort of treading along, sometimes disrupted by change, but often remains status quo. Wedging myself into these systems to procure this material is the first disruptor, and I create works by moving through research of records, cultural and political writings, and working with materials in the studio. The materials that I procure highlight and illuminate systems of repetition, space, rhetoric, and language that in the long run dictate how people participate in society as workers and consumers.

MA: In creating your works, do you think about how corporate infrastructures affect the body? You spoke about the overworked body. In some ways this is visualized through the actors in the diversity training videos. I'm wondering about how the body or embodiment relates to your work, in its creation but also as something that people encounter.

JV: There's this idea that anyone should be able to occupy these spaces, but there are many ways in which racial differences, and whiteness as a construct, make this virtually impossible. And I think the text in the videos, although dated, begins to make clear how the aspirations for capital inherently fall short at correcting discrimination. The texts used in the video are streamed together from a number of diversity training videos and cut together in different patterns and sequences. The scenes used in the video consists of groupings of found footage from these training videos and footage I shot in different office spaces. The staged nature of the footage heightens my awareness of the artificial relationship between the content of the video and the actual workers in real life. And I think that the regulations and compliances within the ideological concepts of various institutions dictate how we act, move, and interact with others. These forms of compliance and the minutiae of these ideological concepts that start off as texts, laws, jurisdiction writing, some form of a script or proposal, become invisible once a material object is produced. It then reveals itself again through the direct action someone might have with architecture, infrastructure, or products—everything really.

MA: I like how you're drawing attention to the texts by overlaying them in the video. It draws attention to that gap between theory and practice. It is sort of echoed in the spatial installation as well. Your displaying of the infrastructure doesn't transform the space. You know it's a gallery, so what you do is place corporate and infrastructural materials within another structure, in this case a museum or gallery.

JV: Exactly. Exactly. These spaces share commonalities both materially and in practice. As an artist who benefits directly and greatly from cultural institutions, I think that there's a way in which I approach these ideas from a sense of care, an interest in seeing art and cultural institutions function differently and more equitably. These intersecting issues of economics and representation are not just theoretical points of interest but are actual conditions that exist in the world through material and aesthetic decision-making that have real consequences.

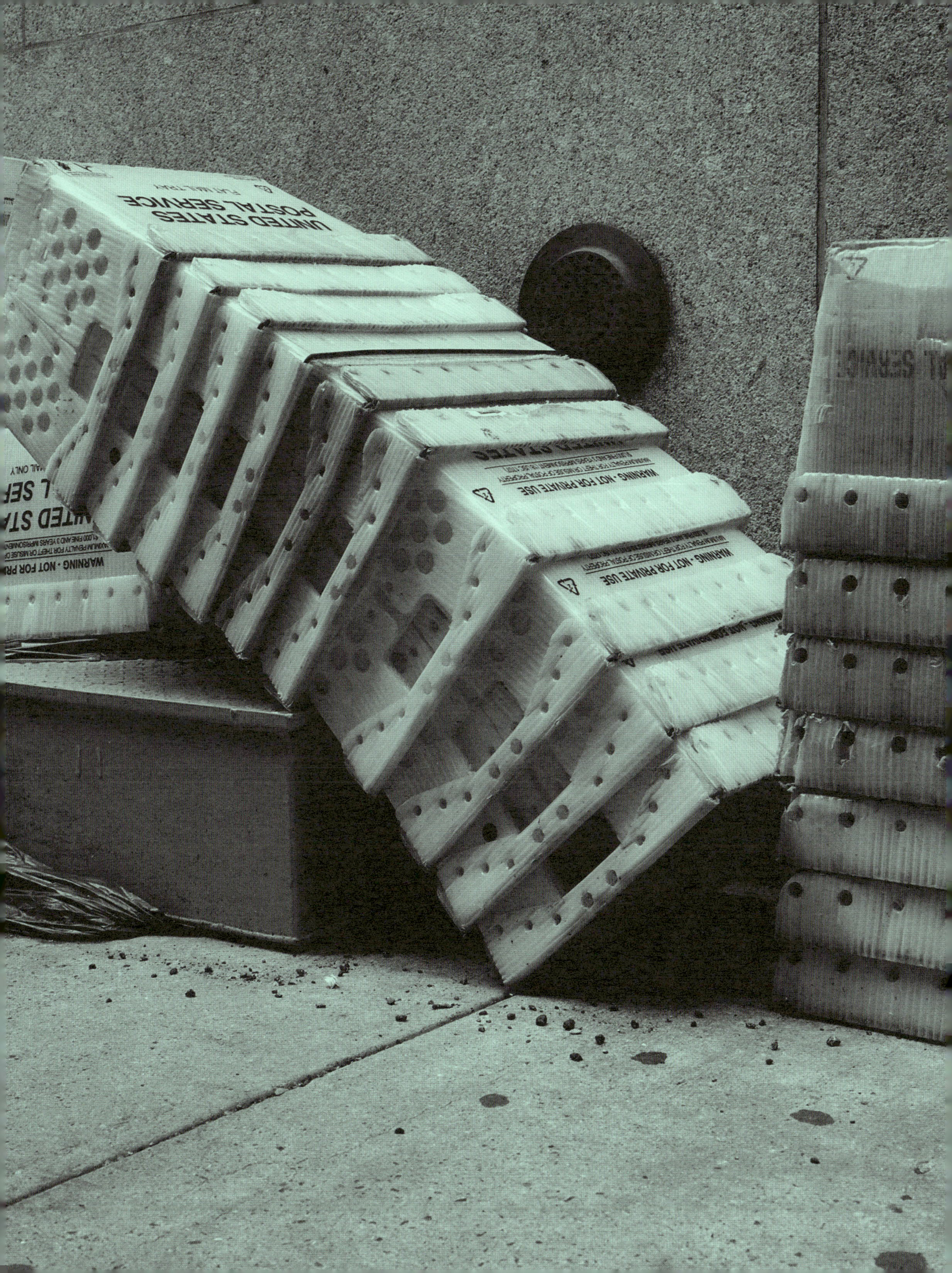
UNITED STATES
POSTAL SERVICE
WARNING - NOT FOR PRIVATE USE
WARNING - NOT FOR PRIVATE USE

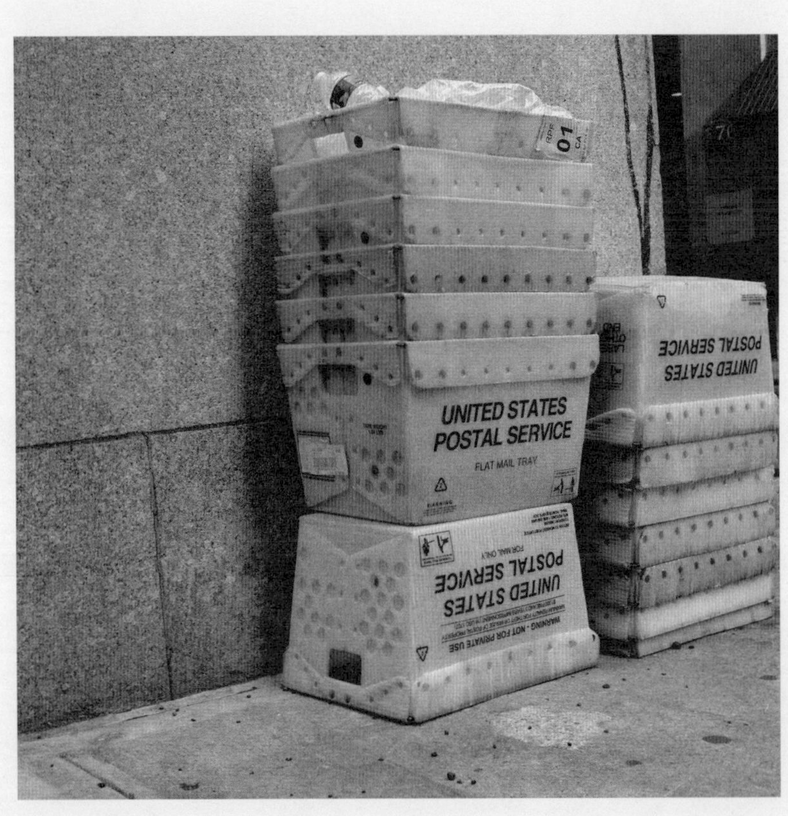
UNITED STATES
POSTAL SERVICE
FLAT MAIL TRAY

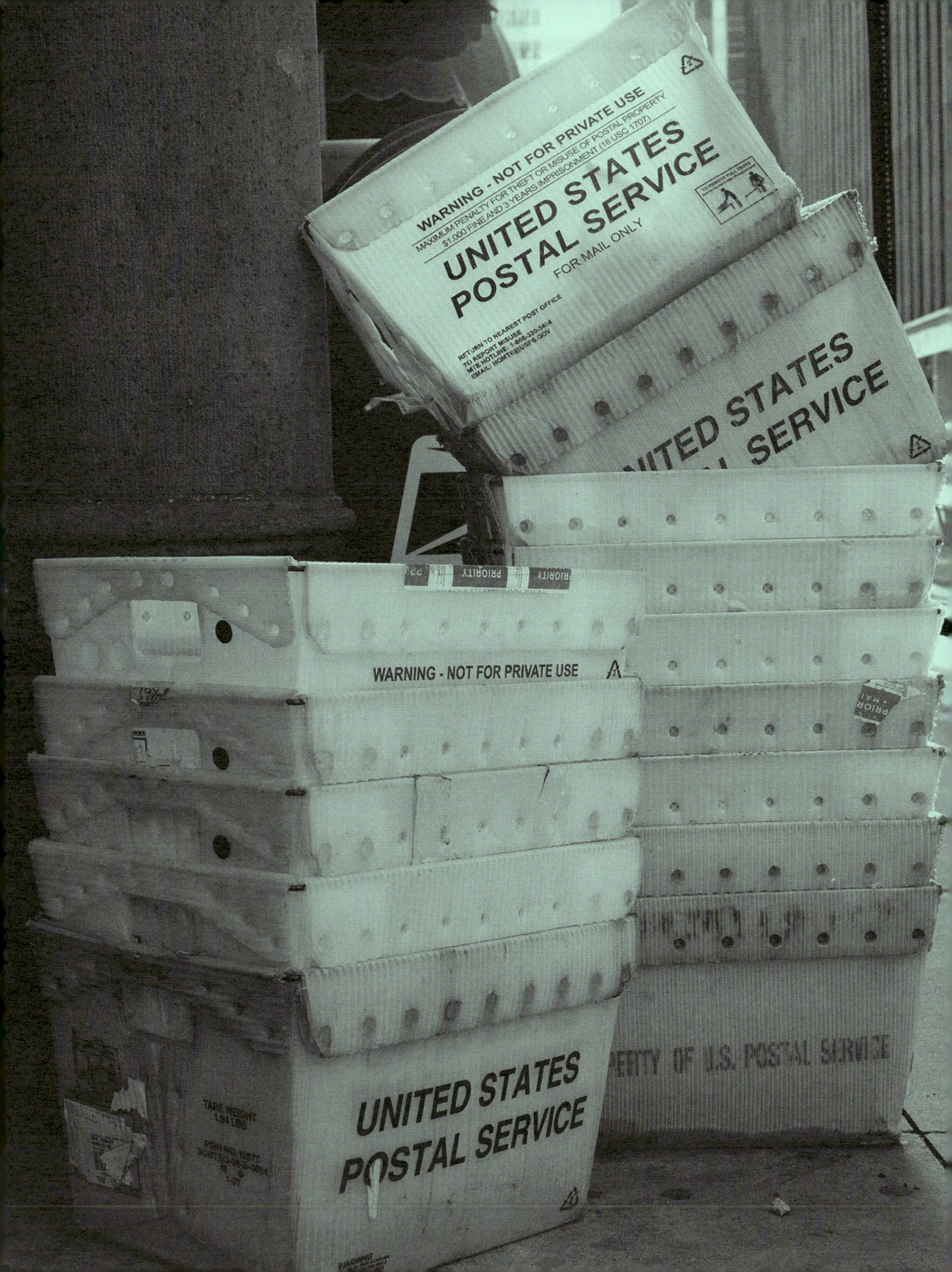

WARNING - NOT FOR PRIVATE USE
UNITED STATES
POSTAL SERVICE
FOR MAIL ONLY
UNITED STATES
POSTAL SERVICE
WARNING - NOT FOR PRIVATE USE
PRIORITY
UNITED STATES
POSTAL SERVICE
PERTY OF U.S. POSTAL SERVICE

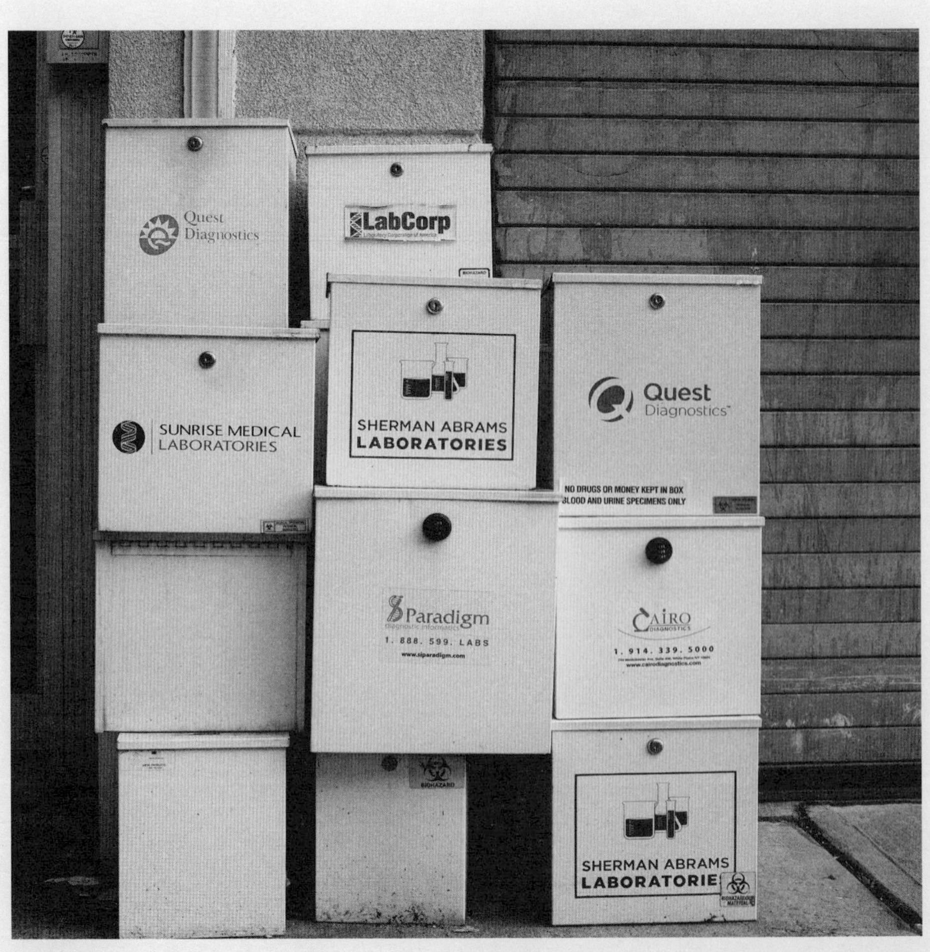
Quest Diagnostics
LabCorp
SUNRISE MEDICAL LABORATORIES
SHERMAN ABRAMS LABORATORIES
Quest Diagnostics
NO DRUGS OR MONEY KEPT IN BOX
BLOOD AND URINE SPECIMENS ONLY
Paradigm
1. 888. 599. LABS
CAIRO DIAGNOSTICS
1. 914. 339. 5000
SHERMAN ABRAMS LABORATORIE

Workspace Environments (2006 – present)

Job # One
2006 – 2007
Institutional building including a lab and individual, closed offices with cement floors.
- 30 employees
- 7 desks
- 7-8 chairs
- various shelving units
- 8 book/collateral shelves
- 1 copy machine
- 1 water cooler

Job # Two
2007 – 2009
Open office space with studio facilities, and a couple of closed offices with doors and carpeted floors.
- 13 employees
- 12-15 desks
- 15-20 chairs
- various shelving units
- 2 copy machines
- 4 conference desks
- 1 fridge
- 1 microwave
- 1 water cooler

Job # Three
2009 – 2010
Institutional space with open office with carpeted floors.
- 20 employees
- 15 cubicles
- 20-30 chairs
- 12-15 freestanding filing cabinets
- 2 copy machines
- 3 conference tables
- 1 water cooler

Job # Four
2012
Open office, 2nd floor of an office building with carpeted floors.
- 8-10 employees
- 1 reception desk
- 4 desks
- 5 chairs
- 1 copy machine
- 1 fridge

Job # Five
2012 – 2014
50th floor of an office building, mainly an open office with designated closed glass offices and conference rooms with cement and carpeted floors.
- 85 employees
- 80 desks
- 80 chairs
- 2 reception desks
- 1 conference desk
- 5 conference room chairs
- 2 copy machines
- 1 fridge
- 1 microwave
- 1 coffee machine
- 1 water cooler
- 2 lunch tables
- 12 lunch seats
- 1 break room television

Job # Six
2014 – 2015
4th floor of an office building with carpeted floors.
- 2-3 employees
- 2 desks
- 2 chairs
- 1 copy machine
- 1 postage machine
- 12 freestanding filing cabinets
- 5-6 book/collateral shelves

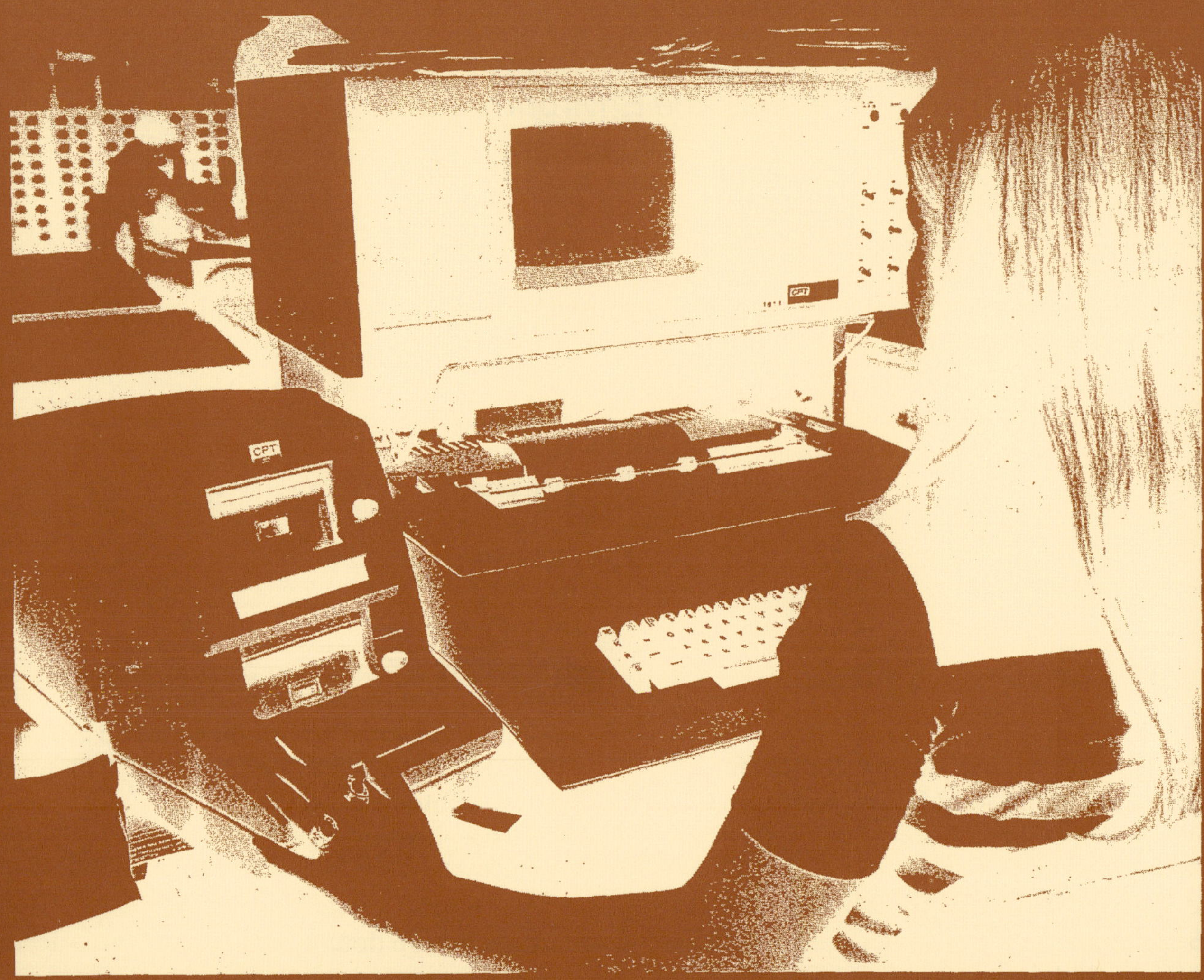

Deanna Kay Dove using automated text-editing typing equipment in the word processing center.

Automation of Accounts Receivable

In March 1977 we began implementing an automated accounts receivable system which eliminates the need for manual posting of payments; issues monthly statements, including delinquency notices, to all debtors; and provides user and management reports for followup and analysis.

Word Processing Center

In July 1977 we established a word processing center which, when fully operational, will serve most of the division. The center, using the latest in automated equipment, can produce more and better work, partly because its typing capability eliminates the peak-and-valley work demands on individual typists. Also video screens and memory apparatus are useful for work involving original compositions requiring extensive revisions and for high-volume, frequently used, standard text material.

1 conference table
6 conference room chairs
2 reception seats
1 small fridge

Job # Seven
2015
Institutional space, with individual closed offices with carpeted and cement floors.
8-10 employees
3 cubicle workstations
4 desks
7 chairs
1 book/collateral shelf
1 table
1 water cooler
1 coffee machine

Job # Eight
2016 – 2019
21st floor of an office building, mainly an open office with designated closed glass offices, conference rooms and carpeted floors.
38 employees
40 standing desks
+5 hot desks
40 desk chairs
1 book/collateral shelf
1 copy machine
2 printers
1 binding machine
1 postage machine
8 framed photos
5 conference tables
22 conference chairs
4 sofa chairs
1 reception desk
2 reception sofa chairs
1 large fridge
2 small fridges
1 dishwasher
1 microwave
3 coffee machines
1 water cooler
12 counter seats
10 lunch seats
2 lunch tables
2 break room televisions

Job # Nine
2019
40th floor of an office building, mainly an open office with designated closed glass offices and conference rooms with carpeted floors.
50 employees
50 desks
50 chairs
5 conference tables
25 conference chairs
2-3 book/collateral shelves
2 copy machines
2 fridges
1 dishwasher
2 microwaves
2 coffee machines
1 water cooler
1 ice machine
1 snack machine
7 lunch tables
20 lunch chairs
1 break room television

Job # Ten
2019 – 2020
Open office floor plan in a coworking building with glass facing doors and walls for all spaces including 4-5 conference rooms with wood floors.
27 employees
28 desks
28 chairs
7 conference tables
20 conference chairs
1 sofa
7 soft seating units
3 carpets
2 shelving units
3 television consoles
5 televisions
1 fridge
1 coffee machine

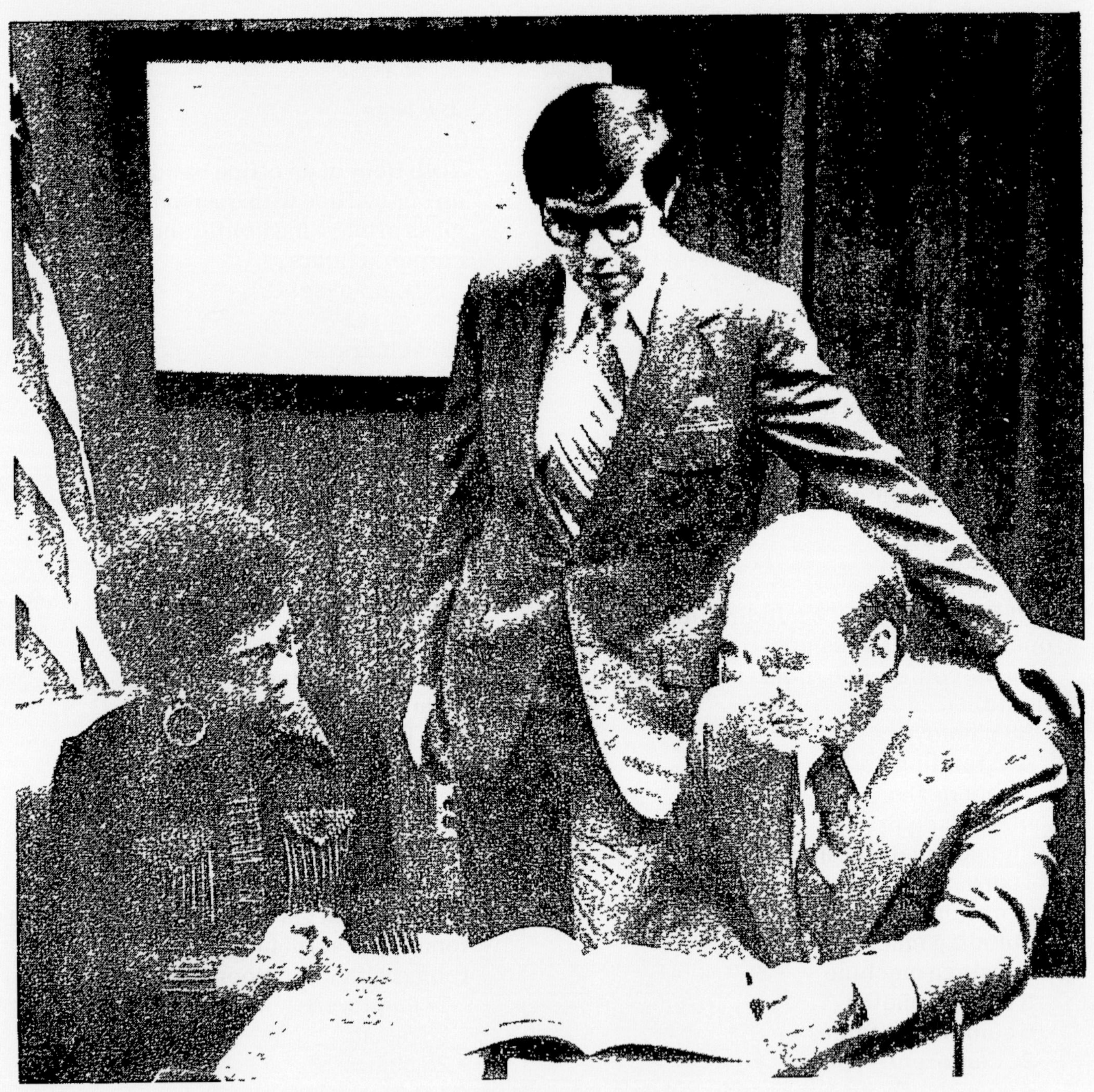

Dr. Mildred Glover, Atlanta University, discusses GAO report in relation to recently issued audit standards with Marvin Colbs, regional manager, Atlanta, and Jim Berry, Atlanta regional office.

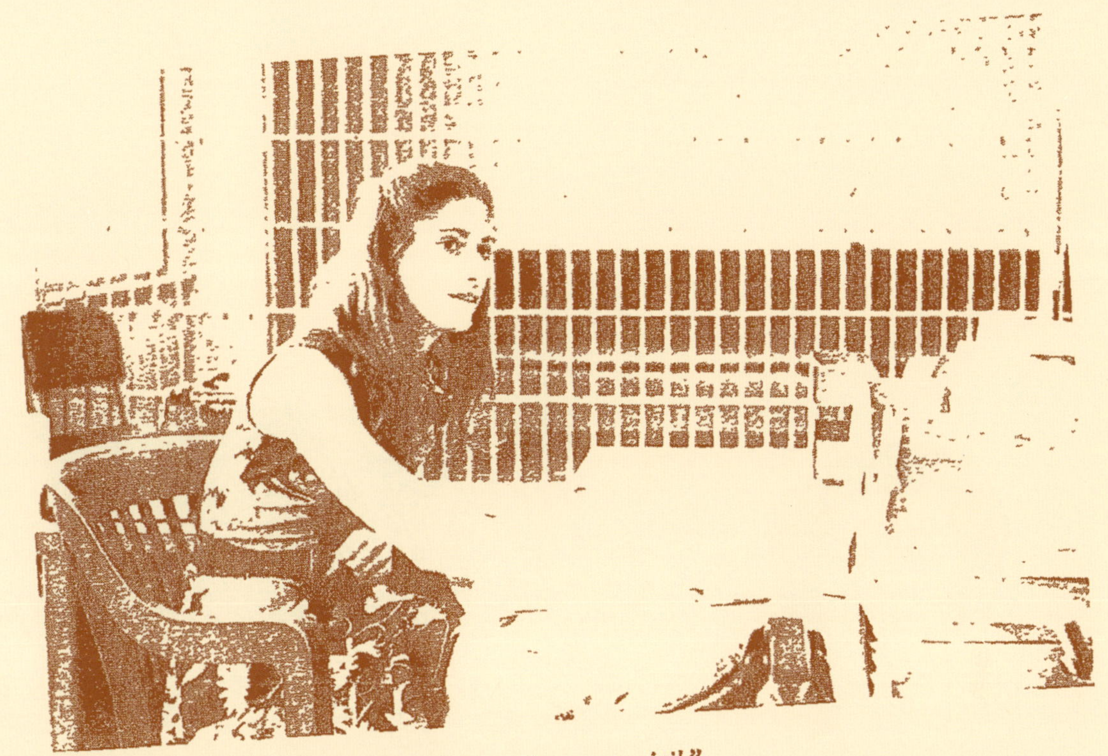

" * * our 'office' was in the back room of a county jail."*

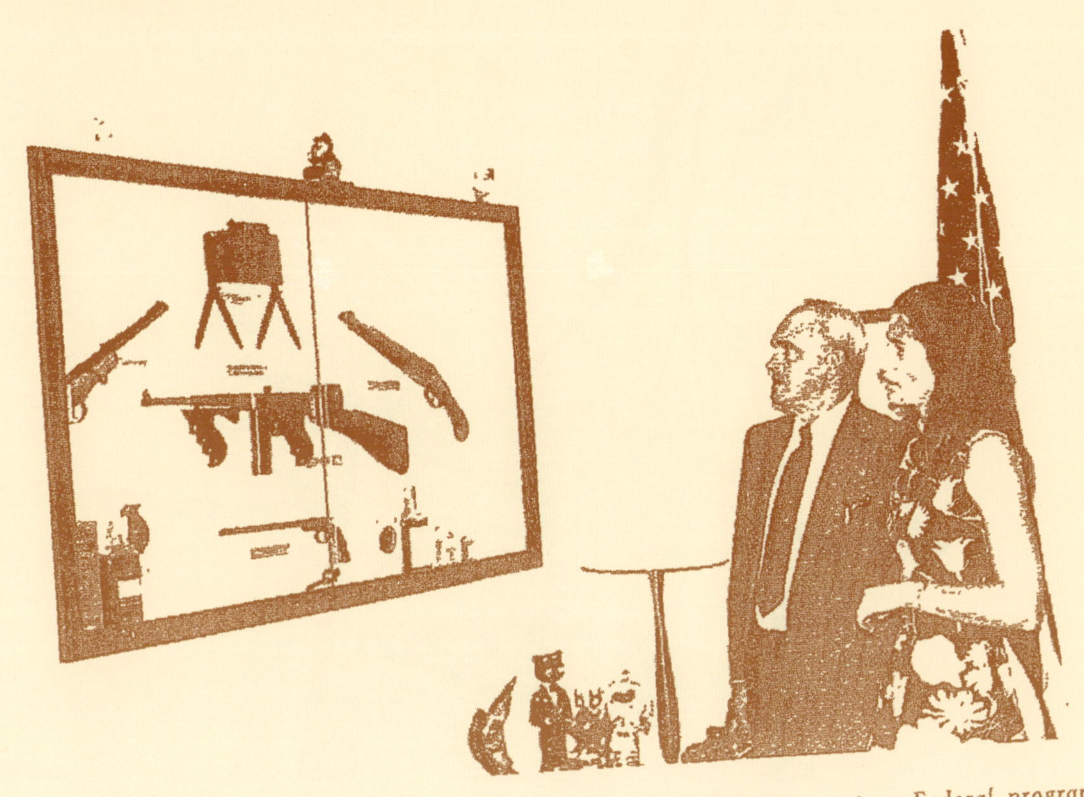

*"[GAO] has provided an opportunity to learn the operations of various Federal programs, such as those carried out by the Cincinnati office of the Bureau of Alcohol, Tobacco and Firearms, Treasury Department, * * *."*

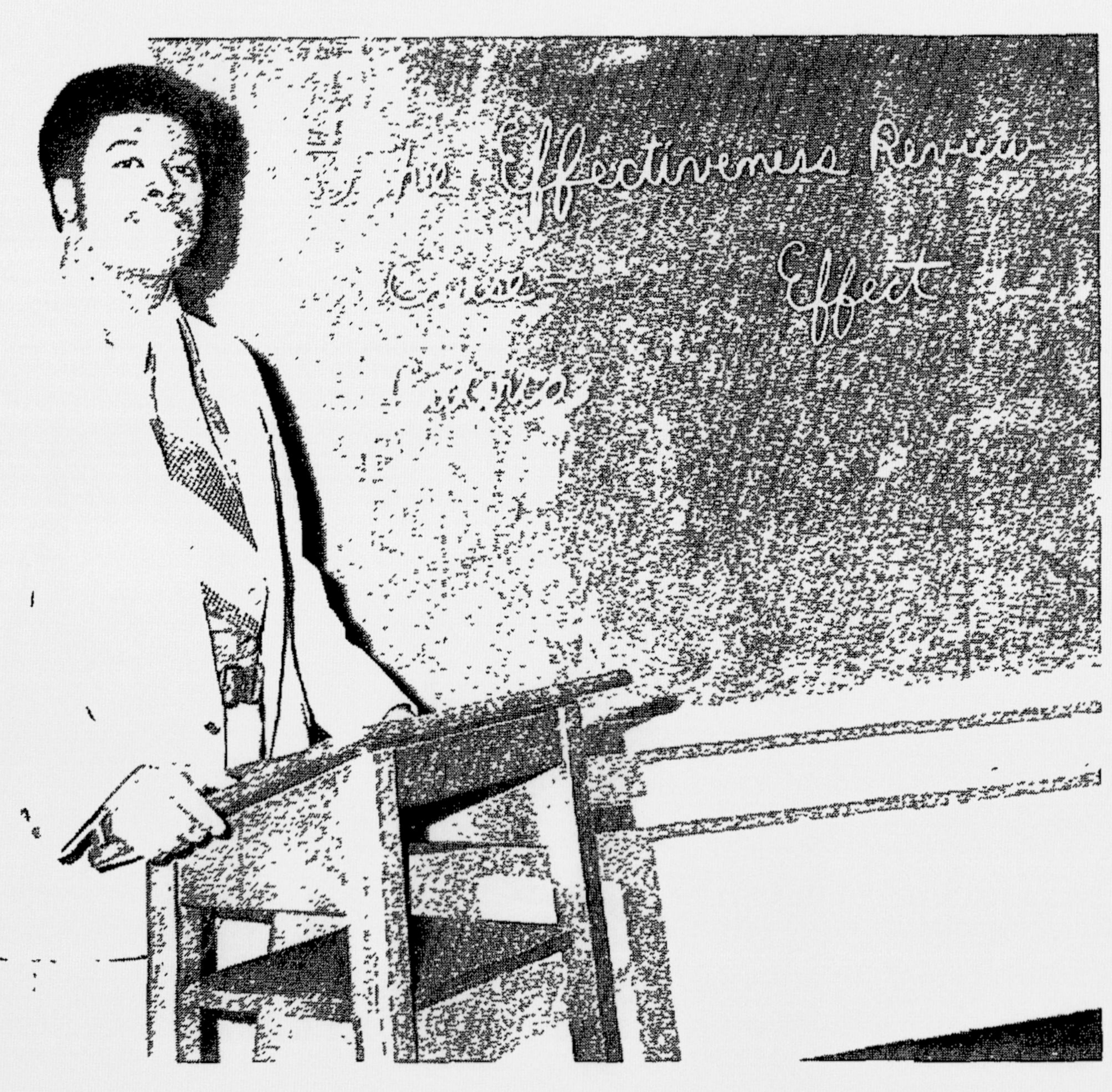

The author discusses the GAO auditors magic words—Criteria, Cause, and Effect.

Job Responsibilities
(2006 – present)

Job # One	2006 – 2007
• Coordinate research activities across multiple organizations • Plan and schedule study meetings with partners, participating sites, and collaborators • Work well with other study personnel, including research personnel and program leadership • Coordinate training and technical assistance activities for clinical staff, including developing agenda and meeting materials • Gather program data for grant reports and presentations • Play an active role in dissemination of findings, including preparation of manuscripts and presentations • Assist with program flyers, posters, brochures, and social media promotions • Prepare reports, agendas, memos, meeting minutes and email correspondence • Reserve meeting spaces • Manage logistics of board meetings • Organize the calendar and coordinate meeting reminders • Provide reception coverage when needed	

Job # Two	2007 – 2009
1. Studio Programs • Work with the manager of studio programs to perform tasks associated with developing course curricula, creating artist teacher/teaching assistant contracts, and related communications as necessary • Work with the manager of studio programs to monitor all studio programs division expenses • Monitor student behavior and carry out discipline, as needed • Work at the front reception area to admit students to the front door, direct students to studios, assist with questions, unlock studios/storage areas as appropriate, and provide general troubleshooting services for students, artist-teachers and teaching assistants • Hire and supervise employees and contractors needed to assist in the operation of the studio programs division including teaching assistants to ensure a diverse and skilled teaching staff. Serve as the education department's primary point of contact to artist teachers and teaching assistants for any questions related to supplies, attendance, permission slips, and studio needs • Market, plan, and implement the annual advanced study trip in collaboration with manager of studio programs • Coordinate program services for students affiliated with program partners • Develop and maintain a rapport with students and their families to help foster a sense of community among the current participants	

Job # Two cont.	2007 – 2009

• Work in partnership with the registrar to assure the maintenance of meticulous, up-to-date records of studio program contacts

• Understand safety and emergency procedures and be prepared to act in the event of a student or facility emergency

• Coordinate communications with field trip sites and organizations

2. Studio Management/Maintenance
• Maintain, equip, and supply all six studios, including both general and program specific equipment and supplies, as well as arranging for equipment maintenance, repair, upgrade, and replacement

• Perform errands associated with securing studio programs equipment and supplies

• Monitor studio supplies in all studio and storage areas

• Receive all supply shipments & distribute to appropriate studios

• Address storage and accessibility issues associated with supplies

• Inspect and lock all studios and close building at conclusion of program day

3. Exhibitions
• Collect and organize student work at the end of each term in preparation for exhibition installation

• Work with exhibitions preparator as necessary to install and de-install exhibitions in a safe and timely manner

• Prepare exhibition labels, wall text, and honor roll prior to each exhibition

• Collect, organize, distribute, and archive, as appropriate, artwork from past exhibitions

4. Outreach
• Maintain communications with contacts at select Chicago Public Schools

• Visit schools and present opportunities to school administrators, teachers and students

• Distribute educational and promotional materials to school contacts prior to each term

• Provide a quarterly summary report on outreach activity to education department staff

Job # Three	2009 – 2010

• File correspondence and donor records into alumni files

• Scan incoming documents into database

• Update closed file database with a detailed inventory of file contents before sending to off-site storage facility

Job # Four	2012

• Operate multi-line telephone system to answer incoming calls

• Direct callers to appropriate personnel

• Assist non-clerical staff with clerical work (i.e. data collection and entry)

• Assist with program flyers, posters, brochures, and social media promotions

• Prepare reports, agendas, memos, meeting minutes and email correspondence

• Assist with the completing and submission of statistics and deposits

• Organize the calendar and coordinate meeting reminders

• Provide reception coverage when needed

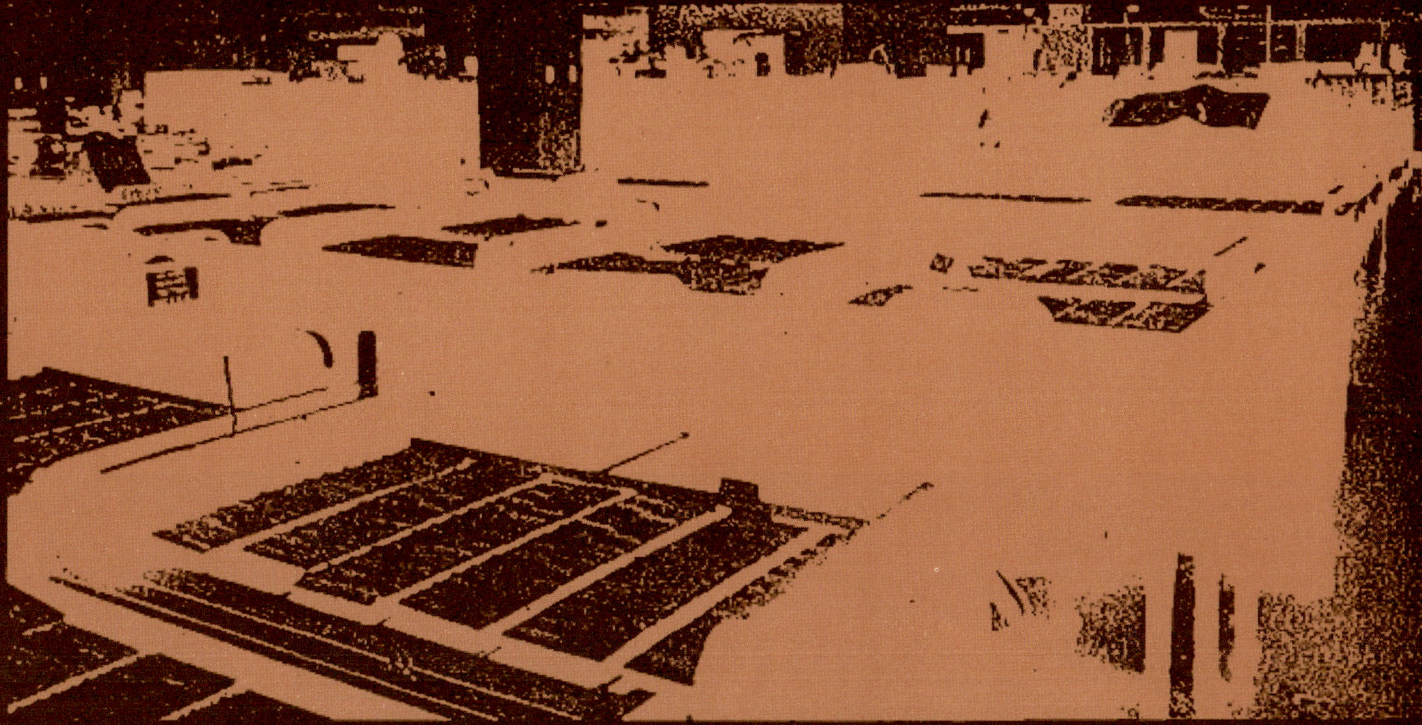

Examiners search card files, to associate correspondence with GAO claim number. These files, requiring over 3,000 square feet of floor space, are being put on microfilm which will be stored in a single cabinet requiring only eight square feet of floor space.

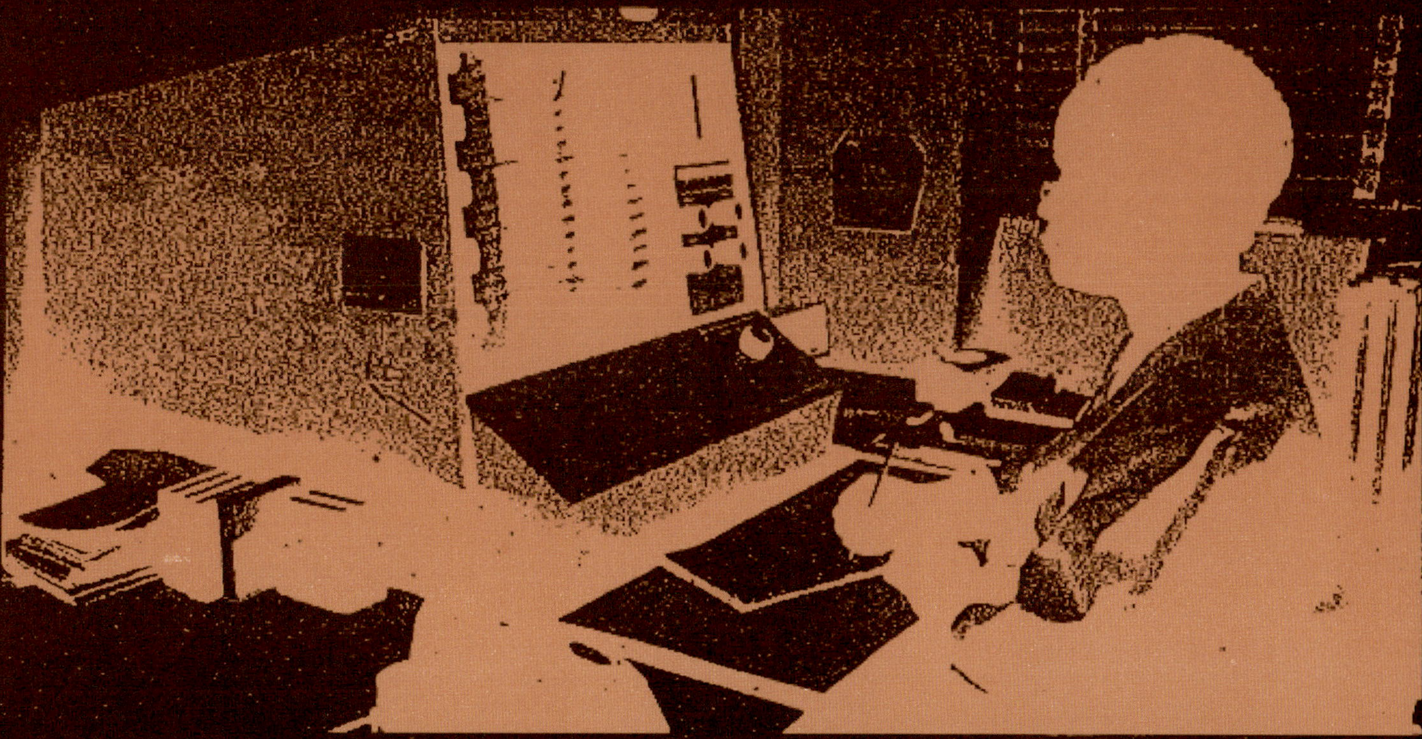

Marion McDonald performing similar search after conversion to microfilm. Note microfilm cartridges at lower left of picture. Each of these cartridges represents about 20,000 records.

Agency Reviews and Assistance

The Federal Claims Collection Act of 1966 and the implementing Claims Collection Standards require agencies to promptly collect debts and, where appropriate, to explore compromises and suspend or termi-

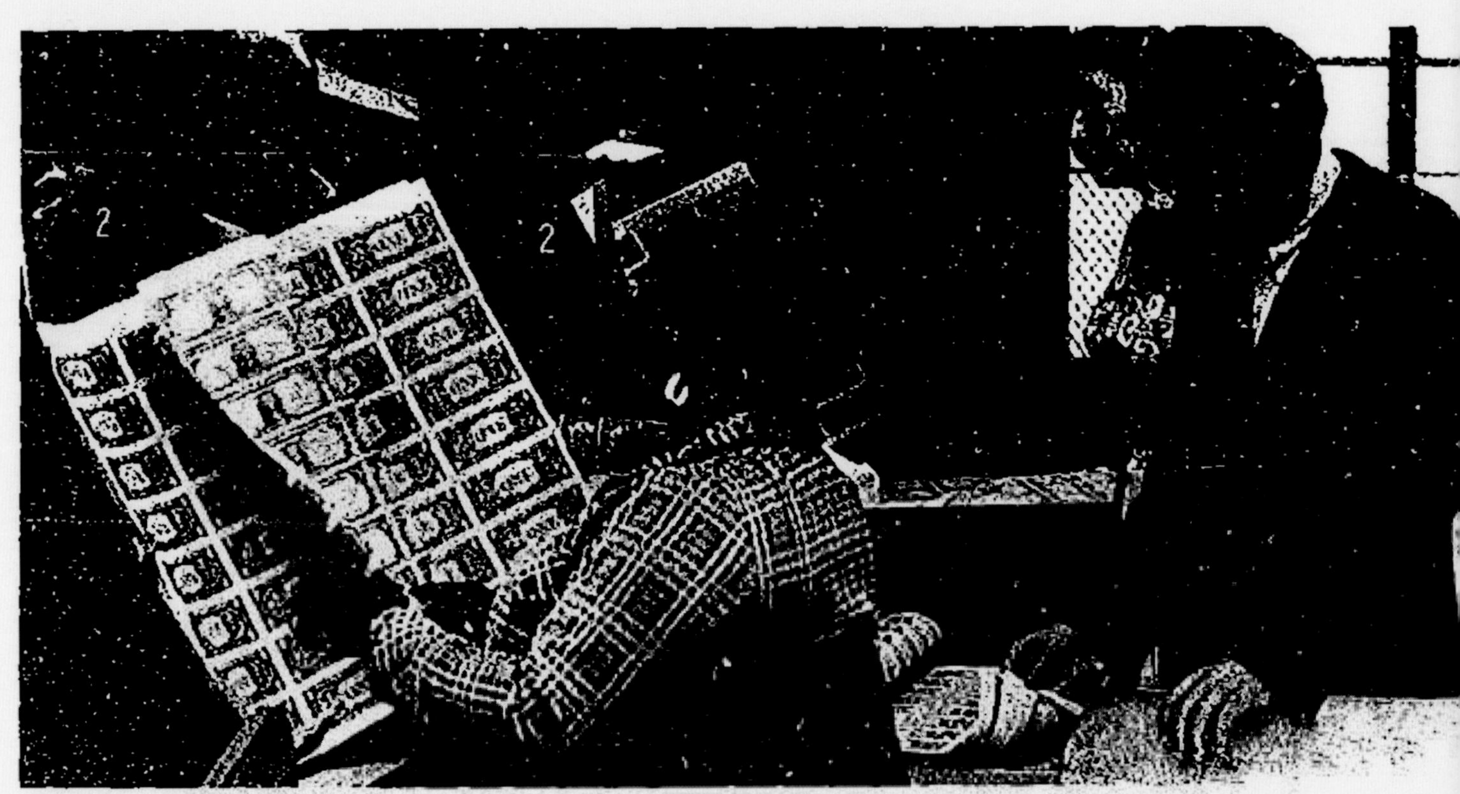

Merle Courtney and Jose Rodriquez observe Bureau of Engraving and Printing employee inspecting new currency.

Job # Five	2012 – 2014

- Schedule interviews and phone screens working directly with candidates and hiring managers
- Arrange travel for visiting candidates
- Update candidate records and job postings in recruiting systems and confirming new hires
- Provide follow-up correspondence to candidates on recruiting status via phone and email
- Track recruiting activities and provide candidate status in a weekly report
- Coordinate the post-interview debrief meetings and provide debrief materials
- Identify opportunities for improving candidate experience and scheduling efficiency
- Assist in the coordination of other recruiting activities

Job # Six	2014 – 2015

- Coordinate and maintain effective office procedures and efficient workflow
- Schedule client meetings, reserve conference rooms, coordinate audio visual equipment and food needs
- Coordinate travel arrangements
- Prepare itineraries and process travel reimbursements in a timely manner
- Maintain Outlook calendar and contacts and monitor crucial due dates
- Answer phones and direct callers as required, receive, register and assist visitors as required
- Monitor incoming emails as directed and when required
- Maintain timely and regular attendance
- Type, revise and proofread general correspondence, memos, legal documents, and reports
- Ensure accuracy and clarity of all work product in a timely manner
- Provide accounting on a daily basis, prepare client billing as required, follow through on all client billing matters
- Perform other duties as necessary and as assigned

Job # Seven	2015

- Provide detailed and high-level secretarial and administrative support
- Coordinate and maintain effective office procedures and efficient workflow, foster an atmosphere of teamwork and cooperation
- Schedule client meetings, reserve conference rooms, coordinate audio visual equipment and food needs

Job # Eight	2016 – 2019

- Answer phones and direct callers as required, receive, register and assist visitors as required
- Perform other duties as necessary and as assigned by supervisor for efficient functioning of the office
- Manage calendars, including prioritizing and scheduling appointments with internal team and external partners
- Proactively manage calendar conflicts and preferences
- Manage all travel arrangements including transportation, hotel, and restaurant reservations
- Edit, print, ship, and/or distribute materials used for presentations or meetings

Job # Eight cont.	2016 – 2019
• Process expense reports, reconcile department invoices, pay orders, and purchases • Coordinate and book staff travel logistics for team • Organize paper and electronic files	

Job # Nine	2019
• Provide database organization/management and reconciliation • Complete ad hoc administrative tasks associated with event planning and execution • Provide conference website updates and regular monitoring on app and website for accuracy • Create evaluation forms used at live events and tally results post event • Schedule meetings with internal associates and external contacts • Attend events and see to client management • Pack and ship conference materials to event venues around the U.S. (lifting boxes up to 30lbs) • Assist with overflow, special projects, assistant back-up coverage and day-to-day tasks • Take inventory of materials periodically and keep conference closet tidy • Prepare registration lists for badges and print badges • Create internal evaluation reports for distribution • Create sponsor follow up reports for distribution • Create run of show documents as needed • Assist with sponsor follow up for deliverables and tracking details • Provide on-site assistance for NYC events • Assist with ARS (Audience Response System) integration and testing prior to live events • Post photos and presentations to website immediately following conference, convert all presentations into PDFs • Review and update presentation decks on PPT for accuracy and formatting • Assist with loading app alerts and presentations	

Job # Ten	2019 – 2020
• Order snacks, lunches, and office supplies • Organize and help with all of the company “All Hands” meetings, and company offsites • Build relationships with facilities staff and provide transparency to employees • Plan team events and celebrations • Manage new hire onboarding • Answer phones and direct callers as required, receive, register and assist visitors as required	

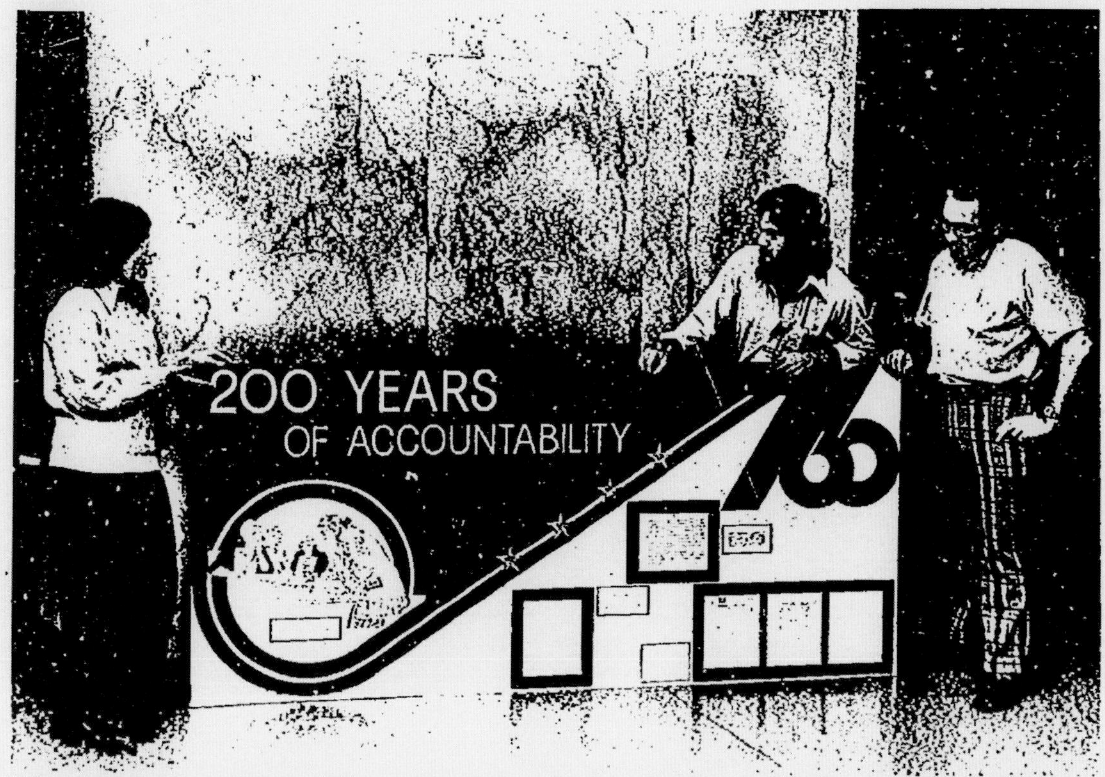

Wendy Mitchell explains one of GAO's Bicentennial displays to Carmelo Ciancio and Bud Garces, other members of GAO's Graphic Services Staff. Ms. Mitchell designed the display.

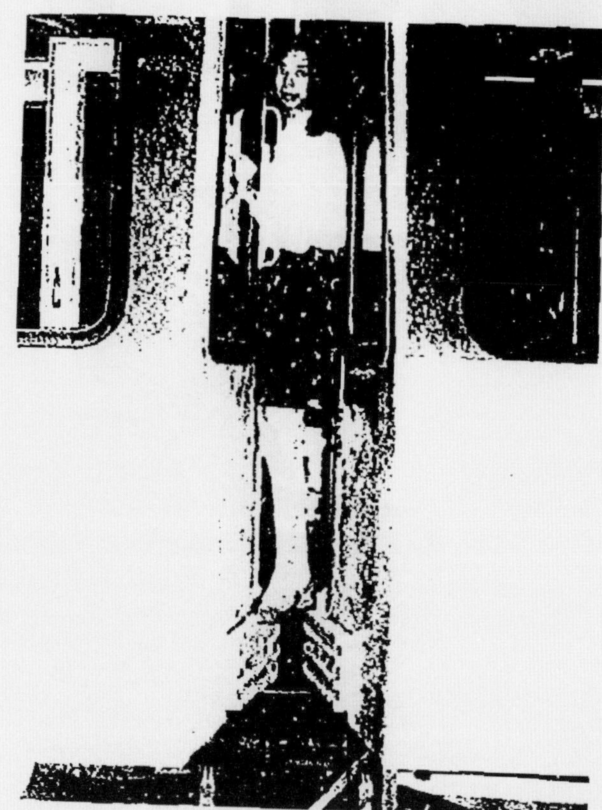

Peggy Frank, a GAO auditor, demonstrating the potential hazard when passing between subway cars operated by the Washington Metropolitan Area Transit Authority.

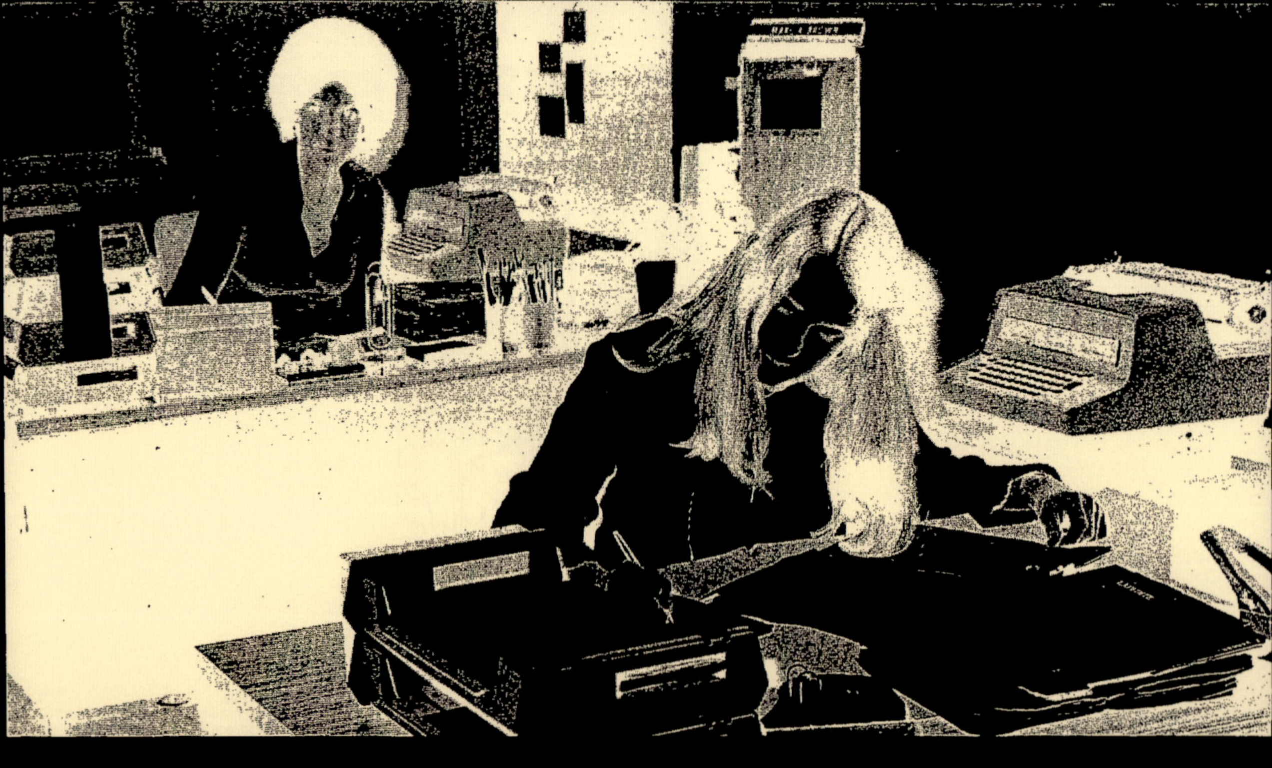

Adjudicators Marcia Brown and Terri Hurst work on "March" judgments.

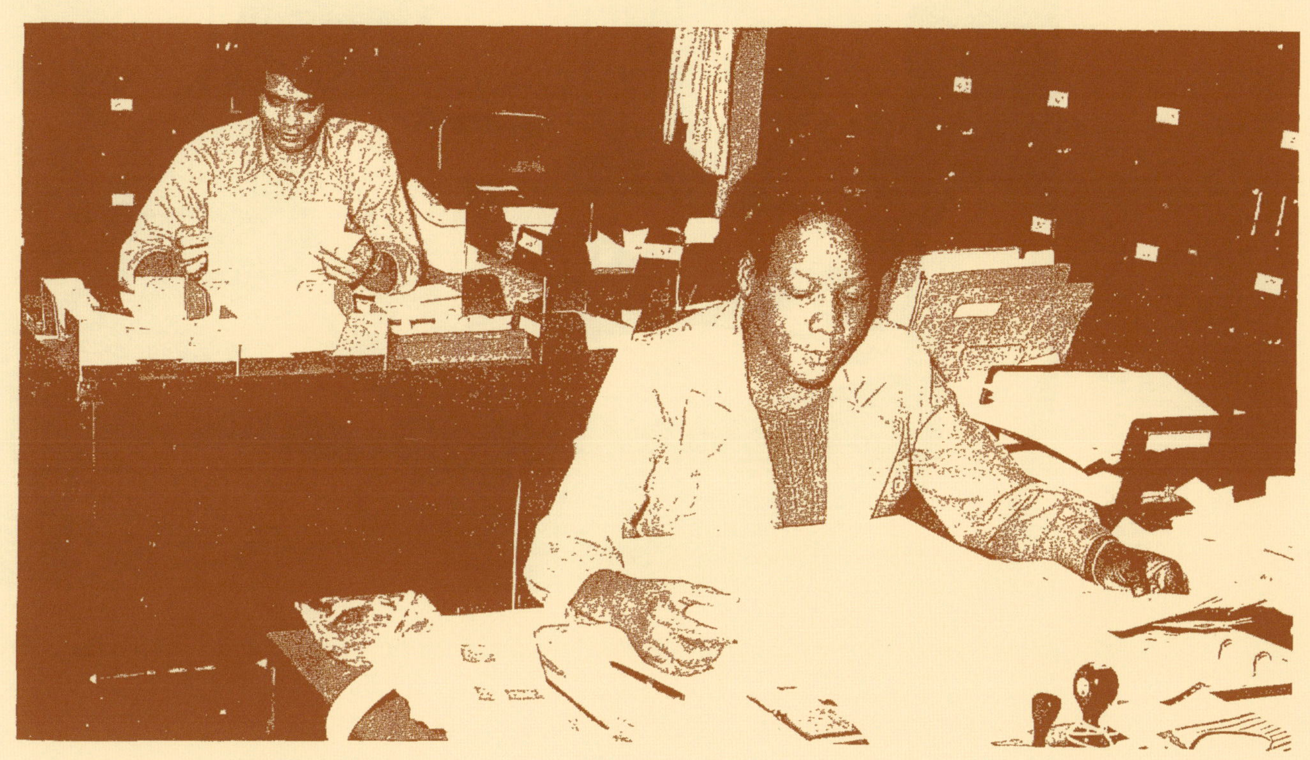

Mary McRae and Larry Gusman review automated accounts receivable reports.

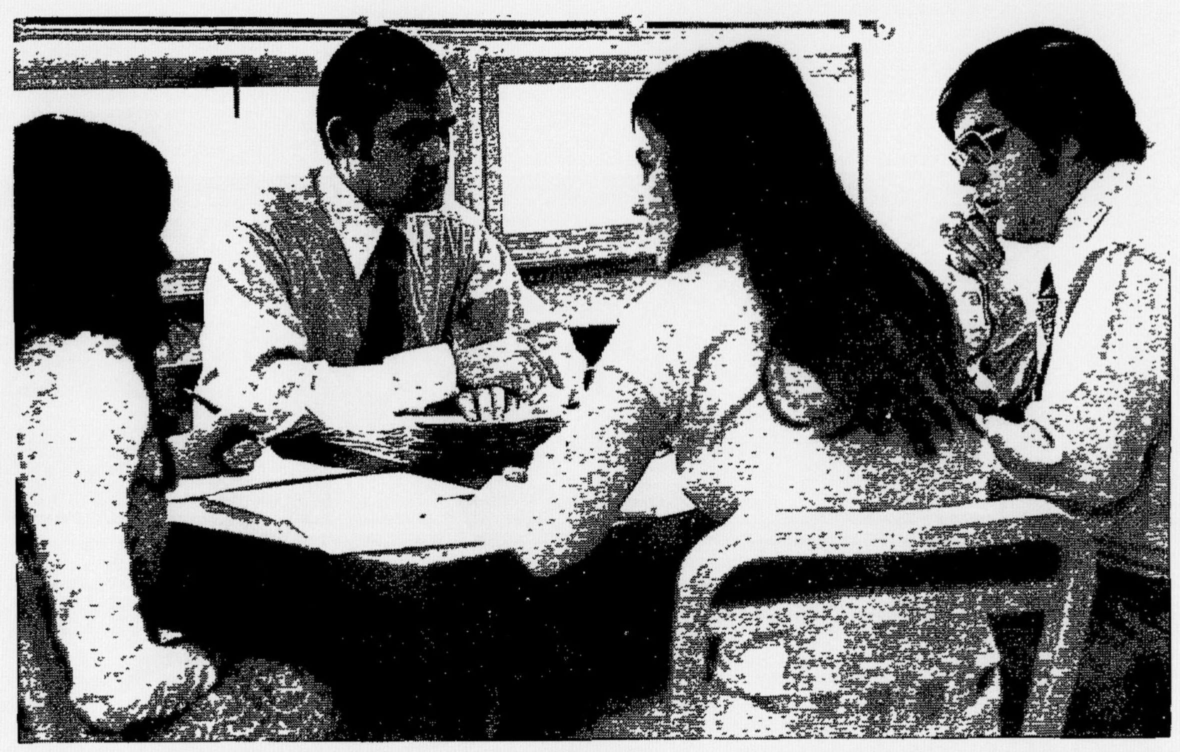

Team members participating in the simulated audit discuss audit objectives. From left: Janis E. Combs, William W. Caywood, Jr., Joan B. Hawkins, and Gary L. Johnson.

Many of the formal and material decisions made during the design and production of this book were taken in response to guidelines and rules set out within three documents issued by the US Government Publishing Office (GPO): the GPO Style Manual, Paper Samples guide, and Paper Standards guide.

The GPO is the Federal Government's official, digital, secure resource for producing, procuring, cataloging, indexing, authenticating, disseminating, and preserving the US Government's official information products. Through the issuance of documents, it sets out rules, structures, and guidelines related to the form and production of all printed materials produced by the Federal Government.

The GPO is also responsible for the production and distribution of information products and services for all three branches of the Federal Government, including US passports for the Department of State and the official publications of Congress, the White House, and other Federal agencies in digital and print formats.

The GPO provides permanent public access to Federal Government information at no charge through www.govinfo.gov and a secure online bookstore.

LAYOUT & TYPE DESIGN

The page layout and type design of this book were informed by the guidelines (constraints) set out in the 2016 version of the GPO Style Manual (the first revision to be issued since 1894).

The GPO Style Manual serves as a guide to the style and form of Federal Government printing and publishing. Essentially, it is a standardization device designed to achieve uniform word and type treatment and aims for economy of word use across all government offices. Its rules point to (what the GPO considers) the most economical manner for the preparation and typesetting of a manuscript.

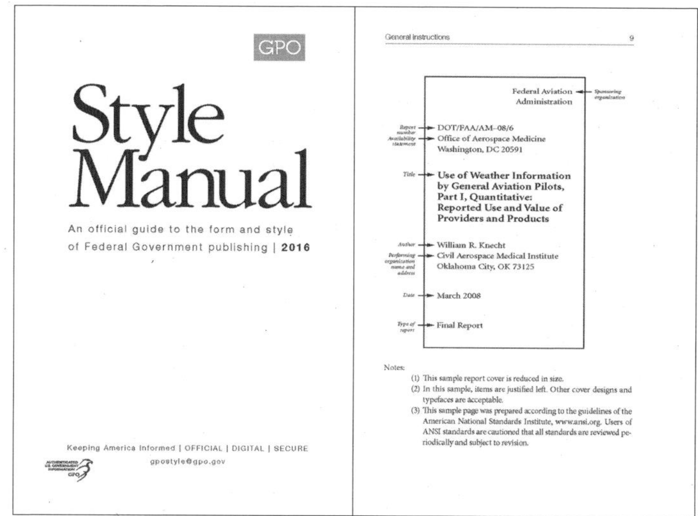

GPO

Style Manual

An official guide to the form and style of Federal Government publishing | 2016

Keeping America Informed | OFFICIAL | DIGITAL | SECURE

gpostyle@gpo.gov

General instructions 9

Federal Aviation Administration ← Sponsoring organization

Report number → DOT/FAA/AM–08/6

Availability statement → Office of Aerospace Medicine
Washington, DC 20591

Title → **Use of Weather Information by General Aviation Pilots, Part I, Quantitative: Reported Use and Value of Providers and Products**

Author → William R. Knecht

Performing organization name and address → Civil Aerospace Medical Institute
Oklahoma City, OK 73125

Date → March 2008

Type of report → Final Report

Notes:

(1) This sample report cover is reduced in size.
(2) In this sample, items are justified left. Other cover designs and typefaces are acceptable.
(3) This sample page was prepared according to the guidelines of the American National Standards Institute, www.ansi.org. Users of ANSI standards are cautioned that all standards are reviewed periodically and subject to revision.

The Style Manual is widely recognized by writers and editors both within and outside the Federal Government as a useful editorial tool. As a result, its influence on the formatting and production of printed material within the US workplace is notable. By choosing to employ this standardization device (alongside the GPO paper guides) as a key to the design and production, this book aims to examine the GPO's assumed authority and point to the institutional control inherent in the issuance of design rules and their influence on the US office environment. This is intended as archeology rather than a critique.

From the Style Manual:
"By act of Congress, the Director of the US Government Publishing Office (GPO) is authorized to determine the form and style of Government printing. The Style Manual is the product of this authorization.

The GPO Style Manual is prepared under the authority of section 1105 of Title 44, USC, which requires the Director to "determine the form and style" of Government printing. The Manual is prepared by the GPO Style Board, composed of proofreading, printing, and Government documents specialists from within GPO, where all major congressional, as well as executive agency publications, are produced.

It should be remembered that the Style Manuals rules cannot be regarded as rigid, for the printed word assumes many shapes and variations in type presentation. An effort has been made to provide complete coverage of those elements that enter into the translation of manuscript into type."

PAPER & COLOR CHOICES

The material choices for this book, its paper, paper weight, and paper finishes, binding, and choice of ink colors were informed by the GPO Paper Samples and Paper Standards guides.

The Paper Samples and Paper Standards contain over seventy approved papers representing a range of stock weights and finishes in coated and uncoated sheets and recommendations for their use within different printing projects. Each sample lists authorized colors, available basis weights, and notes about other optional sheets within each paper grade. The papers are chosen by the Joint Committee on Printing and Publishing (JCP).

The guide is a standardization tool for all Federal Government printing, design, and publishing professionals. Its purpose is to ensure that Federal agencies conform to the JCP's consensus procedures, following rules (statutes) regarding the use of printing papers, limiting choice, and thereby ensuring visual and material consistency and the and ironing out of difference.

There are 14 classes of papers listed in the table of contents. Each item of paper is identified by a paper code that indicates both class and grade. For example, JCP A60, the "A" refers to the class of printing paper and the 60 to the grade "offset book." Similarly, JCP L20, "L" refers to cover paper class and 20 to the "vellum-finish" grade. The four-digit number associated with the FSC prefix is a General Services Administration Federal Supply Catalog designation and is included when available. The use of optical (fluorescent) brighteners is prohibited in those grades with 50% and 100% cotton/linen content, as well as those papers specified for use in optical scanners.

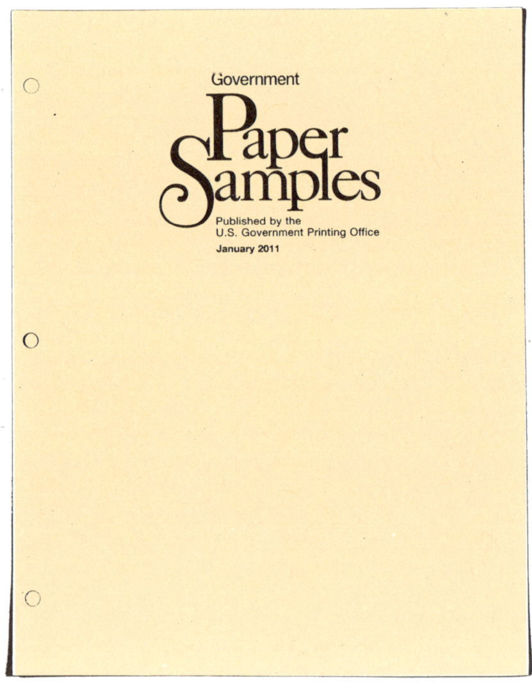

Paper stocks used in this book are as follows:
JCP-Q20 18-point board (cover)
JCP-L20 65lb matt finish cover stock
JCP-D20 70lb matt coated text weight stock
JCP-D10 50lb offset/text weight paper (green and salmon)

From the Paper Standards guide:
“The US Government Publishing Office (GPO) provides Federal agencies with valuable advice and assistance in obtaining their printing needs. One of the ways in which we provide this assistance is in the development and issuance of Government paper standards. The purpose of these standards is to (1) achieve compliance with relevant statutes regarding printing papers; (2) address environmental, workplace safety, and paper longevity issues; and (3) maximize savings in the Government’s paper purchases and, ultimately, your print projects. These standards are available for use by all departments of the Government and their field offices. Some standards are specialty grades with limited availability and have been designated within the standard. Generally, these stocks are procured as mill run quantities. There is maximum flexibility in specifying color, texture, and recycled content. The use of these standards will achieve the greatest possible savings in paper stocks for your agency’s printing needs.”

The GPO Paper Samples guide also specifies a range of color papers for use in the office. The influence of the guide and the paper mills that service the US Government is apparent in the familiarity of these colors. They are the default color papers found in letter and tabloid-sized mixed color reams in US office supply stores. Produced in such vast quantities for the US Government these specific colored papers are then also packaged and sold at a significantly reduced cost to office retail stores. The prime colors are green, yellow, Venetian blue, tan pink, salmon, brown, and black.

Noting and highlighting this structural familiarity, this book has been printed entirely in a selection of these colors, which were converted into PMS spot colors and used (in different sequences) across the book sections.

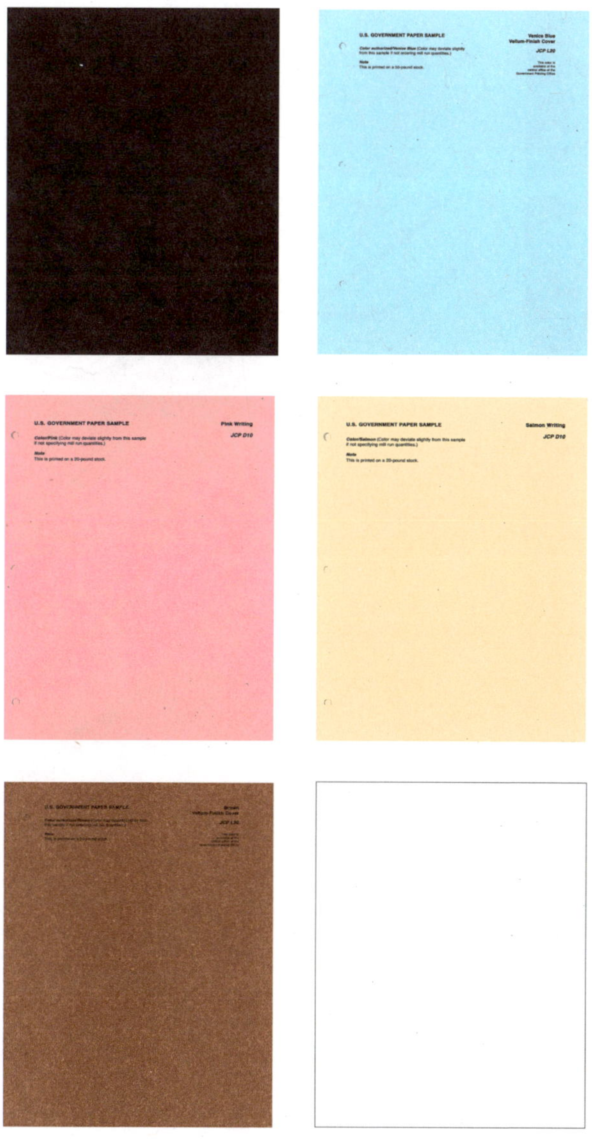

References:
Government Paper Samples 2011, GPO Stock Number: 021-000-00194-5, https://bookstore.gpo.gov/products government-paper-samples-2011

GPO Style Manual; An official guide to the form and style of Federal Government publishing, 2015. https://www.govinfo.gov/features/new-edition-gpo-style-manual

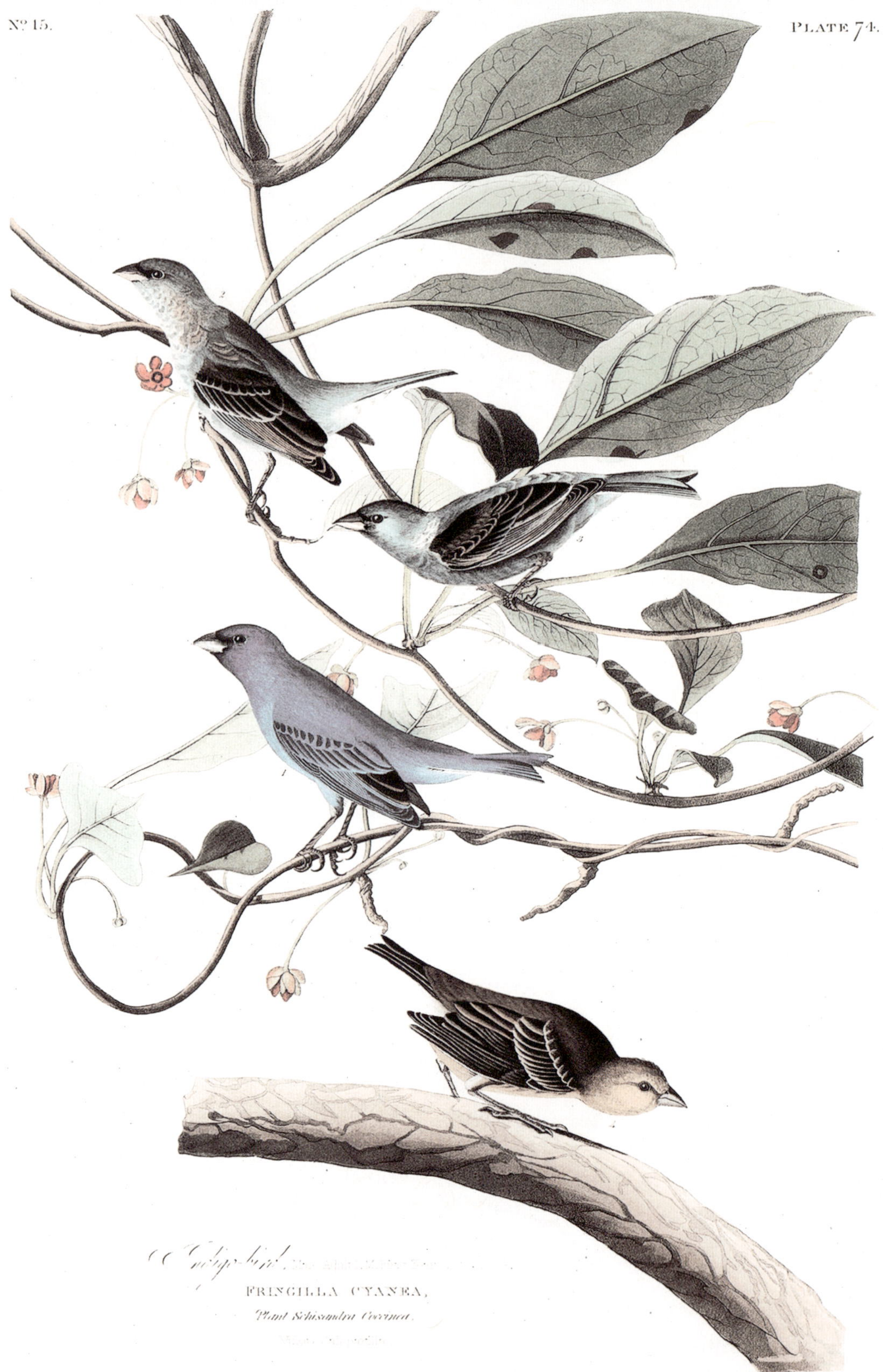

A reproduction of John James Audubon's painting depicting a natural life study of Indigo Birds.

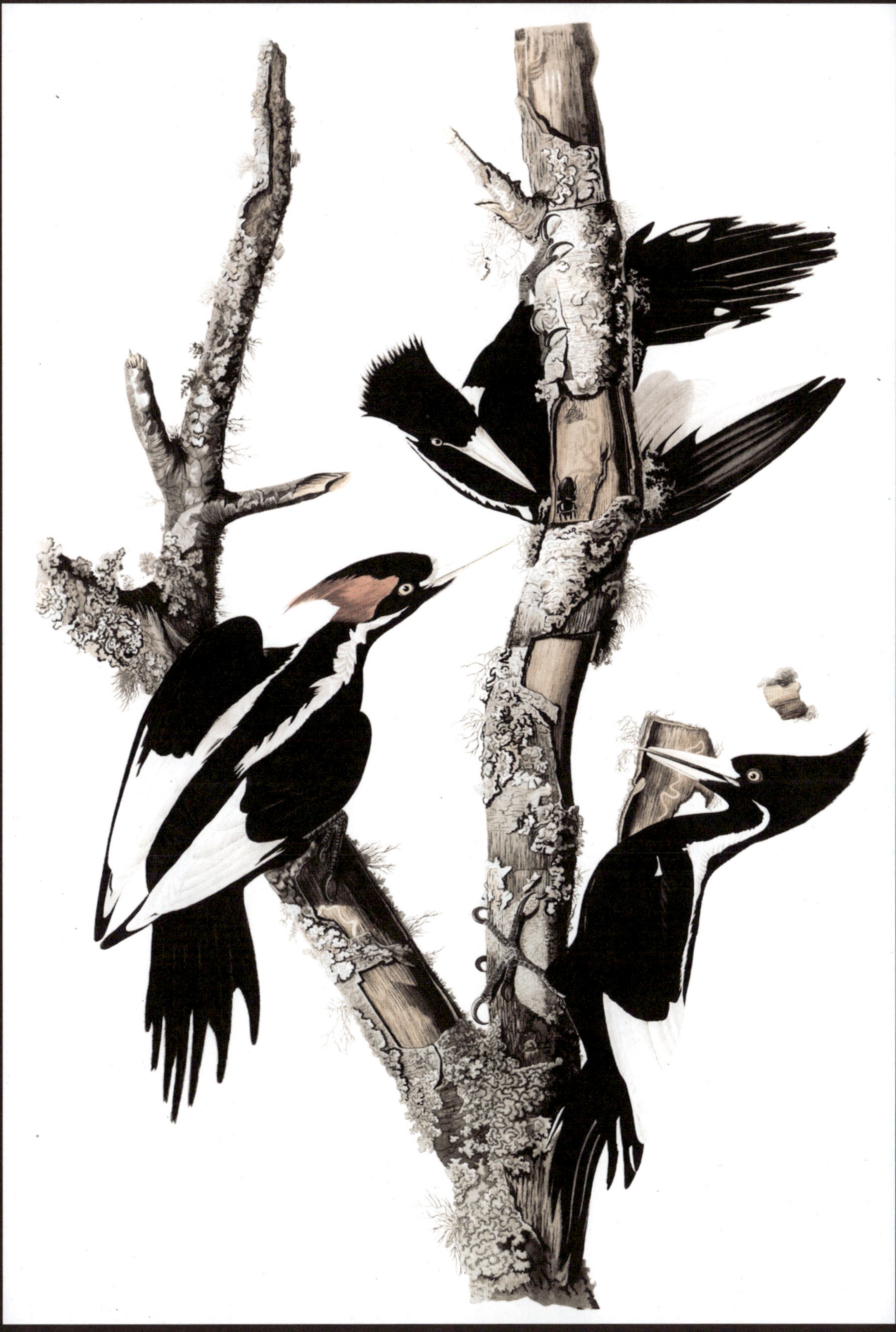

A reproduction of John James Audubon's painting depicting a natural life study of extinct Ivory-billed Woodpeckers.

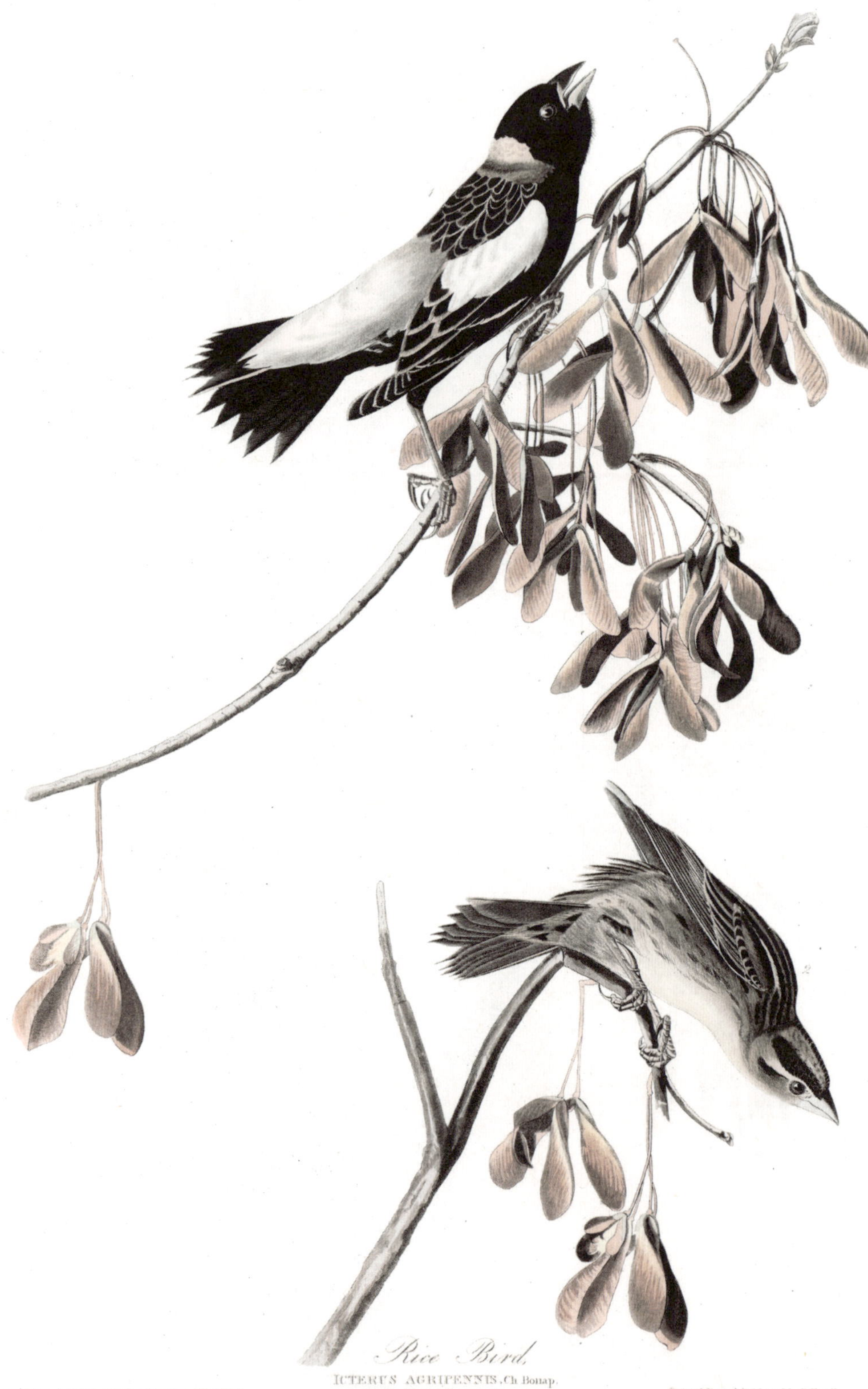

A reproduction of John James Audubon's painting depicting a natural life study of Rice Birds. Birdwatching, or birding, is a recreational activity where observing birds without distraction, noise or free-roaming pets is imperative.

George Floyd tested positive for COVID-19 in April, just over a month before his killing by a police officer in Minneapolis on May 25th, 2020. Black Americans have a rate approximately 5 times that of non-Hispanic white Americans for contracting COVID-19 and experiencing severe illness, regardless of age.[1] Black people who are more likely to be uninsured and lack adequate health insurance.[2] Insurance that doesn't function like insurance to cover the risk of potential injuries and medical expenses, but is instead a monthly payment into a black hole. Even when care can be administered to us, it is after multiple attempts of calling attention to symptoms and injury that oftentimes go ignored until conditions are irreversible. Protests about the murder of George Floyd and the continual murders of other Black people, the systemic racism inherent in American policing, and the racism that remains inscribed in American education, health, housing and economic institutions go on. There is rarely, if at all, a reprieve from the structures that keep us sick and in fear, both in and outside the workplace.

Will the current global pandemic and continued protests against generational racial, economic, health and educational inequalities change how we treat workers and the architecture that houses this work? Some companies will use partitioned walls outfitted with plexiglass to subdivide and replace open concept floor plans in workspaces. Keeping the infrastructure intact that keeps us sick in the first place continues to be the "appropriate" response from this administration and US companies. They are doing just enough to get by without changing anything structurally to improve for the future. Such is the case in adding transparent barriers but not improving worker's health insurance, and ignoring that the majority of workers in low-paying customer-facing jobs, care work, or service work are overwhelmingly people of color, and (in the United States) Black. Structural racism that keeps this infrastructure afloat is also the compliance that keeps these workplaces moving.

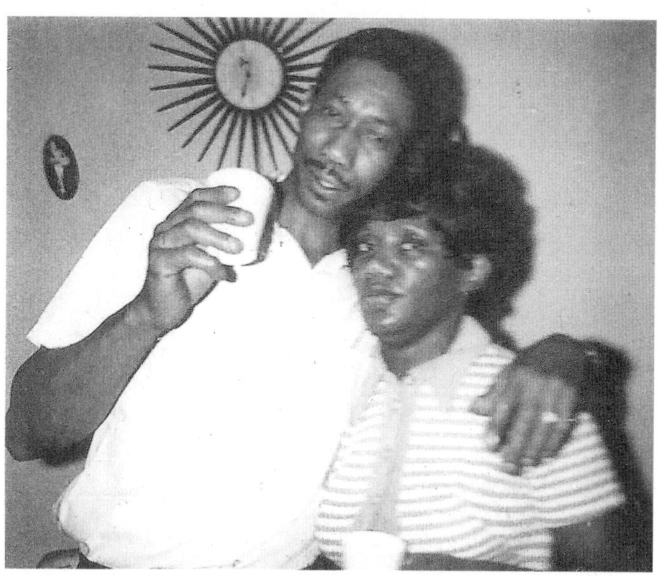

Randolph Jarmon who was a warehouse worker and Martha Jarmon who was a factory worker and later a nursing assistant enjoy their time together outside of the workplace.

Creating *Depreciating Assets* allowed me to react, consider and think through the labored, economic, and racialized experiences that have constituted and continue to make up my experiences in workspaces. The physical format of this book, as outlined in Appendix Three, riffs off the physical, aesthetic and organizational attributes of US government reports and documents. It provides a space to critique who and what is inherently left

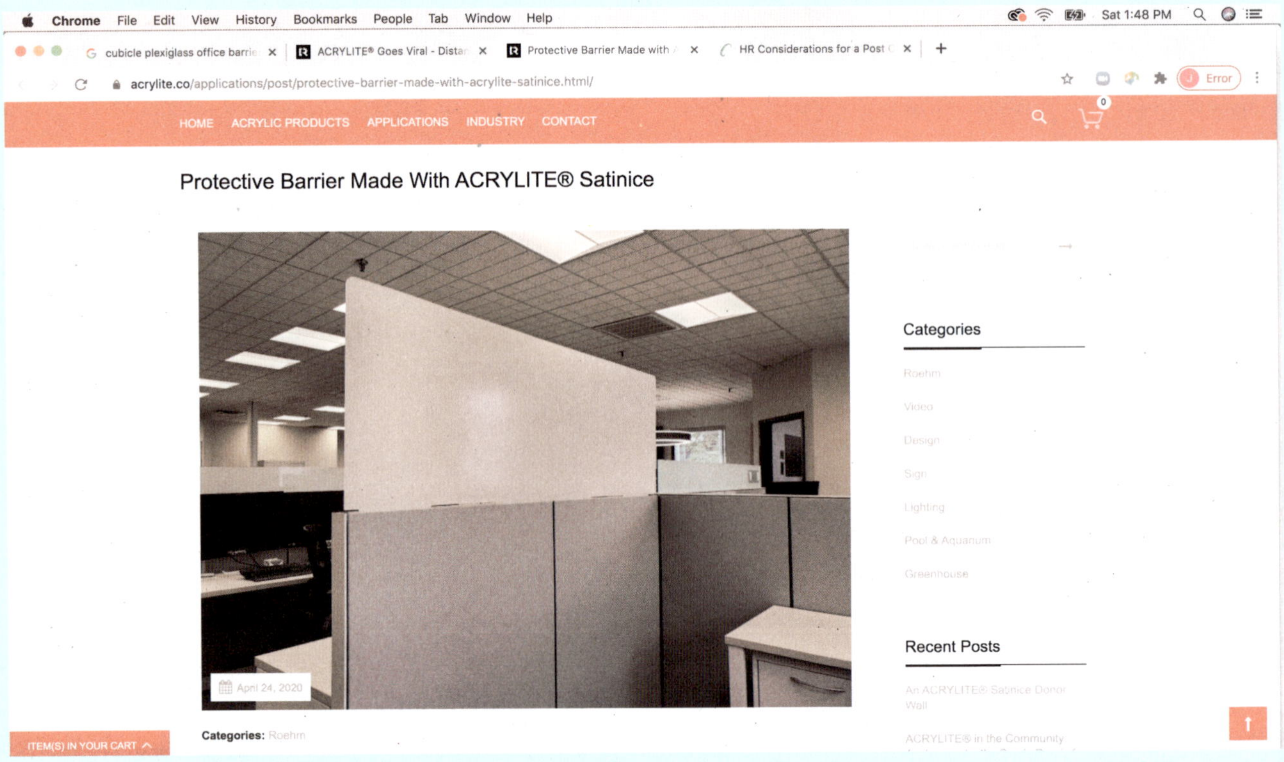

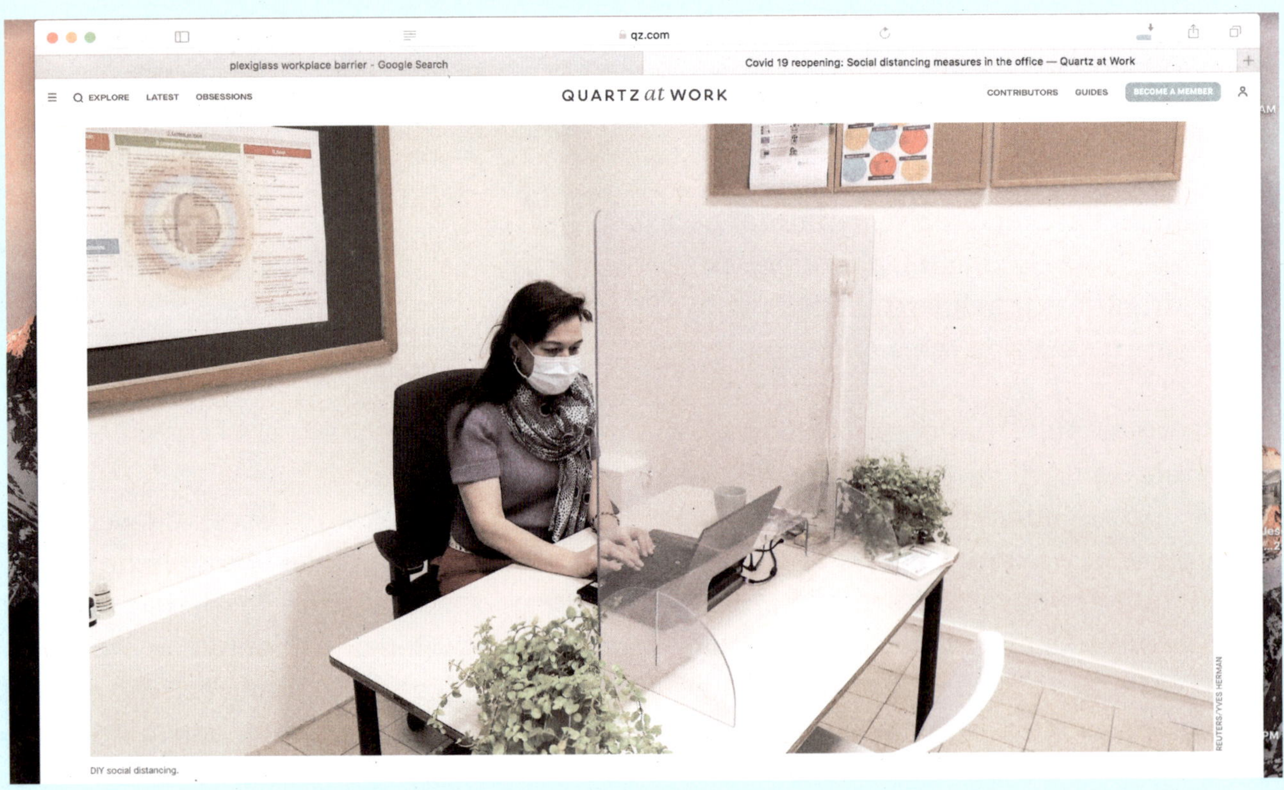

With hasty reopenings of workplaces across the US and a lack of centralized guidance, advertisements for casually built products and mock-ups of DIY safety measures for office and public spaces proliferate on the Internet. Summer 2020.

out—an overlooked relationship to how anti-Black sentiment is prescribed to how economic and labor concerns operate. Off and on since 2006, I have had precarious employment situations that have placed me in various workspaces. These workspaces for the most part had a familiar matrix that existed throughout, sometimes quantified in the architecture alone, other times in the policy and culture that keeps these places running. The modularity of these workspaces alongside the generic nature of the administrative work I was performing revealed overlaps between the interior architecture of these spaces and how workers are treated.

Do minimalist design gestures and open floor plans exist outside conditions of race, class and labor? They don't. They carry and inscribe in them the entrenched social, political and policy concerns that keep institutional inequalities running. "Race is there even when we think it is not. And sometimes it was there all along, but we did not know how to 'see' it." [3] Art institutions ignore this and instead obfuscate their role in creating equitable spaces. We see this in the histories left out of artifacts accumulated (stolen) by institutions; Bauhaus-designed architecture and furniture; canonized minimalist artists who casually omitted the racial, economic and political concerns of the 1960s and 70s in the making of their artworks and are never faulted for it, even in 2020; racial and ethnic difference easily consumed by way of exhibiting particularly figurative artwork by Black artists as spectacle; and pacifying structural racism as a concern of the past.

I will continue to make work, share it and collaborate with others to keep the important work moving.

July, 2020

Endnotes:

1. Centers for Disease Control and Prevention. "COVID-19 in Racial and Ethnic Minority Groups." June 25, 2020. https://www.cdc.gov/coronavirus/2019-ncov/need-extra-precautions/racial-ethnic-minorities.html. Accessed June 26, 2020.

2. Artiga, Samantha, Damico, Anthony and Orgera, Kendal. "Changes in Health Coverage by Race and Ethnicity since the ACA, 2010-2018." Kaiser Family Foundation. March 05, 2020. https://www.kff.org/disparities-policy/issue-brief/changes-in-health-coverage-by-race-and-ethnicity-since-the-aca-2010-2018/. Accessed June 26, 2020.

3. Irene Cheng, et al. "Introduction," *Race and Modern Architecture: A Critical History from the Enlightenment to the Present*. University of Pittsburgh Press, 2020, 11.

Colophon

Depreciating Assets
Jessica Vaughn

Published by Printed Matter, Inc., 2021

First edition of 600 copies

I would like to thank the many people who have talked, listened and thought through the concerns of this project to help make this book possible: Carolyn & Larry Vaughn, Leah Zepeda Vaughn, Sarah Vaughn, Magdalyn Asimakis, Amalle Dublon, Duncan Hamilton, Charlotte Ickes, Caroline Key, Park McArthur, Meg Onli, Gonzalo Reyes Rodriguez, Sadia Shirazi, Tina Zavitsanos and Printed Matter.

ISBN: 978-0-89439-099-9

Design: The Uses of Literacy

Printed and bound by
Standard Form, Canada

Printed Matter, Inc.

Printed Matter, Inc.
231 11th Avenue
New York, NY 10001
www.printedmatter.org

Published as part of Printed Matter's Emerging Artists Publication Series

This publication is made possible with the support of the Jerome Foundation, The Andy Warhol Foundation for the Visual Arts, public funds from the New York City Department of Cultural Affairs in partnership with the City Council, as well as the New York State Council on the Arts with the support of Governor Andrew M. Cuomo and the New York State Legislature.

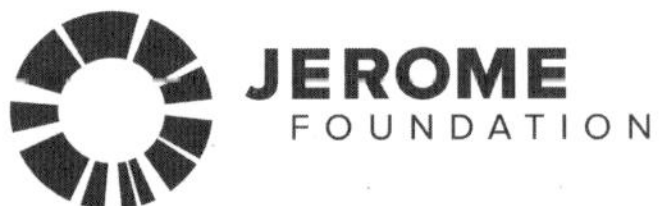

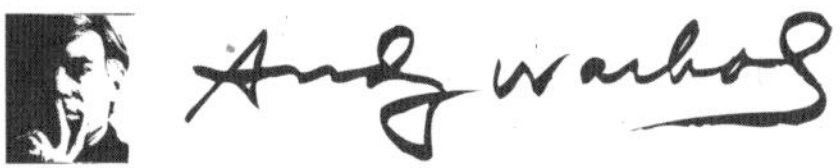

The Andy Warhol Foundation for the Visual Arts

Research for this project was made possible with funding from the Graham Foundation for Advanced Studies in the Fine Arts.

Graham Foundation